TRAVELER

WASHINGTON, D.C.

NATIONAL
GEOGRAPHIC
TRAVELER

WASHINGTON, D.C.

by John Thompson
photography by Richard Nowitz

National Geographic
Washington, D.C.

CONTENTS

■ Pages 2–3: The Jefferson Memorial and cherry blossoms draw crowds on a spring evening.
■ Left: Fireworks light up the monuments and memorials of Washington, D.C.

TRAVELING WITH EYES OPEN

Alert travelers go with a purpose and leave with a benefit. If you travel responsibly, you can help support wildlife conservation, historic preservation, and cultural enrichment in the places you visit. You can enrich your own travel experience as well.

To be a geo-savvy traveler:

- Recognize that your presence has an impact on the places you visit.

- Spend your time and money in ways that sustain local character. (Besides, it's more interesting that way.)

- Value the destination's natural and cultural heritage.

- Respect the local customs and traditions.

- Express appreciation to local people about things you find interesting and unique to the place: its nature and scenery, music and food, historic villages and buildings.

- Vote with your wallet: Support the people who support the place, patronizing businesses that make an effort to celebrate and protect what's special there. Seek out local shops, restaurants, and inns. Use tour operators who love their home—who love taking care of it and showing it off. Avoid businesses that detract from the character of the place.

- Enrich yourself, taking home memories and stories to tell, knowing that you have contributed to the preservation and enhancement of the destination.

That is the type of travel now called geotourism, defined as "tourism that sustains or enhances the geographical character of a place—its environment, culture, aesthetics, heritage, and the well-being of its residents." To learn more, visit National Geographic's Center for Sustainable Destinations at *nationalgeographic.org/sustainability-policy*.

WASHINGTON, D.C.

⌷ ABOUT THE AUTHORS & THE PHOTOGRAPHER

▪ **John M. Thompson** has written or contributed to more than a dozen titles for National Geographic Books, from *Driving Guides to America: Florida* and *Guide to America's Outdoors: Southeast* to *America's Historic Trails* and *Our National Parks: Tours with Ranger*. His other National Geographic publications include the *National Geographic Almanac of American History; Who's Who in American History: Leaders, Visionaries, and Icons Who Shaped Our Nation; The Revolutionary War; Wildlands of the Upper South;* plus *America's Western Edge* and *The Medieval World: An Illustrated Atlas*. He also authored *American Journeys: Weekends Across the U.S.* and two novels, *The Reservoir* and *Love and Lament*, set in post-bellum North Carolina. A former resident of Washington, D.C., he lives in Charlottesville, Virginia.

▪ **Richard Nowitz** was a contract photographer for *National Geographic WORLD* (now *Kids*) magazine and is now a contributing photographer to the National Geographic Image Collection. He has been the principal photographer of more than 20 large-format photo and travel guides; in 1968 he was honored by the Society of American Travel Writers as Travel Photographer of the Year.

▪ **Christopher P. Baker,** the Society of American Travel Writer's 2008 "Travel Journalist of the Year," updated and wrote new features and sidebars for this edition. He is the author of the *National Geographic Traveler* guidebooks to Cuba, Panama, and Dominican Republic, plus Colombia and Costa Rica, both of which he also photographed. He has also been the update editor for six other guidebooks in the *National Geographic Traveler* series, including *Walking Washington, D.C.*, as well as having written and photographed more than 20 other guidebooks to destinations worldwide. He is a regular contributor to such publications as CNN Travel, BBC Travel, *National Geographic Traveler,* and *Robb Report*.

CHARTING YOUR TRIP

Shedding its past reputation as a buttoned-down bureaucratic town, the city of Washington, D.C., buzzes these days with urban life and a cosmopolitan air. Politics still takes center stage. But the fabled monuments, world-class museums, vibrant cultural life, and vast swaths of open parkland make this a city to savor, while the compact layout puts it all within easy reach.

Many people think of Washington, D.C., mostly as the National Mall and the Smithsonian Institution, anchored by the U.S. Capitol at one end and the Lincoln Memorial at the other. But the often overlooked charms of this tiny 68-square-mile (176 sq km) city can best be found in its neighborhoods, each with a distinctive character. **Georgetown** is a favorite for its narrow streets, historic townhomes, and boutiques. **Dupont Circle** and **Adams Morgan** have an eclectic beat, **Capitol Hill** a village ambience. The **14th and U Street** area explodes these days with new restaurants, while the downtown **Penn Quarter** has become a vibrant arts district. Some long-neglected areas are getting a face-lift, thanks to projects like the new Wharf development along the Potomac River and the hip club scene that's grown up on formerly riot-scarred **H Street.**

What doesn't change is Washington's essential character as the nation's capital and the living embodiment of American democracy. Its symbolic center remains the National Mall. Most visits begin here, with a stroll among the monuments, a trip or two to the Smithsonian Institution (which actually consists of more than a dozen museums both on and off the Mall). It helps that so much of what you'll want to see lies in close proximity to the Mall and downtown. Easy access by the Metro system (*wmata.com*) means you can spend a few hours at a time, then return later for more. Keep in mind when touring on the Mall and Capitol Hill that the buildings are farther apart than they may seem on a map.

If You Have a Week

Washington offers so much that seeing everything would be a challenge even for the most intrepid traveler. But you can pack a lot into a week. Consider an itinerary of museums and sightseeing in the morning, with afternoons open to broader exploration of other places in or beyond town.

■ **The Marine Corps War Memorial shows an iconic World War II moment.**

A visit to the **Smithsonian** is mandatory. You'll have to choose, however, which of its museums to see. For a varied taste of the many collections and exhibits, allow a couple of days to explore those clustered around the Mall. **Air and Space, Natural History,** and **American History** draw the biggest crowds, but don't overlook smaller treasures such as the **Freer** and **Sackler Galleries,** with superb displays of Asian objects. The **Hirshhorn** is renowned for its cutting-edge art. Also along the Mall: the vast **National Gallery of Art.** Its two wings are connected underground. Near the Smithsonian museums but not part of them, the **U.S. Holocaust Museum** and the **National Law Enforcement Museum** both offer rich educational experiences. The Smithsonian Metro station and several others close by will put you within a block or two of all these sites.

Dusk is the best time to visit the **Lincoln Memorial,** anchoring the Mall's western end. The light grows softer then, and it's quieter once traffic thins and federal workers have all gone home. Steps away from the Lincoln you'll find the black granite **Vietnam Veterans Memorial** and its wall of names especially moving. A hidden gem, with waterfalls and a serene park setting, is the **Franklin Delano Roosevelt Memorial,** tucked away in a glade alongside the **Tidal Basin.**

Start one day with a visit to the **U.S. Capitol** (book a tour in advance since same-day passes are limited), at the Mall's eastern end. You'll enter through the underground Visitor Center, across the street from the **Supreme Court** (no advance tickets; entrance is on a first-come, first-served basis) and a block from the Capitol South Metro station. Nearby and well worth a look inside is the ornate **Jefferson Building** of the **Library of Congress.** Grab lunch several blocks away at a café or bistro around **Eastern Market** and **Barracks Row.**

NOT TO BE MISSED:

The Library of Congress   **62–63**

Browsing Eastern Market   **66**

The National Mall, monuments, Smithsonian, and springtime cherry blossoms   69–106

A view of the White House from Lafayette Square   116

Strolling Georgetown   150–154

The Phillips Collection   166–169

Trying ethnic restaurants in lively Adams Morgan   175

Lunch or tea in the gardens at Hillwood Estate   187–188

A visit to Mount Vernon with a stop in Old Town, Alexandria, Virginia   224–226

Visitor Information

Advance planning and reservations are always a good idea, ensuring you don't waste precious time. In the busiest tourist seasons (April through August), when lines can be long, it's often mandatory.

Destination DC *(washington.org)* is a one-site directory of good information. You can request or download the free 112-page Official Visitor's Guide, which is updated twice a year. The **D.C. Tourist Information Center** *(509 9th St., N.W.,*

tel 202-347-7201, dcchamber.org) has free maps and city guides. It's open weekdays from 8:30 a.m. to 5:30 p.m.

If you like discovering hidden points of interest, check out the neighborhood walking tours developed by **Cultural Tourism DC** *(culturaltourismdc.org).* And for tips on the ever changing restaurant scene and nightlife, browse the online site of *Washingtonian* magazine *(washingtonian.com).*

Come dinnertime, you'll discover that Washington has become a foodie town with a diverse range of choices—from well-priced ethnic restaurants to pricey temples of gastronomy. And do try to take in a play or other performance while you're here. A local favorite are the bold, contemporary stagings of the classics by the **Shakespeare Theater Company,** in the downtown Penn Quarter. The **Kennedy Center,** in the Foggy Bottom neighborhood, offers opera, theater, and ballet as well as free concerts daily at 6 p.m. A heavy influx of young people to Washington in recent years has also given rise to comedy clubs and open-mic events at venues such as the popular café cum bookstore **Busboys & Poets** in Washington, D.C., and Shirlington, Virginia.

If You Have More Time

Plan to reserve one morning or afternoon for a trip to **Mount Vernon,** George Washington's plantation house on the banks of the Potomac River. It's in Virginia, 16 miles (25 km) south of Washington; you can get there by Metro, then bus. For a

Pack Your Walking Shoes, or Hop a Bus

Like most world-class cities, Washington is best discovered one step at a time. Indeed, D.C. is a place made for walking. In January 2021, *USA Today* ranked Washington, D.C., the most walkable, pedestrian-friendly city in the United States. At first glance, the city's low structural heights and neoclassical dominance in federal buildings seem to make for a homogenized urban landscape. But upon closer inspection, this compact capital city has a welcoming human scale and a wealth of architectural styles. It's also a refreshingly green city, with thousands of acres of easily accessed federal parkland that is exquisitely landscaped and immune to development.

But even the most devoted on-foot explorer needs to sit back and just look around now and then. The city's fleet of red and gray **DC Circulator buses** *(dccirculator.com)* are just the ticket. They make frequent circuits around the National Mall and along four other routes. It's $1 each time you hop on. You can pay by cash (exact change), Metro's SmarTrip card, or WMATA regional bus pass *(wmata.com/fares)*.

pleasant all-day excursion, combine a visit to Mount Vernon with several hours in colonial-era **Old Town, Alexandria,** halfway between Washington and Mount Vernon. The **Mount Vernon Trail** along the Virginia side of the Potomac gives Washington a great recreational artery for biking, jogging, or strolling. From the section that lies near Rosslyn you'll get awesome views of the D.C. skyline and its famous landmarks. Close by is **Arlington National Cemetery,** easily accessible by Metro.

Back in Washington, D.C., other good ideas for convenient and memorable outings include the **C & O Canal trail,** which runs through Georgetown on its way to Maryland; a summer baseball game at **Nationals Park;** and the popular **National Zoo. Hillwood Estate Museum and Gardens,** with a remarkable collection of Russian art and icons, is in the same Upper Northwest neighborhood as the zoo and has a nice café that serves both lunch and tea (reservations advised).

For an afternoon of shopping head to Georgetown or up **Wisconsin Avenue** to the enclave of swanky shops around Chevy Chase and Mazza Gallerie. And don't

THEY (WHO) SEEK TO ESTABLISH
SYSTEMS OF GOVERNMENT BASED ON
THE REGIMENTATION OF ALL HUMAN
BEINGS BY A HANDFUL OF INDIVIDUAL
RULERS... CALL THIS A NEW ORDER.
IT IS NOT NEW AND IT IS NOT ORDER.

■ **The FDR Memorial also remembers the Depression-era president's lovable dog, Fala.**

overlook the city's museum shops when you're downtown; many of them offer distinctive items that make great gifts or souvenirs. The **National Building Museum** has one of the best selections in town.

If you find yourself craving a bit of relief from Washington, consider blocking out a day for a trip to Annapolis or Baltimore. Getting to either place from Washington usually takes less than an hour's drive. But traffic in the metropolitan area can be horrendous, especially during rush hour, so plan accordingly. **Annapolis,** 30 miles (48 km) east of Washington via U.S. 50, is great for rambling. A maze of streets surrounding the **Maryland State House** feature historic homes, high-class antique shops, and a seaside dock of restaurants serving the region's famous crab cakes. **Baltimore,** in revitalizing itself over the last three decades, has managed to preserve a friendly folksiness beneath its urban veneer. You'll find world-class arts, several science museums, and a vibrant **Inner Harbor**—but also bars in **Fells Point** that ring with acoustic guitar music and joints that serve breakfast all day. Get there from Washington by driving north on I-95 or, even better, via an under-an-hour ride on an Amtrak train from **Union Station** in Washington, D.C. ■

Metro Tips

Washington's subway system is easy to navigate. Plan your routes by visiting *wmata.com*. At the stations, stand to the right on the escalators so that those in a hurry can pass up or down on the left. The farecard machines have step-by-step illustrated instructions. Buy your farecard with a small bill; change is in coins only. Long-term SmarTrip cards can be bought with a credit card and value can be added. You can ask the station manager (usually in the glass kiosk) for help if you have any difficulty.

HISTORY & CULTURE

■ The gold-leaf eagle has landed—
atop Union Station.
**Opposite: The Main Reading Room, in
the Library of Congress**

WASHINGTON TODAY

A heady self-confidence is blossoming in Washington, D.C., as the city boldly demonstrates it is a city, not some unclassifiable zone dubbed the District of Columbia—a term that appears in speeches but never in conversation.

To natives and longtime transplants, home is just Dee-Cee, thank you, or Wahr-shington in soft Southern-accented tones slightly edged by the oddly Elizabethan flint of dialects around the Chesapeake Bay. Washington never forgets that the government is the reason this once marshy lowland was reclaimed and the federal city was planted at a bend in the Potomac River. Yet the city defiantly transcends its role as a bland backdrop to the grandeur of the monuments, museums, and great American history hereabouts. Those things are why many people come—but not why they stay.

The map looks as if something took a ragged bite out of the once perfect 100-square-mile (259 sq km) diamond-shaped District. That happened in 1846, when Virginia reclaimed its share of the land donated to create the capital. The remaining 68 square miles (176 sq km), originally part of Maryland, make an intimate city of 689,545 people (2020 U.S. Census), a whopping 14.9 percent increase since the 2010 census.

The other physical dimension of the intimate city is up, and in Washington ambition soars higher than architecture. No building stands taller than the Capitol dome; in the densest part of town—the K Street canyon populated by lawyers and lobbyists—offices top out at the 12th floor. This architectural homage to the Capitol means the typical Washington street has one of the biggest skies in urban America. It makes walking a pleasure in a city designed with walkers in mind, with wide avenues and breathtaking sight lines anchored by Pierre-Charles L'Enfant's ceremonial circles. Turn a corner and you might see the upper quarter of the Washington Monument peeking above the modest roofline of a modern office building—a juxtaposition of the monumental capital and the working city that is quintessentially Washington.

The dual nature of the city's soul is reflected in myriad ways as power Washington and workaday Washington mingle serendipitously. Spend time shopping in Georgetown, lunching near Connecticut Avenue, or talking politics on Pennsylvania Avenue,

---

EXPERIENCE:
Take a Bus or Trolley Tour

A good way to begin your visit is with a general tour. It will help you get your bearings, introduce you to places you might not get to on your own, and give you a clue as to where you may want to spend more time later. **Big Bus Tours** (tel 877-332-8689, bigbustours.com), authorized by the National Park Service, has the National Heroes Tour, the official tour of the National Mall which also goes to Arlington National Cemetery and the Pentagon. For specialty tours and great views from open-top double-decker buses, check out **DC Tours** (dctours.us). **Old Town Trolley** (tel 202-832-9800, trolleytours.com) offers two-hour narrated tours.

■ The Capitol Reflecting Pool mirrors the U.S. Capitol and a statue of Ulysses S. Grant.

and you'll be startled to see motorcycle police appear out of nowhere and block traffic. Next you'll hear the sirens, then comes the speeding motorcade: the President on his way to some engagement, or perhaps some dignitary being whisked across town. Then the police vanish—maestros of that Washington ballet of the blacktop, the rolling blockade.

Washingtonians always know when someone important has moved down the block. Suddenly fit-looking men and women in plain clothes wearing earpieces linger about. In Glover Park, trying to guess which neighbor's house conceals the entrance to a secret FBI tunnel under the old Soviet Embassy has been a favorite parlor game.

Not that the privilege of being the nation's capital isn't sometimes a burden. The lack of a vote in Congress is a sore point. Washingtonians pay $2 billion a year in federal income taxes yet have no say in how the money is spent. Repeated attempts to repeal that have failed. In November 2016, 86 percent of D.C. residents voted for statehood. On June 26, 2020, the Democrat-controlled U.S. House of Representatives passed the "Washington, D.C. Admission Act," creating the State of Washington, D.C., plus a much reduced and separate, constitutionally-required Federal District, but the bill died in the Republican-controlled Senate.

As Washington strides into the future, its aspirations rise in glass and limestone amid the marble totems of its past. Construction cranes hover throughout the downtown like a new kind of Washington monument while layers of scaffolding signal exciting new uses of old spaces: a buzzing 7th Street corridor, luxury hotel rooms inside the 19th-century Tariff Building, and welcome makeovers of august institutions such as the Smithsonian's Air & Space Museum and District Wharf.

> **District residents take infinite comfort that Ben's Chili Bowl on U Street continues to purvey the best chili dogs in the free world.**

Preservation guidelines are intended to ensure that development travesties don't mar the best of the old; still, there's always a fear that shiny new facades and high rents will doom quirky neighborhood joints. A buttoned-down town like Washington needs as many of these places as it can get. District residents take infinite comfort that Ben's Chili Bowl on U Street continues to purvey the best chili dogs in the free world. Around Ben's, the street that was once known as the "Black Broadway," where native son Duke Ellington played, throbs again with energy beneath the soulful gaze of Ellington himself—painted larger than life on an alley mural (1213 U St., N.W.) also featuring the Obamas and other African-American heroes.

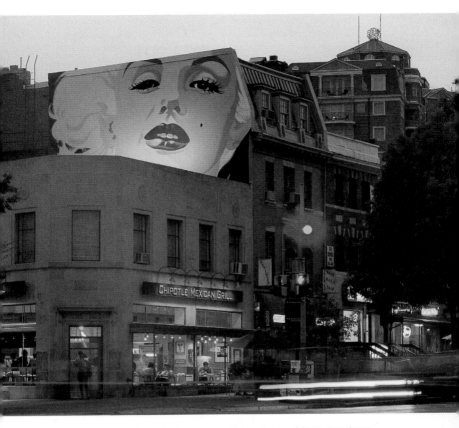

■ **Marilyn Monroe is a regular on the busy corner of Calvert Street and Connecticut Avenue.**

Postcard Washington is a vision of famous buildings, but the people make the city. Contrary to reputation, this is not a population of transients, a capital of people from someplace else getting ready to leave. When a presidential administration changes, or a new Congress is seated, only a few thousand people arrive to replace the few thousand on their way out.

Most Washingtonians don't work for the government. Many settled here for opportunities in technology, education, public policy, international affairs, and journalism. A large core of native Washingtonians, particularly African-American families, moved here from the South generations ago when jobs in the federal government afforded one of the few avenues of advancement for blacks. Now about 45 percent of the population is black, 37 percent white. The growing Asian and Hispanic communities are about 10 percent.

In the late 1990s Washingtonians began to hear real estate agents use a surprising word to describe the city: "Hot!" Suburban traffic congestion, falling crime, and an improving economy merged to make city living fashionable again. Decades of population loss subsided, replaced by slight annual gains. The newcomers are busy restoring row houses in once neglected neighborhoods and filling new condo complexes, with the ease of the Metro at their doorstep.

Even longtime Washingtonians still savor monumental Washington. They stand at the top of the Capitol steps and try again to absorb the perfect landscape geometry lesson that is the Mall. They visit their favorite Smithsonian exhibits religiously and take in the latest additions and remakes, often after the crowds are gone. They wait to see the Washington Monument at sundown, when the marble turns rose and gold.

But Washingtonians would just as soon leave the Mall and zip out to the National Arboretum in Northeast to study the exquisite bonsai tree exhibition. Or take the kids on an excursion to the remains of the Civil War forts that once ringed the city. Or catch a home baseball game since the national pastime returned to the capital in 2005 after a 34-year hiatus. Or disappear into the wilds of Rock Creek Park, where you can forget you are in a major city. It is places like these—beyond the Mall—where the

■ **Follow the beat at the beautifully landscaped Meridian Park (16th and Euclid Streets).**

Who Lives Here

To the people who call it home, Washington isn't just tiny D.C.—but the entire Washington Metropolitan Area, which includes parts of Virginia and Maryland. Total population: 5.4 million. Greater Washington has one of the most affluent, diverse, and educated populations in the United States.

• Some 51 percent of residents 25 and older have a bachelor's degree, 25 percent an advanced degree. D.C. has 50 local colleges and universities.

• The area's median household income is the country's highest: $91,414 (2020).

• Diplomatic missions of 174 countries work at embassies in D.C., most of which are near Dupont Circle, Kalorama, and along Massachusetts Avenue—on Embassy Row.

• According to a *Wall Street Journal* survey, Washington tied with Seattle as the No. 1 "youth magnet."

heart of the living city beats in four quadrants. The perfect coda to seeing the Lincoln Memorial is a visit to the Frederick Douglass house in Anacostia. During the Potomac springtime, when the perfume of Southern blooms intoxicates even the most hopeless workaholic, by all means go to see the cherry blossoms suspended like pink breath around the Tidal Basin—but also don't miss the less crowded and still spectacular blossom display at Dumbarton Oaks in Georgetown.

Spanish will get you as far as English in the Adams Morgan neighborhood, where club music blares until 2 a.m. The cuisine in this multicultural part of town runs from Ethiopian and Salvadoran to Vietnamese and Caribbean; there are even dishes from the top of the world at the Himalayan Heritage restaurant. Hop the Metro to the Southwest waterfront and find the latest Pulitzer Prize–winning play at the renovated Arena Stage or the freshest catch from the Chesapeake being hawked on the Maine Avenue docks.

It's in the neighborhoods that Washington comes most clearly into perspective. Make your way up the hill in Anacostia that John Wilkes Booth crossed when escaping after he assassinated Abraham Lincoln, and take in the view from the historic Frederick

> **Spanish will get you as far as English in the Adams Morgan neighborhood, where club music blares until 2 a.m.**

Douglass house. Or find a perch on the Brookland heights occupied by the Basilica of the National Shrine of the Immaculate Conception. Washington, D.C., spreads out before you—the low downtown skyline slipping into rings of row house neighborhoods stretched along the long lines of L'Enfant's broad boulevards.

And there, too, are the white dome and the obelisk—still grand at this distance, but not so dominating, and part of a larger picture. ∎

HISTORY OF WASHINGTON

George Washington, Pierre-Charles L'Enfant, and the many others involved knew they were engaged in something momentous when they set out to design the capital of the United States in the late 1700s. In an age when preplanned cities of this scale were unheard of, here was a chance to lay out a worldwide center of culture, commerce, learning, and government.

Doing It on Purpose

Seven years had passed since the Revolutionary War when, in July 1790, Congress agreed on the location of a new capital. Until that time, citizens of the new nation had identified primarily with their home state, thinking of themselves as Virginians or New Yorkers rather than Americans. Local ties would continue to command the loyalties of many, but it was clear that establishing the seat of a central government was essential to holding the loosely joined republic together.

One key was to avoid the mistakes of the European empires that had failed the very people who were here now. This was to be a government of the people, so the placement and design of the capital would set the tone for a federal government that aspired to be strong but not domineering. The capital, by extension, must be grand yet welcoming.

The first step in that tall order was to pick an appropriate virgin tract. With the 13 Colonies strewn the length of the eastern seaboard, it was logical to locate the capital about halfway down. In a classic display of democratic compromise, Secretary of the Treasury Alexander Hamilton agreed to urge northern states to vote for a southern capital if Virginia Representative James Madison would support federal assumption of state war debts (he did). So despite occupying the approximate midpoint of the coast, Washington was deemed a "Southern" town from the outset, a characterization that had much to do with the fact that Washington lay 60 miles (96 km) south of the Mason-Dixon Line—the Maryland-Pennsylvania border that divides North and South.

As for the precise size and the location of the new city, Congress left President Washington somewhat in the dark. The representatives decreed only that the capital was not to exceed 10 miles square (26 sq km), and that it must be positioned on the Potomac River between the mouth of the Eastern Branch (now called the Anacostia

Smith on the Potomac

Journeying far from Jamestown, Capt. John Smith and his men sailed up the Potomac River in June 1608. It was part of two trips, totaling nearly 3,000 miles (4,800 km), to explore the Chesapeake Bay and surrounding waterways. On the Potomac they went as far as Great Falls, Virginia. From late winter through August, fish such as herring and sturgeon swam upriver. Smith wrote: "Neither better fish, more plenty, not more variety for small fish had any of us ever seen in a place." Along the "Patowmeck" the men saw several villages of Indians—probably Algonquin—on the shore of what is now George Washington Memorial Parkway; one village occupied present-day Theodore Roosevelt Island.

■ A statue of George Washington stands inside the U.S. Capitol.

River) and Conococheague Creek, some 70 miles (112 km) upriver. The rest was up to Washington.

In January of 1791, Washington selected a swatch of land at the highest navigable point on the Potomac River, where it was joined by the Eastern Branch. The site was partly a marriage of convenience: The preexisting river-port towns of Alexandria, Virginia, and Georgetown, Maryland, could easily receive shipments of the lumber and other supplies the city would need to sustain construction.

Laid out in a square carved from Maryland (mostly) and Virginia, the capital was named "City of Washington" to honor America's first president. Surveyor Andrew Ellicott and Benjamin Banneker—his self-taught, freeborn black assistant—delimited a square 10 miles (26 sq km) on a side, with the corners pointing in the cardinal directions. Though President Washington had trained as a surveyor, like any good leader he was quick to recognize those moments when he needed expert advice. For his chief engineer he chose a well-connected young Frenchman who had fought against the British

■ **The ruins of the U.S. Capitol following British attempts to burn the building during the War of 1812**

during the Revolutionary War and had gone on to design a temporary headquarters for the federal government in New York. The idea of creating an important city out of nothing appealed mightily to the brilliant Pierre-Charles L'Enfant—and apparently daunted him not at all. Angling for the job, he wrote these words to President Washington in 1789: "No nation, perhaps, had ever before the opportunity offered them of deliberately deciding on the spot where their Capital City should be fixed."

L'Enfant got the job. Throughout 1791, he could be seen standing high atop Jenkins Hill (now Capitol Hill) or striding the woods of Tiber Creek (modern-day Constitution Avenue), his surveying instruments in hand, measuring distances and elevations. By contrast, L'Enfant's motivation—a vision of a grand city of broad avenues, monumental government edifices, and stirring vistas—remained invisible to all but himself. "I see the capital city as something more than a place to live and work," he wrote. "I see it as a symbol ... [W]e should plan now with the realization that a great nation is going to rise on this continent ... Right now, we have a chance which no nation has ever given itself ... How can America plan for less than greatness?"

> **Standing a mile apart but joined by Pennsylvania Avenue, the Capitol Building and the President's House formed a barbell.**

L'Enfant Terrible

L'Enfant's extraordinary prescience and pride were voiced at a time when the country's most populous city, Philadelphia, claimed only 28,522 residents. Yet here was L'Enfant, imagining a capital of 800,000 citizens—larger than many of the European cities such as Paris that had served as his models.

As it turned out, L'Enfant was dead-on: At its population peak in 1950, Washington was home to about 802,000 people. (That number is now estimated to be 690.000.)

Standing a mile apart but joined by Pennsylvania Avenue, the Capitol Building and the President's House formed a barbell. This was the core of L'Enfant's design. (The presidential residence would not be officially named the White House until 1901.) Several broad streets would radiate from these two powerhouses, signifying their accessibility. The avenues would unspool at length before ending at circular intersections atop hills, creating views of "magnificent distances."

The Capitol would divide the city into quadrants, while a grid of numbered and lettered streets would be superimposed on the radiating avenues. The Mall, extending about 1 mile (1.6 km) west from the Capitol to the Potomac River, would be a grand esplanade similar to the one L'Enfant had beheld in Marly, near Versailles. The Frenchman foresaw fine baroque houses lining it on either side.

Within a year, L'Enfant had been fired by President Washington for insubordination and refusal to compromise. Still, his plan was largely enacted: Trees and buildings may veil a few hoped-for views of "magnificent distances," yet Dupont and Scott Circles, among others, display the beauty of the original design.

Despite its ambitious origin, the city hardly sprang up overnight. Congressmen arriving for the Inaugural session in 1800 looked out upon a dismal scene. The streets were muddy. Mosquitoes and snakes bred in abundance. Hogs and cattle roamed at will, while the unfinished Capitol and President's House had spawned attendant clusters of huts and shacks resembling refugee villages. One newly minted statesman dubbed this hardship post "a mud-hole equal to the great Serbonian bog."

With no property tax on government buildings, the city relied on real estate speculation for funding. Yet buyers were scarce: By 1800, less than 10 percent of city lots had been sold. Washington grew from 8,208 people by 1810 to 18,826 by 1830, a rate far below the national average. Gazing upon these wide, uncluttered avenues going nowhere, Charles Dickens would dub Washington "the City of Magnificent Intentions."

War Comes to Washington

The War of 1812 proved to be a turning point in the city's fortunes, which mirrored those of the country at large. In August 1814, with the British victory sealed,

redcoats landed in Maryland and marched on Washington, where they torched the Capitol, the President's House, and all federal buildings except the old Blodgett's Hotel, which housed both the Post Office and the Patent Office at the time.

> **Though slavery would not be outlawed in the city until 1862, by 1830 Washington had more free blacks than slaves.**

Afterward, Congress came close to voting that the capital be relocated. But with local bankers promising to help rebuild the city—and galvanized by the strong sense of community in adversity—Washington dug in and bounced back. President Madison repaired to the Octagon House—a friend's nearby residence—Congress moved to the Patent Office (and from there to a temporary building on the site of the present-day Supreme Court), and life went on.

The third of the District lying west and south of the river was ceded back to Virginia in 1846. Not only did the federal government have no need for the land on that side of the Potomac River, but Alexandria—having lost political advantages by its inclusion in the District—had petitioned the state to re-embrace it. This reduced Washington City to a parcel of land covering just 68 square miles (176 sq km).

■ **Fugitive slaves fleeing Eastern Maryland**

A Second City

History's most bitter irony may be that this bastion of freedom was built on slave labor. Beginning in the 1790s, plantation owners in Maryland and Virginia were paid for the use of their slaves to supplement the meager supply of skilled workers constructing the capital. In a parallel development, the city became a magnet for the disenfranchised. Situated at the northern extreme of the upper South, Washington was a natural gateway for runaway slaves. Though slavery would not be outlawed in the city until 1862, by 1830 Washington had more free blacks than slaves. A "second city"—one composed largely of African Americans—sprang to life within the federal city.

Lacking a permanently entrenched society but rich with a transient mix of foreigners and congressmen, Washington was more tolerant of blacks than were other Southern cities. From 1807 to 1861, more than 15 private black schools flourished in the district.

Occasionally, however, race riots erupted. On the heels of the Nat Turner Rebellion in 1831, the Snow Riot of 1835 was ignited by two unrelated events: A slave allegedly tried to murder the widow of the U.S. Capitol designer, William Thornton, and a white physician was arrested for possession of abolitionist tracts, whose publication or distribution was forbidden in D.C.

Rebuffed from lynching the doctor, a white mob turned its fury on Mr. Beverly Snow, the free black owner of a local restaurant. Snow escaped, but roving bands attacked black churches, schools, restaurants, and tenements for the next week. Before long the city had tightened its black codes—discriminatory laws governing the behavior of free blacks.

In the 1830s and '40s, Congress heard numerous petitions to banish slavery in

■ The Lincoln Memorial at night

Washington—the only place over which it exercised total control. Each time, shamefully, Georgetown's Southern-leaning aristocracy joined with the pro-slavery segment of Congress to keep the issue from being seriously debated.

In April 1848, 77 Washington slaves boarded the schooner *Pearl* at a city wharf and tried to escape to freedom down the Potomac River. Captured within a day, the slaves—many of them privileged house servants with only a few years' bondage remaining—were sold off to agents in Louisiana and Georgia. The deep passions stirred by the affair led the House of Representatives to pass a resolution that year calling for an end to the slave trade in Washington.

The resolution was nothing but paper. Slavery itself continued. Free blacks were only marginally better off. Black or white, poor neighborhoods were plagued by violent crime. The seedier areas of town included Swampoodle (now the area north of Massachusetts and New Jersey Avenues) and Murder Bay (today's Federal Triangle). The latter—located between President's Park (the Ellipse) and the fetid Washington City Canal (since covered by Constitution Avenue)—was especially notorious. "Crime, filth, and poverty seem to vie with each other in a career of degradation and death," a police superintendent characterized Murder Bay in 1866. "Whole families ... are crowded into mere apologies for shanties."

Brother Against Brother

Monumental Washington started to take shape in the years leading up to the Civil War. Work began on the Washington Monument in 1848, but within six years funds had dried up, the monument was mired in political controversy, and construction was suspended with the building just 152 feet (46 m) tall. By the time work resumed in 1880, white marble from the original quarry was no longer available; the white marble furnished by the second quarry has weathered differently from the base, yielding the two-tone tower in evidence today.

The distinctive red-sandstone Smithsonian Castle rose beside the Mall in 1855, paving the way for several national museums. A forerunner to the National Theatre was in place on Pennsylvania Avenue by 1835. The Willard and other fine hotels popped up in the neighborhood by the 1850s. Amid the statuary and posh town houses of Lafayette Square, the President's House had settled into a state of manorial dignity, complete with greenhouses, flower gardens, and fruit trees.

Destined to tower above it all, the Capitol's cast-iron dome (replacing its wood dome of 1822) was under way by the Civil War's outbreak in April 1861. Despite an absence of building funds during that conflict, Lincoln ordered the Capitol's construction to go forward as a sign that the Union would endure.

Considered a remote and somewhat sleepy town before the Civil War, Washington now entered the national consciousness as the staging ground for Union forces and the embattled capital of a divided nation. With the Confederate capital of Richmond, Virginia, just 100 miles (160 km) distant, the war's major battles—Fredericksburg, Antietam, Gettysburg—formed an arc within easy striking distance of Washington. The first and second battles of Bull Run, for example, took place just 30 miles (48 km) west of city limits.

To keep the Rebels at bay should they outflank the Union Army, a ring of 68 forts was hastily thrown up around Washington. These installations proved their worth in July 1864, when a large Confederate force led by Gen. Jubal Early dashed through Maryland and reached the city's northern portal of Fort Stevens. Early's assault was repulsed within a day, but it gave the president a vivid taste of combat: Observing the skirmish from the fort's parapet, the 6-foot-4-inch (1.93 m) top-hatted Lincoln made such a tempting target for enemy sharpshooters that a Union officer reprimanded him, "Get down, you damn fool, before you get shot!" The words were out of his mouth before the speaker—Lt. Col. (and future Supreme Court justice) Oliver Wendell Holmes, Jr.—realized he was upbraiding the president.

> **The distinctive red-sandstone Smithsonian Castle rose beside the Mall in 1855, paving the way for several national museums.**

Washington was eventually overwhelmed—by its own troops. Bone-weary soldiers arrived by ship and rail, thronging the streets, falling asleep on vacant lots and sidewalks. Horse-drawn guns and caissons rutted the muddy streets; livestock grazed on the Mall; a bakery and barracks opened in the Capitol.

With more than 4,000 prostitutes in residence, a newspaper reported, the "majority of the women on the streets were openly disreputable." Troops under Gen. Joseph Hooker were such constant patrons of the red-light district southeast of the Treasury Department that the area was dubbed "Hooker's Division." An epiphet was born.

As battle casualties poured into Washington, the city scrambled to treat as many as 50,000 sick or injured soldiers at once. Practically every church, public building, and large private home in the city was pressed into service as military housing.

Happy Days Again

The population explosion unleashed by the war—during which the city grew from 60,000 to 140,000 inhabitants, including 40,000 former slaves—continued to boom in peacetime. Freedmen's Village in Arlington and Barry Farm in Anacostia received federal aid to house northward-migrating blacks.

With the help of radical Republicans bent on Reconstruction, black Washington enjoyed a sudden (if short-lived) heyday in the late 1860s and early 1870s. Howard University and the nation's first black high school—both staffed by top-notch instructors turning out well-educated graduates—were founded during this period. At the same time, blacks moved into jobs as officials and clerks, launched newspapers and other businesses, and mingled in white society.

Washington had elected its own mayors and aldermen since 1820. With the city in debt and officials apprehensive about the power of the newly granted black vote, Congress scrapped that system in 1871 and replaced it with a territorial government headed by a presidentially appointed governor. The new city government included boards of public works and health; a nonvoting delegate to Congress; an elected house of delegates; and a president-appointed council, with Frederick Douglass one of three blacks among its 11 members.

President Ulysses S. Grant wanted to hand the governorship of this newborn political

Politics as Unusual

If it is true that all politics is local, Washington is no exception. Washingtonians, fueled by the injustice of being deprived of full congressional representation, often obsessively focus on local politics.

Except for a brief flowering of self-governance from 1812 to 1871, Congress and the president long controlled the city government and appointed its officials. In 1970, Washington was finally allowed to send a delegate to the House of Representatives but without major voting authority.

In 1973 civil rights and home rule activists won Washington the right to elect its own mayor and city council. But Congress retained the right to interfere in local government whenever it deemed necessary. That happened in 1995: With district finances in a shambles, Congress created a presidentially appointed D.C. financial control board that took over the city reins for a while.

After the 1998 mayoral election of Anthony Williams, previously the city's chief financial officer, the health of the city improved dramatically and the control board eventually released its grip on Washington.

After Adrian Fenty took office in 2007, he launched an ambitious program of improvements that included major reform of the city's public schools, new recreational facilities, and economic development. He was defeated in re-election by Vincent Gray, whose single term was plagued by hiring and campaign finance scandals. In 2014, D.C. council member Muriel Bowser defeated Gray to win two terms as mayor.

entity to his crony Alexander R. "Boss" Shepherd. He backed down when the city's conservative old guard protested his choice, but Shepherd wormed his way into power nonetheless: He was named vice president of public works, a post that allowed him to run the entire city.

"How is our new governor like a sheep?" went a riddle popular at the time.

"He is led by A. Shepherd" was the answer.

By hook but mostly by crook, Boss Shepherd led the way for the next three years. During his reign the city added miles of sewers, water lines, gas lines, sidewalks, and roads, as well as 60,000 trees and more than 1,000 houses and buildings. Most important, Shepherd saw to it that miles upon miles of streets were leveled and paved. Working people adored him for the jobs and civic improvements; blue bloods despised him for raising their taxes.

> **In Washington as in many other American cities, the final quarter of the 19th century was a fin de siècle free-for-all.**

As it turned out, citizens were amply justified in feeling fleeced. Authorized to spend $4 million on the city, Shepherd approved the expenditure of $20 million instead. This put the city in hock but landed Shepherd in a mansion on Farragut Square, two blocks from the White House.

Armed with Grant's tacit approval, Shepherd bullied the city into submission. When the Baltimore & Ohio Railroad delayed removing its tracks from the Capitol grounds, Shepherd loyalists materialized at midnight to rip up the offending ties and rails. He invited critics of such tactics to "git up and git."

Shepherd's undoing was the financial panic of 1873. The next year, Congress dissolved the territorial government and installed three presidentially appointed commissioners. The Organic Act of 1878 abolished home rule for good, giving the three commissioners "near-absolute power." It also set up the system whereby the district receives an annual operating subsidy from the federal government for the costs that the federal presence places on the city. The federal government now employs some 283,000 people, about 15 percent of the region's workforce, and suburban commuters hold many of these jobs.

Into the 20th Century

In Washington as in many other American cities, the final quarter of the 19th century was a fin de siècle free-for-all. Hotels, public buildings, and arriviste villas mushroomed along the city's main avenues. Though industry was confined to a handful of gristmills and breweries in Georgetown and Foggy Bottom, Washington's main employer—the federal government—provided thousands of jobs. In addition to the clerks needed to run the many newly born government agencies, construction workers were in demand to complete the long-delayed Washington Monument (1884), to construct the Library of Congress (1897), and to erect many other buildings that are city landmarks today. The National Zoological Park (1889) and Rock Creek Park (1890) were also created, putting the pleasures of nature within easy reach of downtown museums and monuments.

Even as official Washington flourished, the city was nurturing seeds of discontent. Thousands of poor people had gravitated to the capital, lured by the simple notion that the president's adoptive hometown would welcome them as well. Rarely was that the case. Washington's alleys, home to more than 17,000 residents, were notorious incubators of filth, crime, and disease. Most of these alleys would ultimately be torn down or gentrified, driving the poor underclass from one neighborhood to another.

To help the growing city realize the beauty envisioned by L'Enfant, in 1901 Senator James McMillan proposed a commission that would upgrade the Mall, expand the White House and the park system, and place judicial and congressional office buildings facing the Capitol. McMillan recruited four brilliant designers—architects Charles McKim and Daniel Burnham, landscape architect Frederick Law Olmsted, and sculptor Augustus Saint-Gaudens—whose plans, drawn up free of charge, would be transformed into reality by the U.S. Army Corps of Engineers.

With Burnham leading the way, the city beautification began to take shape. Railroad tracks crisscrossing the Mall were torn out. The Mall was extended to stretch all the way from the Capitol to the site of a planned memorial to Abraham Lincoln at its far west end. Gardens, fountains, and a reflecting pool were slated for the Mall as well. An opulent tram station—Union Station—designed by Burnham himself, rose north of the Capitol.

Not every aspect of the plan was enacted, yet it furnished a blueprint for future growth of the city core. It's fair to say that the McMillan Plan made possible the Mall's current status as a national showpiece.

Struggles for Freedom

During the 1910s, the city's population swelled again as workers flooded in to support America's role in World War I. By decade's end, nearly 450,000 people called Washington home—a 32 percent increase since 1910. The Mall, which had begun to feel like a park, became a vast parking lot for hundreds of new automobiles that suddenly appeared in Washington.

With the proliferation of relief agencies during the Great Depression and President Franklin D. Roosevelt's New Deal, the number of workers on Washington's federal payroll rose from 70,261 in June 1933 to 108,673 in June 1935. Construction added many new facades to the cityscape: the Supreme Court building, the Federal Triangle buildings, the Library of Congress Annex (now called the John Adams Building), the Longworth House Office Building, and nearly 5,000 houses, apartment buildings, and office buildings.

As the city focused its efforts on winning World War II, the early 1940s brought yet another influx of new Washingtonians. Thousands of female office workers and servicemen descended on the city, and many of them stayed on after the war. By 1950, the district's population would peak at just over 800,000.

Once again, the National Mall became a warehouse for the nation's wartime needs. A beehive of "tempos"—temporary government office buildings made of cement and asbestos board—were built along both sides of the Mall, adding to those thrown up during World War I.

> **In 1945, Washington found itself the capital of the most powerful nation on Earth. It had evolved from a small Southern town.**

In 1945, Washington found itself the capital of the most powerful nation on Earth. It had evolved from a small Southern town. In little more than half a century it had become a world leader. The city seemed to be flexing its new muscles, spearheading a Cold War against communism worldwide. On a local level, however, the story of Washington was increasingly a tale of two cities. More and more, white and black Washingtonians led separate lives in separate parts of town. Throughout the 1940s,

The March on Washington for Jobs and Freedom filled the National Mall in August 1963.

D.C.'s schools, parks, playgrounds, restaurants, theaters, and water fountains remained as segregated as those in any Southern town.

Then, in 1954, came the U.S. Supreme Court ruling, in *Brown* v. *Board of Education,* that "separate but equal education facilities are inherently unequal." The ensuing rapid integration of D.C. public schools served as a model for the nation.

In the late 1950s, blacks outnumbered whites for the first time in Washington history. The far reaches of the city's Northeast and Southeast quadrants had drawn a raft of new residents since World War II, most of them from rural backgrounds. Now, with whites leaving the crowded city for the suburbs, middle-class blacks moved en masse into such upper Northeast neighborhoods as Fort Totten and Brookland. From 1950 to 1975, the city's black population rose from 35 percent to more than 70.

With the appointment of Walter Washington as mayor-commissioner in 1967, black Washington gained a degree of control over its affairs for the first time since the dissolution of the territorial government nearly a hundred years earlier. Congress, however, retained final say over city governance—a power it continues to wield. This has created a troubling and inequitable political quirk: Washingtonians are the only modern Americans who suffer "taxation without representation," as some city vehicle licenses protest. D.C. voters can elect only a nonvoting delegate (as opposed to representatives) to Congress, yet that body has veto power over Washington's laws and budgets—a bone of lingering local contention and resentment.

The People's Parade Ground

The National Mall—the country's unofficial forum—has long been a rallying point for social causes. The women's suffrage movement, for example, demonstrated here in the 1910s; two decades later, thousands of Bonus Marchers descended on the Capitol to demand veterans' benefits, only to be run off by Gen. Douglas MacArthur's cavalry.

On August 28, 1963, more than 200,000 people marched on Washington to demand jobs and freedom for blacks. The event culminated in the rousing "I Have a Dream" speech delivered by Dr. Martin Luther King, Jr., on the steps of the Lincoln Memorial.

Television cameras caught the historic moment, which was seen by millions of people across the nation.

This progress was tragically interrupted in April 1968, when Dr. King fell to an assassin's bullet on a motel balcony in Memphis, Tennessee. Around the country, grief erupted in spasms of violence. In Washington, rioting and looting broke out near the intersection of 14th and U Streets in Northwest and spread outward from there. Eventually the conflagration gutted 57 blocks in the heart of the city, crippling the once thriving retail district downtown. Twelve people died and several hundred were injured amid the chaos.

It took 4,000 U.S. Army and National Guard troops three days to restore the peace. But the scars, emotional and physical, lingered for years. Not until the late 1990s did some areas recover. The U Street corridor, for instance, has been spruced up and now draws visitors from all backgrounds.

A Fresh Start

The seeds of the city's rejuvenation had been planted several years before the 1968 riots. In 1961, President John F. Kennedy and his wife, Jackie, initiated improvements to the city core. They applied a mix of historic preservation and urban renewal to Lafayette Square and to the part of Pennsylvania Avenue from the White House to the Capitol.

A few years later, the landscape received another official face-lift, this time from Lady Bird Johnson and her "Beautify America" campaign, which added tulips, daffodils, and flowering trees and shrubs to the banks of Rock Creek and the Potomac River.

1971 was a pivotal year in the city's growing emphasis on aesthetics. The Mall's temporary structures were finally removed to make way for Constitution Gardens—a 50-acre (20 ha) park north of the Reflecting Pool—and the John F. Kennedy Center for the Performing Arts opened on the Potomac River just off the Theodore Roosevelt Memorial Bridge. Inscribed on a wall of the Kennedy Center are the words of arts patron JFK: "This country cannot afford to be materially rich and spiritually poor."

Yet poverty is still an ugly reality of Washington. As of 2021, median household income for the District was $139,500, but the income gap between the city's poor and wealthy residents is one of the widest of major U.S. cities, with whites averaging $150,380

A Makeover for the Mall

Laid out in 1791 as part of the master plan for the nation's capital, the Mall, 2 miles (3.2 km) long, was never designed for the level of use it gets today. Every year about 36 million people visit the Mall, including 10 million from overseas. It is the city's most heavily visited area.

In July 2010, the National Park Service released plans for a $700 million makeover. The improvements included new landscaping, paved pathways, and a visitor center for the Vietnam Veterans Memorial.

The Reflecting Pool near the Lincoln Memorial was once again filled with water, after a $34 million rehabilitation. Both the pool and its surrounds were upgraded, with concrete sidewalks replacing gravel paths. The marble D.C. War Memorial was restored, and the seawalls of the Tidal Basin around the Jefferson Memorial were stabilized. And in May 2014, a complete restoration of the Washington Monument was completed followed damage caused by a 5.8-magnitude earthquake and Hurricane Irene, two days apart in August 2011.

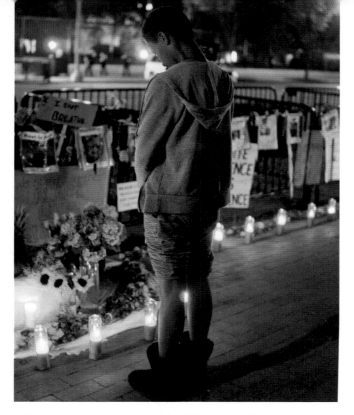

■ **Black Lives Matter protests in front of the White House in 2020**

and blacks $67,850. Meanwhile, during the attack of September 11, 2001, Islamic terrorists flew an American Airlines plane into the Pentagon; United Airlines flight 73—which had targeted the White House—crashed in Pennsylvania after passengers overpowered the hijackers. Thereafter security throughout the city was massively increased.

Poking fun at Washington politics has become a national pastime, yet the city possesses a beauty, grandeur, and cultural richness that can win over even the most hardened cynic. Many Americans have a soft spot for the nation's capital and relish an opportunity to visit. Indeed, a record crowd of 1.5 million flocked to the National Mall on January 20, 2009, to witness Barack Obama being sworn in as the country's president; another one million appeared for his second Inaugural in 2013. Only one-third that number attended Donald Trump's inauguration on January 20, 2017, followed next day by the largest-ever mass protest in U.S. history as more than 470,000 attended the Women's March on Washington to protest sexism. Trump's contentious term in office ended ignominiously after Democratic nominee Joe Biden defeated the incumbent president in the November 2020 election. Thereafter, Trump waged a campaign to subvert the election, culminating on January 6, 2021, in a violent assault by his supporters against a joint session of the U.S. Congress as it prepared to formalize Biden's victory. ■

CITY ON THE RIVER

Most people don't think of Washington as a riverside city, yet the Potomac is the wildest watercourse running through any major metropolis in the United States. Explore Washington by water, and you'll leave a world of traffic, concrete, and crowds for a realm where turtles bask on logs, an osprey wings low with a fish flashing in its talons, and your neighbor glides by in a scull.

The Potomac River (nicknamed the Nation's River) has been the heart of Washington since Georgetown was founded as a shipping center in 1751. By the 1790s the harbor was exporting more tobacco than any other port in the country. Later, the Chesapeake & Ohio Canal (whose towpath you can still amble) connected Georgetown to villages inland, fueling both their growth and that of the capital city.

With affluence came effluence: The Potomac was declared unfit for bathing as early as 1894, and even touching the bacteria-laden water was deemed unwise as late as 1971. Political commentator Patrick Buchanan, a native son, used the river's pollution to make a political statement: "Just as there's garbage that pollutes the Potomac River, there is garbage polluting our culture. We need an Environmental Protection Agency to clean it up."

The 1970s saw a concerted, community-wide effort to clean up the river. Today, the fish are back, the birds have returned, and the water bobs with all manner of recreational craft: canoes, kayaks, rowing shells, sailboats, and—alas—Jet Skis.

At water level, the city takes on a different cast. Near the shore a great blue heron freezes in mid-stride, waiting for a fish. In the safety of mid-river, bass break the surface to feed on hatching bugs. Keen-eyed ospreys peer down from shaggy nests, screaming if you venture too close, while bald eagles soar high above.

EXPERIENCE: Seeing Washington by Water

Many visitors take to the river aboard narrated cruises for sweeping views of the city or sign up for an even more leisurely trip to Mount Vernon. Meal and moonlight cruises are available; schedules vary daily and seasonally. Options include **Capitol River Cruises** (tel 301-460-7447, capitolrivercruises.com); and luxury **City Cruises by Hornblower** (tel 800-459-8105, cityexperiences.com), whose options include a 2-hour buffet brunch cruise. **Potomac Riverboat Company** (tel 703-684-0580, potomacriverboatco.com) offers cruises as well as a water taxi service that will ferry you to a day of shopping at National Harbor (down the Potomac in Maryland) or an evening baseball game at Nationals Park. For something really cool, cruise the Potomac on *Providence*, a reproduction of Capt. John Paul Jones' 18th-century sloop operated by the **Tall Ship Providence Foundation** (tel 703-772-8483, tallshipprovidence.org). **Embark DC Boat Tours** (tel 202-570-2410, embarkdc.com) offers private skippered speedboat trips.

Or spend a few hours quietly skimming the river by canoe, kayak, or rowing shell. Rent from **Thompson Boat Center** (2900 Virginia Ave., N.W., tel 202-337-9642, thompsonboatcenter.com) or **The Wharf Boathouse** (700 Water St., N.W., tel 202-337-9642, boatingindc.com.com). **Atlantic Kayak** (tel 301-292-6455, atlantickayak.com) offers rentals as well as instruction and guided tours.

GEORGETOWN

M STREET

Francis Scott
Key Bridge
WHITEHURST
FWY.
Potomac
Riverboat

PENN. AVE.

GEORGE WASHINGTON MEM. PKWY.

29

Washington
Harbour
Thompson
Boat Center
Watergate

Theodore
Roosevelt I.

Theodore
Roosevelt
Mem. Bridge

Kennedy Center

50

237

50

CONSTITUTION   AVENUE

Marine Corps
War Memorial

Lincoln
Memorial

WWII
Memorial

Washington Monument

INDEPENDENCE AVE.

50

Arlington
House

Arlington
Memorial
Bridge

F.D.R.
Memorial

Tidal Basin

Cherry
Blossoms

1

395

WATER ST.

9TH ST.

Columbia
Island

110

ARLINGTON
NATIONAL
CEMETERY

Jefferson
Memorial

The Wharf
Boathouse

Water Street
docks

Embark DC
Boat Tours

27

BOUNDARY DR.

MEMORIAL

PARKWAY

395

EAST
POTOMAC
PARK

WASHINGTON

Air Force
Memorial

Pentagon
Memorial

Pentagon

27

14th
Street
Bridges

Fort
McNair

244

395

A R L I N G T O N

Gravelly
Point

Potomac

Hains
Point

Anacostia
Naval
Station

V
I
R
G
I
N
I
A

GEORGE WASHINGTON MEM. PKWY.

Ronald
Reagan
Washington
National
Airport

Anacostia

WASHINGTON, D.C.

120

Giving the wildlife a run
for their money, Washington's
iconic landmarks appear both
grander and more intimate from
the water. You can get especially
close-up views of the Lincoln Memorial, Kennedy Center, and Jefferson
Memorial. And with water sightseeing
comes outstanding photo ops.

As you glide beneath one of the
nine graceful arches of Memorial Bridge,
Robert E. Lee's home, Arlington House,
looms above Arlington Cemetery on the
river's Virginia shore.

Opposite Washington Harbour, the
heavily wooded, 88-acre (36 ha) Theodore Roosevelt Island makes a delightfully
natural destination teeming with geese,
snapping turtles, and beavers—and perfect for a great-outdoors picnic lunch.

Mount Vernon Trail

1

DAINGERFIELD
ISLAND

Bolling
Air Force
Base

295

ALEXANDRIA

400

0   1 kilometer

0   1/2 miles

Naval
Research
Lab

OLD TOWN

Tall Ship Providence

KING ST.

To
National
Harbor

DUKE ST.

To
Mount
Vernon

THE ARTS

Despite being the birthplace of many gifted musicians and actors—among them John Philip Sousa, Duke Ellington, Helen Hayes, and Pearl Bailey—an artistic community of note did not really coalesce here until 1971, when the John F. Kennedy Center for the Performing Arts welcomed its first music and theater patrons. Today, Washington is a leading center of the arts worldwide.

Classical Music

One of the nation's finest orchestral companies, the National Symphony Orchestra (NSO) was officially incorporated in 1931. At the opening of the Kennedy Center 40 years later, the NSO premiered Leonard Bernstein's "Mass," a work commissioned for the occasion. The orchestra now has a busy year-round season that includes local performances in the Kennedy Center Concert Hall, tours in this country and abroad, televised Independence Day and Memorial Day concerts on the West Lawn of the U.S. Capitol, and programs for visiting heads of state and music festivals.

Branching out in recent years, the NSO has expanded its programs to include more contemporary music as well as classical favorites. After six years under Christoph Eschenbach, in 2018, the orchestra tapped Gianandrea Noseda to infuse new energy as music director.

From a regional company struggling to make its name in 1956, the Washington National Opera has evolved into a world-class organization playing to sellout audiences in the Opera House at the Kennedy Center: It now stages up to eight operas a year. The opera is under the artistic direction of Francesca Zambello, whose theatrical honors include three Olivier Awards. A commitment to staging new American operas and epic-scale productions, bringing out lesser known important works, and nurturing young talent keeps this company in the mainstream of the opera world.

Music lovers in Washington can find a concert any night of the week, whether performed by a D.C.-based or visiting group. The Kennedy Center has hosted renowned companies from around the world, including the Berlin Philharmonic Orchestra, the Metropolitan Opera, and La Scala, while the Millennium Stage program brings free daily performances of all sorts of musical genres to the Kennedy Center's Grand Foyer.

> **Music lovers in Washington can find a concert any night of the week, whether performed by a D.C.-based or visiting group.**

Just north of Washington, near the Grosvenor–Strathmore Metro stop, the Music Center at Strathmore features the Baltimore Symphony Orchestra, the National Philharmonic, and other arts performance groups. A converted mansion and an 11-acre (4.4 ha) setting make for pleasant surroundings. In the heart of the city, Lisner Auditorium at George Washington University is a comfortable 1,490-seat hall, and other area universities feature music by local and guest artists. Downtown churches and museums often schedule musical events: Concerts at the National Gallery of Art, the Phillips

■ **A ballerina performs the Washington Ballet's *Carmen* at the Kennedy Center.**

■ **D.C. native and jazz maestro Duke Ellington gazes from a painting on sale at Eastern Market.**

Collection, and the Library of Congress can be wonderfully intimate occasions. The 670-seat auditorium at the National Academy of Sciences, with its excellent acoustics, occasionally offers free concerts, often of new music. Another small venue, the Folger Shakespeare Library, presents medieval, Renaissance, and baroque music in an Elizabethan setting.

Many music aficionados consider the District of Columbia to be the nation's capital of choral music. The Choral Arts Society of Washington, under artistic director and maestro Scott Tucker, regularly performs in concert with the National Symphony Orchestra and touring orchestras.

Popular Music

Washington has historically excelled at military band music. The U.S. Marine Band received a great boost in 1868 when a local 13-year-old boy signed up as an apprentice. His name was John Philip Sousa, and within 12 years he would assume leadership of the band. Dismayed by the band's outdated and poorly arranged music, Sousa sent off to Europe for scores by Wagner, Berlioz, and other modern composers of the day. He also began writing music of his own. Demanding excellence from others as well as from himself, Sousa drilled the band into shape. Many members quit within a year, but those who stayed became a well-honed and disciplined unit. In 1892 Sousa formed his own band and toured the United States and abroad. His tuneful lifetime outpouring ultimately included 140 original military marches, among them "The Washington Post" march (1889) and "The Stars and Stripes Forever" (1896).

Heart-poundingly patriotic performances of the illustrious U.S. Marine Band and other military combos are staged free of charge on summer evenings, alfresco, at the Sylvan Theater (on the grounds of the Washington Monument) and on the West Terrace of the Capitol. Alternatively, you might enjoy an evening tattoo at the Marine Barracks on Capitol Hill.

Another local musician who made good was jazz legend Edward Kennedy "Duke" Ellington. Born at 1217 22nd Street in 1899 and raised in the Shaw neighborhood, Ellington studied classical music with a neighbor who taught music at Dunbar High School. At 24 he headed off to New York City—and thence into the Big Band and Jazz Hall of Fame. Washington jazz has enjoyed a devoted following ever since. After the Howard Theatre opened at 7th and T Streets in 1910, it marqueed such standouts as W. C. Handy, Fletcher Henderson, Bessie Smith, and Count Basie. Duke Ellington and Pearl Bailey were among the local talents who debuted at the Howard. Another star-studded black showcase, the 1922 Lincoln Theater on U Street closed for a short while but reopened as a movie theater in the 1970s; renovated in 1994, the 1,250-seat theater today features a mixture of concerts, dance recitals, plays, and movies.

Blues Alley in Georgetown has long worn the crown as the best place in town to catch big-name jazz acts. This comfortable den has low ceilings, high cover charges, and a serious and sophisticated clientele. Other reliable spots for hearing live jazz include JoJo Restaurant & Bar in Adams Morgan and Mr. Henry's in the Lincoln Park neighborhood. Meanwhile, on 12th Street, N.E., the homey Alice's Jazz & Cultural Society is ground zero for straight-ahead jazz. The National Gallery of Art offers free jazz Friday evenings in the summer. The Kennedy Center and other venues also host a range of jazz performers.

> **Blues Alley in Georgetown has long worn the crown as the best place in town to catch big-name jazz acts.**

An endless number of options exist for rock and other popular music. These range from headliner concerts at the 20,000-seat Capitol One Arena downtown to eclectic local acts (and some up-and-coming national ones) at popular hangouts such as the 9:30 Club on V Street and the Black Cat on 14th Street. Acoustic folk and bluegrass have also carved out solid niches in the Washington area; the Birchmere in Alexandria, which nurtured Grammy-winner Mary Chapin Carpenter and bluegrass pioneers The Seldom Scene, is the top choice. The Eighteenth Street Lounge, in its new location on Blagden Alley, in Shaw, also dishes up funk, reggae, and Latin sounds.

Theater

Home to dozens of active theaters, the Washington metro area can boast more playhouses than any city besides New York. Most prominent is the Kennedy Center, with two large theaters: The 1,100-seat Eisenhower Theater is a plush venue for touring productions of dramas and comedies, while the adjacent 2,350-seat Opera House presents musicals and performances of the Washington Ballet and other dance troupes.

A theater has operated continuously on the Pennsylvania Avenue site of the National Theatre, rebuilt in the early 1920s, since 1835. In 1845 fire destroyed the building during a performance of *Beauty and the Beast*—the first of five such conflagrations in the theater's history. Until 1873, blacks were confined to the balcony; after that they were not admitted at all. Finally, in 1948, local civil rights activists campaigned to desegregate the National.

John Wilkes Booth, Jenny Lind, Helen Hayes, John Barrymore, Sarah Bernhardt, Vivien Leigh, and Katharine Hepburn have all trod the boards of the National, which has premiered such groundbreaking productions as *West Side Story* and *M. Butterfly*. It continues its tradition of offering big glittery Broadway and pre-Broadway productions.

Half a block away on 13th Street, the Warner Theatre opened in 1924 as a silent-movie palace and vaudeville stage. From 1945 to the late 1960s, it presented movies only. It then deteriorated, as did much of downtown Washington, but stayed alive with a menu of porn films and rock concerts. After closing for three years, the Warner reopened in 1992 with its rococo finery intact. It now offers a mix of musical performances and live comedy.

> **Ford's Theatre had been in business for only four years when, in 1865, it became notorious as the scene of Lincoln's assassination.**

About three blocks east of the Warner, on 10th Street, is the city's most famous theater. Ford's Theatre had been in business for only four years when, in 1865, it became notorious as the scene of Lincoln's assassination. Restored to its 1860s appearance, it now offers plays and musicals as well as spring and summer walking tours led by actors playing characters from Civil War Washington.

Probably the city's best program of serious and innovative drama is offered at Arena Stage, on the waterfront in Southwest Washington. Since its 1950 founding, Arena has pioneered the resident theater movement. Arena Stage also owns the distinction of being the first playhouse outside New York City to win a Tony Award. James Earl Jones, Ned Beatty, Jane Alexander, and other notable actors cut their teeth here. After a major face-lift, Arena moved back to its historic spaces in fall 2010, with new state-of-the-art capabilities in three separate theaters.

After 20 praiseworthy years in its original home at the Folger Shakespeare Library on Capitol Hill, the Shakespeare Theatre Company moved downtown in 1992 to the larger, 451-seat Michael R. Kelin Theatre on 7th Street. In 2007, the much acclaimed company

EXPERIENCE: Engage the City's Intellectual Life

Think about it. With a well-educated and culturally savvy population, Washington supports an abundance of activities for the curious-minded. Many events are free, but advance tickets may be required.

For 40 years, patrons have turned out in large numbers for lectures and other programs organized by **Smithsonian Associates** (smithsonianassociates.org). **"National Geographic Live"** (national geographic.com/events) features presentations by leading explorers, scientists, photographers, and authors.

Literary types may want to plan a visit that coincides with the **National Book Festival** (loc.gov/bookfest); it attracts thousands of people to the Mall every fall for appearances by numerous authors. For readings and book signings year-round—often by nationally known figures—check the events calendars of **Politics and Prose** bookstore (tel 202-364-1919, politics-prose.com) and **East City Bookshop** (tel 202-290-1636, eastcity bookshop.com). Civic affairs and progressive politics top the bill at **Busboys & Poets** (tel 202-387-7638, busboysandpoets.com). **E Street Cinema** (555 11th St., N.W., tel 202-783-9494, landmarktheatres.com) screens independent and foreign-language films, documentaries, and classic revivals.

All the city's museums and cultural institutions offer special events. At the **National Archives** (see pp. 142–143), for example, you can see free historic films, hear a historian read excerpts from a new book on the Civil War, or attend a seminar on researching your family's history.

expanded its facilities further to include the 775-seat Sidney Harman Hall at 6th and F Streets. The group also stages a summer Shakespeare play presented free to the public.

Known for its bold and eclectic contemporary plays, Studio Theatre at 14th and P Streets in the Logan Circle neighborhood has claimed many Helen Hayes awards in its three decades of existence. These homegrown awards for theatrical excellence recognize the formative contributions to local drama of Hayes, a Washington native who first appeared on a D.C. stage at the age of six and later won an Academy Award for her portrayal of the title character in 1932's *The Sin of Madelon Claudet.*

Definitive productions of Stephen Sondheim shows, such as *Sweeney Todd,* and other lively works are the hallmark of the Signature Theatre group. After 17 successful years operating in a converted auto garage, the group moved to a new theater in suburban Arlington's Shirlington Village.

Drawing strong material from political proceedings on Capitol Hill, comedy is growing more popular around town. The Capitol Steps, founded by congressional staffers, offer witty, well-polished songs and skits every Friday and Saturday night at the Ronald Reagan Building on Pennsylvania Avenue. The Connecticut Avenue comedy club DC Improv features headliners as well as promising locals doing traditional stand-up.

Fine Arts

In a city of monumental buildings and larger-than-life statuary created by some of the nation's finest architects and sculptors, D.C. art has tended to be powerful and realistic, depicting powerful people and real events. With a preponderance of these pieces being commissioned—and with many of them requiring committee approval—it's a wonder the city holds so many truly fine works of art.

■ **The interior of the East Building of the National Gallery of Art**

The U.S. Capitol, for example, is a trove of officially sanctioned art. Its chief muralist, Italian artist Constantino Brumidi (1805–1880), was known as the Michelangelo of the Capitol; his 1865 "Apotheosis of George Washington" graces the ceiling of the Rotunda. Acclaimed artist John Trumbull (1756–1843) painted the eight large historical scenes hanging in the Rotunda.

Much of the city's great painting and sculpture is housed in established museums: the National Gallery of Art, the National Portrait Gallery, the Phillips Collection. Significant works of art created on-site in Washington have tended to be in portraiture and outdoor sculpture.

Early painting in Washington was documentary as well as aesthetic: Public figures, it was agreed, should have their portraits painted for posterity. Thus locals such as George Washington and James Madison sat for eminent portrait painter Gilbert Stuart (1755–1828), who lived in Philadelphia and Boston. Another leading portrait painter of the time, Charles Willson Peale (1741–1827), completed seven life paintings of George Washington, as well as portraits of Benjamin Franklin, Thomas Jefferson, and John Adams. His son Rembrandt Peale (1778–1860) parlayed his family connections into a precocious start in portrait painting: At age 17 he produced a life portrait of George Washington. The younger Peale studied under his father, whose neoclassical style exerted a strong influence; Rembrandt Peale's 1805 portrait of Jefferson, now owned by the New-York Historical Society, is considered his masterpiece—and our best likeness of the third president.

The White House, too, has a Rembrandt Peale oil of Jefferson, as well as other fine portraits. The Reception Rooms of the Department of State hold several portraits by the Peales, Stuart, and Thomas Sully (1783–1872). Other places to look for early Washington faces include the National Portrait Gallery and the National Gallery of Art.

What did the city look like in its infancy? Thanks to the efforts of several minor artists, we have a fairly good idea. Sketches by surveyors and architects show the lay of the land around the Capitol, the White House, and other government buildings as they were going up. Views of Washington by painter George Jacob Beck depict the Georgetown waterfront in the 1790s as a Constable-style landscape, where a country lane stands sprinkled with little houses.

City views by August Kollner in the 1830s show a Potomac busy with sailboats and the new steamboats. The latter owed their existence to engineer and painter Robert Fulton (1765–1815), who in 1807 invented the first commercially successful steamboat; in the early 1800s Fulton had stayed with friends who owned a country estate that would become the Kalorama neighborhood, and he painted its pastoral scenes.

An 1832 lithograph of the west front of the Capitol by Hudson River artist Thomas Doughty (1793–1856) shows the important building in a decidedly bucolic setting; the wooded hills and cultivated fields around Jenkins Hill (now Capitol Hill) make the government structure seem almost comically out of place. Washington's rural aspect would continue to be emphasized as late as the 1880s in the sketches and drawings of isolated cabins by DeLancey W. Gill (1859–1940), an illustrator for the Smithsonian Institution's Bureau of American Ethnology. Perhaps these were in wistful lament for a town changing into a city?

An artists' salon blossomed in Washington at the turn of the 20th century. It met at the studio-home of painter and playwright Alice Pike Barney (1857–1931), at 2306 Massachusetts Avenue, next to what is now the Latvian Embassy. Overlooking Sheridan Circle, Barney's Studio House became the venue for poetry readings, plays, art shows, and other creative undertakings of the sort now associated with a multitude of Dupont addresses. Barney helped establish the Sylvan Theatre on the Mall. Both George Bernard Shaw and Alice Roosevelt Longworth sat for portraits in oil by her hand.

Nowadays many of the homes of the rich and au courant are graced by abstract art turned out by Washington Color School artists, who rose to prominence in the 1960s. Gene Davis (1920–1985), known for his boldly striped canvases, worked as a White House correspondent during the Truman years before settling down to abstract art. Sam Gilliam (1933–) stepped into the limelight with his "drape paintings" in the late

Music Under the Stars

From Sheryl Crow to Al Jarreau, *Mama Mia!* to "Prairie Home Companion," enjoy top performers of all genres at Wolf Trap National Park *(wolftrap .org)*, off the Dulles Toll Road or Route 7 in Virginia. The open-air amphitheater with covered stage, built on a sloping meadow, holds 4,000; many patrons prefer cheaper lawn seating and picnicking with friends. Two restored barns offer opera in the summer, other programs in off-summer months. There's round-trip bus service from the West Falls Church–VT/UVA Metro station.

1960s—stained, unframed canvases thrown over sawhorses and furniture, hung from ceiling beams, or draped on walls. The *Washington Post* described a 1999 show of his glass-enclosed collages of acrylic on birch plywood as "cubist African kimono sculptures." Gilliam's work has been commissioned for the Washington Convention Center and Ronald Reagan National Airport. He has also been honored with solo exhibitions and other showcases.

Literature

In more than two centuries as the nation's capital, Washington has inspired many writers to capture this power spot in prose or verse. Washington novels often aspire to capitalize on their setting by taking on the city's major industry: politics. The first classic "Washington novel"—an insider's look at the political machinations of the federal government—was probably *The Gilded Age*, an 1873 satire of political and financial shenanigans co-authored by Mark Twain and newspaper editor Charles Dudley Warner. It was followed in 1880 by *Democracy, an American Novel,* a mysterious and anonymously written exposé that became wildly popular for blowing the lid off corruption in the Grant Administration. Not until the author's death in 1918 would it be revealed that *Democracy* had been written by Henry Adams.

For history enthusiasts, Margaret Leech's *Reveille in Washington,* which won the Pulitzer Prize in 1942, offers an intimate portrait of the city during the Civil War. Many people regard it as the best book ever written about D.C. Allen Drury's *Advice and Consent* (1959) broke new ground for its startling portrayal of backroom politics.

The late Gore Vidal, the erudite author of *Washington, D.C.: A Novel* (1967) and more than 25 other books, spent much of his childhood inhaling politics at the Rock Creek Park home of his grandfather, Thomas P. Gore, a populist senator from Oklahoma. Vidal's most popular work, *Lincoln* (1984), painted a balanced and humane portrait of a president who had been only canonized until then. Vidal's novel *1876* puts recent political history into perspective. In that year, Republican Rutherford B. Hayes stole the election from Democrat Samuel J. Tilden, who had won the popular vote.

> **Washington novels often aspire to capitalize on their setting by taking on the city's major industry: politics.**

Edward P. Jones (1950-), who grew up in Washington and still lives here, may be the city's modern laureate. He won the Pulitzer Prize in 2004 for his novel *The Known World,* based on free black people who owned slaves. He has published many stories with characters inspired by daily life in Washington. Another African-American author, Marita Golden (1950-), found a rich setting for her novel *Long Distance Life* in the city's Columbia Heights neighborhood.

For a hilarious tale set in Washington during 1976, when the country was celebrating its Bicentennial, read Porter Shreve's (1966-) *When the White House Was Ours.* Published in 2008, it chronicles a family's attempt to create an alternative school in the nation's capital—modeled loosely on the author's own family.

Amid the flurry of political books emanating from Washington, some well-known pundits about town, like public television's Jim Lehrer and *Washington Post* columnist David Ignatius also, turn their attention to other genres, such as Westerns, mysteries,

STORIES IN STONE

Filled with monumental architecture and heroic statuary, Washington sometimes transcends words. The pediment of the Supreme Court's west facade, for example, shows Liberty holding the scales of justice. The scene on the pediment of the National Archives uses winged horses, rams, and papyrus flowers as classical symbols of aspiration.

As you walk around Washington, you'll encounter more equestrian statues than you'd see in any other North American city. These sculptures—most of them depicting military men astride horses in various stances—came into vogue in the late 19th century, when the nation's compulsion to honor its Civil War heroes dovetailed with the rapid growth of its capital city. As for equine symbolism, by the way, it's a myth that a horse with one hoof raised denotes its rider was wounded in battle; nor is it true that two hooves in the air suggests the rider died in battle.

Befitting its wartime role as the Federal capital, Washington bristles with Union generals in bronze. Only one Confederate officer was so honored: Even then, the statue of Brig. Gen. Albert Pike (*3rd & D Sts.*) recognized his service not as a soldier but as a Mason. Nonetheless, it was toppled and destroyed by protestors in June 2020, in the wake of the murder of George Floyd, while the statue of a Confederate soldier that stood at Prince and South Washington Streets in Old Town Alexandria was removed the same week.

Washington's late 19th-century renaissance in statuary also coincided with America's emergence as an environment favorable to artists. A nation of growing affluence and power demanded artists to document its glory. As a result, many world-renowned sculptors have work on display in Washington. One of them is Augustus Saint-Gaudens (1848–1907), a Dublin-born artist who grew up in New York City. His 1890 Adams Memorial, commissioned by author Henry Adams to honor his wife, Clover, is one of the most beautiful, moving, and remote pieces of sculpture in Washington: The cast-bronze grave marker is in a grove of

A 19-foot-high (5.8 m) marble statue of Lincoln dominates the Lincoln Memorial.

Japanese yews in Rock Creek Cemetery.

The most famous sculpture in Washington, if not the entire country, is Daniel Chester French's 1922 marble figure of Lincoln, who sits in brooding majesty 19 feet high (5.7 m) inside the rectangular marble Lincoln Memorial at the east end of the Memorial Bridge. Lincoln clenches his left hand to show strength and resolve; his right lies open to signal compassion.

What does it take to get memorialized in the nation's capital? First, you must form a citizens' group to petition Congress. A vote must then be taken, a sculptor commissioned, an approval granted by the Commission of Fine Arts, and funds raised. Only a fraction of proposals make the long journey from paper to stone.

For a guide to more than 400 of the city's outdoor sculptures, take a look at James M. Goode's *Outdoor Sculpture of Washington, D.C.* (Smithsonian Institution Press, 1974).

■ **Kramer Books & Afterwords Café is a literary landmark just north of Dupont Circle.**

and political thrillers. Local authors continue to turn out lots of books on historical figures and events. Recent examples include Scott Berg's book on D.C.'s visionary planner Pierre-Charles L'Enfant (*Grand Avenues,* 2008), Kirsten Downey's thorough biography of Frances Perkins (*Woman Behind the New Deal,* 2009), and David Taylor's look at the WPA Writers' Project during the Great Depression (*Soul of a People,* 2009).

Reporters have used journalism as a springboard to literary fame. Bob Woodward and Carl Bernstein are the best known. The 1976 film version of their book *All the President's Men* has become a classic. Another newspaperman turned literary lion, Ward Just has written several acclaimed works with a Washington-centric focus. His novel *Echo House* (1997) presents a portrait of D.C. government over eight decades and three generations.

Poets, too, have been central in the city's literary life. Walt Whitman, who helped care for Union soldiers in Washington during the Civil War, wrote one of his greatest poems here: the moving elegy to Lincoln, "When Lilacs Last in the Dooryard Bloom'd." Ironically, 1865 was the same year Whitman was fired from his job as a clerk in the Indian Bureau. The charge: writing offensive poetry.

Poetry has a strong presence in Washington in part because U.S. poet laureates are based at the Library of Congress. The latest, Joy Harjo, follows eminent poets such as Tracy K. Smith, Juan Felipe Herrera, and Charles Wright.

Architecture

Conceived as a grand capital, Washington has attained a unifying look about its core. One of the main proponents of a neoclassical-style capital was architect-philosopherstatesman Thomas Jefferson. The great buildings and monuments, harking back to ancient Greek and Roman models, were designed to impress with their massiveness and their references to earlier democracies. Weighty columns of marble and pediments embellished with allegorical scenes are the general rule for these early (and many later) federal buildings.

Precious few 18th-century buildings remain. The White House and the Capitol were started in the early 1790s, but both were burned in 1814—and both have undergone many alterations and renovations since they were rebuilt. The Capitol recalls the Pantheon in Rome, begun in 27 B.C. as a temple for worshiping the gods. A less grandiose style was chosen for the executive mansion: Its Georgian format was popular in many manor houses of the day, among them Mount Vernon, Woodlawn, and Gunston Hall, all in Virginia. All three estates feature porticoes, cornices, steep roofs pierced by several chimneys, and almost perfect symmetry.

The federal style flourished in tandem with Washington's growth in the 19th century. Alexandria and Georgetown, already well established, built scores of elegant brick town houses and row houses for prosperous local merchants. Residences from the early 1800s tend to be unadorned, while those built after the Civil War betray unmistakable Victoriana: They sport rosettes, urns, swags, and decorative ironwork. The finest examples of the federal style in Washington are the 1800 Octagon (1799 New York Ave., N.W.) and the 1816 Tudor Place (1644 31st St., N.W.). The latter, despite its name, blends neoclassical and federal elements. Conceived as private homes by Capitol designer William Thornton, both are now national historic landmarks.

Arts in the Park

Established in 1891 as the Chautauqua movement swept America, **Glen Echo Park** *(glenechopark.org)* provided an open-air setting for speakers, preachers, and entertainers. It later became an amusement park, and today features arts and crafts activities and a restored 1921 carousel. Most popular, however, are the social dances in the historic Spanish Ballroom and Bumper Car Pavilion. Waltz, swing, salsa, square, contra—the styles vary, with live music and classes of all levels offered. You'll mingle with people of all ages and levels of experience. The website has directions to the park, which is in Maryland, 12 miles (19 km) from D.C.

Other building styles began to appear later in the 1800s, but architects risked opprobrium if they strayed too far from the city's neoclassicism. Completed in 1887, the handsome redbrick Pension Building (now the National Building Museum) has a breathtakingly cavernous interior. It was nearly razed in the 1960s.

Next to the West Wing of the White House, the Eisenhower Executive Office Building—the world's largest office building at the time of its 1888 construction—was ridiculed and likewise threatened with demolition. Harry S. Truman, for one, called it the "greatest monstrosity in America." But the gilded age building, with its mansard roofs and hundreds of window pediments and columns, is now recognized as an outstanding American example of French Second Empire–style architecture.

Daring and exuberant, the Old Post Office (1899) was likewise slated for obliteration until it was saved in the late 1970s and converted into a retail-office complex. Popular in the first half of the 20th century, the beaux arts style, with its use of columns and other classical elements, meshed well in Washington. Union Station (1908) by

Since its 1988 restoration, Union Station has been a shopping, dining, and partying hub.

Daniel Burnham and John Russell Pope's National Archives (1935) and National Gallery of Art (1941) are grand without ostentation.

Many downtown buildings were razed in the mid-20th century and replaced with concrete cubes, a few of them noteworthy. Though boxy, Edward Durell Stone's National Geographic Society 17th Street building (1964) and Kennedy Center (1971) have an interplay of columns and white stone well suited to Washington.

Other architectural styles have made their way onto Washington streets, but even these bear details of their forerunners. Architect I. M. Pei's radically modernist East Building (1978) of the National Gallery of Art, for instance, is faced with the same pink marble as the neoclassical West Building (1941).

Washington's sense of openness derives largely from an absence of skyscrapers. In general, no city building is allowed to rise more than 20 feet (6 m) higher than the width of the street on which it stands. In the end, this rule is what helps keep Washington, D.C., refreshingly timeless. ■

On Washington's most prominent hill: grand marble halls of law, justice, and knowledge—plus inviting parks, markets, and gardens

CAPITOL HILL

■ Look up: The Capitol Rotunda ceiling gleams like the heavens.

CAPITOL HILL

"A pedestal waiting for a monument" city planner Pierre-Charles L'Enfant called the swell of land then known as Jenkins Hill, on the city's southeastern side. Today beautiful monuments grace this hill, including the Capitol and the Supreme Court. Humanizing the grandeur of marble buildings and plazas are tree-lined residential streets. The heart of Washington, Capitol Hill is a good place to begin your tour.

■ **Spruced-up historic row houses cluster in the desirable Capitol Hill neighborhood.**

For nearly a century, the Capitol was the only government building on "the hill." To the east spread an orderly neighborhood of brick row houses. But by the end of the 19th century, the Library of Congress's Jefferson Building had risen across from the Capitol, followed shortly by architect Daniel H. Burnham's imposing Union Station and adjacent City Post Office.

The early 1900s saw construction of the Cannon Building (1908) and Russell Building (1909), the first House and Senate office buildings. In the 1930s, the Supreme Court, the Folger Shakespeare Library, and the Adams Building of the Library of Congress added more density to Capitol Hill.

Plan on getting some exercise—the area was designed on a grand scale. Walking gives you a chance to savor the magnificent architecture from various points. As you walk, bear in mind that these buildings are historical museums and working halls of democracy. Touring them gives you a sense of the great enterprise upon which the Founding Fathers embarked.

By the mid-20th century, much of the residential area was in decline as middle-class families abandoned the city for the suburbs. Then in the 1970s, urban pioneers, lured by low real estate values and the convenient location, began moving in and revitalizing the area. With Eastern Market *(7th & C Sts., S.E.)* as an anchor, Capitol Hill became a vibrant neighborhood once again. Today, commercial development is spreading rapidly from Eastern Market to Barracks Row on 8th Street, which offers a selection of small shops and a wide range of restaurants. To learn more about this fascinating neighborhood, follow the poster-size signs along the designated Heritage Trail. The first sign is at the Eastern Market Metro station plaza *(7th St. & Pennsylvania Ave., S.E.)*. ■

U.S. CAPITOL

One of the most recognized landmarks in the world, the white marble U.S. Capitol, rising at the National Mall's east end, defines the center of Washington. South, East, and North Capitol Streets and the Mall radiate outward in the cardinal directions, dividing the city into quadrants. In this vaulted location, presidents are inaugurated, national issues debated, and new laws made.

Paintings by John Trumbull (1756–1843), gracing the echoing cavern of the Capitol's imposing Rotunda, depict pivotal moments in the American Revolution.

U.S. Capitol

Map p. 51

Capitol Hill, bet. Independence & Constitution Aves.

202-226-8000

Metro: Capitol South, Union Station; Bus: 32–36, 39, 96–97, P6, Circulator

visitthecapitol.gov

Evolution

The Capitol you see today looks almost nothing like its original conception. Some half dozen major designers and architects put their visions and efforts into the final image. The egos of architects, engineers, and congressmen often clashed; funding grew scarce at times; and disputes drove major players into resigning their positions.

The city's planner, Pierre-Charles L'Enfant, stubbornly refused to come up with an architectural plan for the Capitol, declaring that he had it "in his head." His dismissal in 1792 led to a national competition to design the building. The 16 known entries were so poor that the contest had to be extended. An amateur architect named William Thornton finally came up with a winning design—a Pantheon-like dome flanked by symmetrical wings for the Senate and the House. George Washington laid the cornerstone in 1793.

Though greatly modifying and extending the design over the years, later architects generally

INSIDER TIP:

Eat your picnic before getting in line to go into the Capitol; no food or liquids (or empty water bottles) are allowed in.

—CAROLINE HICKEY
*National Geographic
Travel Books editor*

followed the basic layout. They also incorporated the Corinthian pilasters, seven-bay portico, balustrade, and other neoclassical details Thornton had envisioned.

In 1800 the government moved from Philadelphia to Washington, and President John Adams addressed the Congress in the Capitol's brick-and-sandstone north wing, the only completed part of the building. During these early years, Thornton resigned, and two out of the three other architects were fired over their attempted design alterations. Fortunately, in 1803 the government hired the brilliant British architect

Benjamin Henry Latrobe, and his collaboration with President Thomas Jefferson, himself an amateur architect, made for substantial progress.

Then in August 1814, British troops marched on Washington, and torched many buildings, including the Capitol. The fire destroyed much of the building's interior, though the walls remained standing.

For the next few years, Latrobe worked at restoring the damage. Cost overruns and a dispute about vaulting the ceilings of the House and Senate Chambers finally led to his resignation. Boston architect Charles Bulfinch stepped in. He served until 1830, completing the building with a copper-covered wooden dome and an east portico.

By 1850, an expanding Congress had outgrown its chambers, necessitating the addition of grand wings to the original building. The Capitol expansion project was still under way when the Civil War broke out. Construction

EXPERIENCE: Watching Congress in Action

If you're looking to see a bit of the long and complicated process of lawmaking, you can visit the **House** or **Senate Gallery** when either body is in session. Tour passes are required and can be obtained through your senator or representative, or on the Capitol Visitor Center's website (*visitthecapitol.gov*). Passes for international visitors are also available online or at the appointment desks on the upper level of the visitor center. Some congressional offices offer staff-led tours to constituent groups of up to 15 people. Check the website for contact details as well as policies on security and etiquette.

Because of heavy demand, you should reserve well in advance. Congress is usually in recess during August and fall elections, and the visitor center is closed on Sundays and major holidays. Plan to arrive at least 45 minutes before your scheduled tour; take the confirmation number you'll receive by e-mail with you.

If you just want to view the visitor center exhibits or have lunch at the restaurant, tickets are not required.

Capitol Views

One of the earliest travel books about America was written by Frances Trollope, mother of English writer Anthony Trollope and herself a prolific novelist. In her popular *Domestic Manners of the Americans* (1832), which she wrote after spending three years in the fledgling United States, she found much to disparage. But she was impressed by the Capitol: "None of us, I believe, expected to see so imposing a structure on that side of the Atlantic. I am ill at describing buildings, but the beauty and majesty of the American capitol might defy an abler pen than mine to do it justice. It stands so finely too, high, and alone ... The view from the capitol commands the city and many miles around, and it is itself an object of imposing beauty to the whole country adjoining."

went on, culminating in the addition of the current cast-iron dome, which replaced a leaky, wooden predecessor.

On December 2, 1863, the magnificent nine-million-pound (4,082 tonne) dome, rising from a circular portico, was crowned with "Freedom," the 19.5-foot-tall (6 m) bronze figure of a woman dressed in flowing robes. The original plan was that she would wear a liberty cap, something worn by freed slaves in ancient Greece. Secretary of War Jefferson Davis—president of the Confederacy by the time the statue was placed atop the Capitol—objected, saying the cap was "inappropriate to a people who were born free." A helmet with eagle feathers was substituted. Renowned landscape architect Frederick Law Olmsted designed and landscaped the grounds in the late 1880s to early 1890s.

Congress again outgrew the building in the early 1900s, scattering to the nearby Senate and House office buildings. An addition in 1958–1962 added 32 feet (9.7 m) to the east front.

Touring the Capitol

A modern Capitol Visitor Center on the building's east front now serves as the gateway for all tours. Book in advance *(visit thecapitol.gov)* or, if you are an American citizen, through the offices of your senator or representative. Or call the Office of Visitor Services *(tel 202-226-8000)*. A limited number of same-day passes are issued at the information desk on the Capitol's lower level. Visitor hours are 8:30 a.m.–4:30 p.m. Monday–Saturday. Begin your tour with the 13-minute film explaining the role of Congress. In the exhibition hall, an 11-foot-high (3.3 m) touchable model shows a cross section of the Capitol dome at one-twentieth the size. Original documents and artifacts tell the story of the Capitol and the U.S. Congress.

Among the sites you will see on the tour, the **Rotunda** soars 180 feet (55 m) to a round ceiling fresco, "The Apotheosis of Washington" (1865), by Italian-American artist Constantino Brumidi. A berobed George Washington stares down from on high, surrounded by a swirl of clouds and figures that represent the 13 Colonies and American democracy. Encircling the Rotunda, a 300-foot-long (91 m) frieze depicts more than 400 years of American history, from Columbus to the Wright brothers. The four huge scenes from the American Revolution were painted by Washington's aide-de-camp John Trumbull. A small white marble stone marks the center of the Rotunda's floor, where noted Americans such as Abraham Lincoln and John F. Kennedy have lain in state.

South of the Rotunda, the **National Statuary Hall** is where the House of Representatives met from 1807 to 1857. In 1864 Congress invited each state to send statues of two prominent citizens. Some have been replaced with more contemporary figures. Among the notables are Dwight Eisenhower (Kansas), Will Rogers (Oklahoma), Hellen Keller (Alabama), and King Kamehameha I (Hawaii).

North of the Rotunda is the **Old Senate Chamber,** which served the Senate at various times in the 1800s. Here such famous men as Clay, Webster, and John C. Calhoun hotly debated the issues of slavery and economics prior to the Civil War. Today the Senate uses this chamber for closed-door conferences, including a 1999 session on the impeachment trial of President Bill Clinton.

On the first floor, directly beneath the Rotunda, is the **Crypt.** George and Martha Washington were to be entombed here, but family members objected, so the two remain at Mount Vernon, in Virginia. Ringing the room, 40 Doric sandstone columns help support the Rotunda. Gutzon Borglum, the sculptor who carved Mount Rushmore, created the marble head of Lincoln displayed here. The statue's missing left ear symbolizes the slain president's incomplete life.

■ **Statue of the Shoshone warrior Washakie at the U.S. Capitol Building**

North of the Crypt, through the small Senate Rotunda and to the right, stands the **Old Supreme Court Chamber.** The Senate originally met in this vaulted room designed by Latrobe; the Supreme Court used it from 1810 to 1860.

In the early 1970s, restorers armed with mid-19th-century descriptions set out to return the chamber to its earlier appearance. Half of the furnishings here, including justices' desks and chairs, are original.

On the first floor of the north wing, the colorful Brumidi Corridors boast a wealth of frescoes and other paintings by Constantino Brumidi, who worked in the Capitol for 25 years in the late 1800s. Sometimes called the Michelangelo of the Capitol, Brumidi based his designs for the corridors on the Raphael loggia in the Vatican, where he had done some restoration work. The historical scenes and heroes, along with depictions of flora and fauna in trompe l'oeil frames, provide a rich summary of early America. Later paintings include scenes of

Senate Chamber

■ The heart of American democracy, the U.S. Capitol is also the geographic center of Washington; the city's four quadrants radiate from the middle of the building.

U.S. Capitol

West Front

the first moon landing and a tribute to the crew that died in the 1986 explosion of the *Challenger* space shuttle.

On the other side of the Crypt, in the south wing, are the **First Floor House Corridors** containing more statuary as well as murals by contemporary American artist Allyn Cox. Among the scenes depicted are the Capitol in flames in 1814 and wounded Union soldiers lying in a makeshift hospital in the Rotunda.

The **Congressional Chambers** are in the Capitol's wings (the House south, the Senate north). The 435 House representatives are not assigned specific seats, though Democrats traditionally sit to the Speaker's right, Republicans to the left. The same arrangement holds for the more stately Senate, but here desks are based on seniority. ■

When a white light shines in the dome, Congress is in session.

Rotunda

Capitol Visitor Center

National Statuary Hall (Old House Chambers)

House Chamber

POLITICS AT WORK

Regardless of the outcome of a bill, the process is interesting and illuminating to watch. You will get to observe how the blueprint for government, the Constitution of the United States of America—hashed out in a steamy room centuries ago—is applied to issues today. Seeing how constitutional democracy plays out can't help but take you back to the early days of the still young United States.

■ Former President George W. Bush delivers his State of the Union speech before a joint session of Congress in 2005.

In the summer of 1787, following the successful rebellion of the 13 Colonies against England and the loosely structured "Confederation" period, 55 leaders from the newly independent states met in Philadelphia's State House (now Independence Hall) to revise the Articles of Confederation, the country's first constitution.

Trying to strike a delicate balance between sufficient government power to rule a nation yet allow adequate liberty for its citizens, the delegates decided to toss the Articles and create a new document. The result: the

Constitution of the United States of America. This constitution could not become the law of the land by fiat, so the founders asked that it be ratified by the people of the 13 independent states. There were many heated state conventions, some producing violence, others producing eloquent words, that have helped Supreme Court justices determine the meaning of this concise plan for the government we have today—living up to its preamble: "We the People of the United States ..."

From the beginning Congress met to air differences and reach hard fought compromises. The reason the capital is in Washington, for instance, is because of the Compromise of 1790, in which northern congressmen and senators got their southern counterparts to approve funding our first national debt in return for placing the nation's capital in the south on the Potomac River, not far from George Washington's home.

From the First Congress came the traditions of national debt and logrolling. And anyone who has tuned into C-SPAN knows that political debate and compromise continue to be integral ingredients in making laws.

While the work done on the House or Senate floor is well publicized, much of the real work of Congress goes on behind the scenes in committees and subcommittees, which meet on most days when the legislature is in session. If you visit you might be able to watch as the Environmental Protection Agency administrator is grilled about pollution enforcement, attend confirmation hearings for a newly nominated federal judge, or listen as the future of space exploration is debated.

If a bill is good and has powerful friends on the committee, it will be recommended to the House or Senate for debate and vote. Of the thousands of bills introduced every year, only a small percentage make it to the

---

INSIDER TIP:

Whenever I pass the Capitol, D.C.'s most iconic and magisterial building, I feel the presence of a force that sets the agenda, like it or not, of the country. The Capitol is so approachable—its visitor center is the gateway to the nation's story.

—KEITH BELLOWS
*National Geographic Traveler
magazine editor in chief*

---

floor of the House or Senate to be voted on.

If passed, the bill is then sent to the other chamber, referred to committee, and so on. If the bill makes it through the tortured path to passage in that chamber, then a "Conference" committee is set up to settle differences between the two bills. The Senate and House vote again on the revised bill, and if that compromise bill passes, it goes to the president for signature—or veto. If a president's veto is overridden by a two-thirds vote in both the House and Senate, then the bill becomes law over the president's objections.

EXPERIENCE: Following the Lawmaking Process

An exciting part of visiting "official" Washington is getting a peek inside the political process. But even if you have a chance to observe Congress in session, it's not always clear exactly what's going on, or what the end result might be. Briefing yourself on the day's agenda and what bills are under consideration can help you make better sense of it all. The Library of Congress offers a comprehensive online source of legislative information. The old "Thomas" website (named for Thomas Jefferson) has now been revamped as **congress.gov.** The site provides the full

text, related details, and status of all bills in the current Congress, as well as those dating back to 1973. You can browse legislation by sponsor, for example, to find out what your senator or representative has been doing. Streaming video follows any floor proceedings that may be under way. Look under "Current Legislative Activities" to find out what's hot.

If a bill has been enacted into law, you can read the full text on the website. For a quick tutorial on the legislative process, click on "More about Congress.gov" at the bottom of the page.

SUPREME COURT

This imposing neoclassical building east of the Capitol makes a simple yet powerful statement with its wide marble stairway and its lofty portico rising on 32 Corinthian columns. An architrave just below the pediment bears the inscription "Equal Justice Under Law."

The Supreme Court's four-word pediment inscription is an echo of Justice John Marshall Harlan's famous dissenting opinion in 1896 in *Plessy* v. *Ferguson*: "In view of the Constitution, in the eye of the law, there is in this country no superior, dominant, ruling class of citizens. There is no caste here ... [A]ll citizens are equal before the law."

Here the nation's highest tribunal arbitrates cases involving the Constitution or the nation's laws. In this court of final appeal, decisions have been handed down that have profoundly influenced the country. In 2000 the Court showed its muscle again by effectively settling the controversial U.S. presidential race.

Surprisingly, the Supreme Court did not have its own building until 1935. Before then it sat in various places within the Capitol. In 1929, Chief Justice William Howard Taft, the only U.S. president (1909–1913) to serve on the Court (1921–1930), urged Congress to authorize the erection of a Supreme Court building. The formal edifice designed by Cass Gilbert was constructed with 27,400 pieces of marble. Every feature lends a sense of gravity and dignity, from the 6.5-ton (5.8 tonne) bronze doors to the seated marble giants out front—"Contemplation of Justice" (left) and "Guardian of Law" (right).

Touring the Court

You enter through one of the doors that flank the building's

■ A stone's throw from the Capitol, the neoclassical Supreme Court, with its courtyard of marble, was completed in 1935.

main staircase and lead to the **Great Hall** and its long line of busts depicting former chief justices. At the end of the hall lies the actual courtroom.

When the court is not in session you can visit the chamber and learn about court procedure by attending a lecture given on the half hour. In the nation's most important courtroom stand the chairs of the nine justices, their height varying according to how tall the justice is (so they all appear the same height when seated). Along the sides of the room rise 24 veined marble columns, above which sculpted marble panels depict such lawgivers as Moses, Confucius, and Napoleon.

When the court is in session *(Mon.–Wed. Oct.–April)*, you can listen to oral arguments by lining up on the plaza in front of the building. Seating begins at 9:30 a.m., and you must go through two security checkpoints. Some cases attract crowds, with people even sleeping outside the court to ensure a place inside. You may have a better chance with the other line—for those who just want to hear a three-minute sample of the case.

More than 10,000 petitions asking the Supreme Court to overturn a lower-court ruling arrive annually. Only about 100 make it to the argument stage. Each side is given 30 minutes to argue its case; the justices then write their opinions.

From the Great Hall, go down a flight of stairs to the small theater on the **Ground Floor;** a 24-minute film details

the workings of the Court and includes interviews with current justices. The floor also has several exhibits. On the south side the Warren Court (1953–1969), presided over by Chief Justice Earl Warren, still sits in session in a stone and aluminum sculpture. The Warren Court's progressive opinions included the outlawing of school segregation.

At the floor's east end is a statue of the great fourth Chief

Supreme Court

- Map p. 51
- 1st & E. Capitol Sts., N.E.
- 202-479-3000
- Closed Sat.–Sun.
- Metro: Capitol South, Union Station; Bus: 97, A11, Circulator

supremecourt.gov

Milestones for Women

When Justice Elena Kagan, the former dean of Harvard Law School, joined the Supreme Court in August 2010, it marked the first time that three women sat on the High Court at the same time. The chief justice—currently John G. Roberts—and eight associate justices, nominated by the president and confirmed by a majority vote in the Senate, are appointed for life terms. To date, only five of the 115 Supreme Court justices have been women. The first, Sandra Day O'Connor, was nominated by President Reagan; she retired in 2006. President Clinton named Ruth Bader Ginsburg (1933–2020) to the Court in 1993. President Obama nominated Sonia M. Sotomayor and Kagan, and President Trump appointed Amy Coney Barrett in 2020.

Justice, John Marshall, who served 1801–1835. He is considered responsible for our system of constitutional law, including the doctrine of judicial review (*Marbury v. Madison,* 1803), by which the Court can declare acts of Congress unconstitutional. Follow signs for a view of two marble-and-bronze spiral staircases; the ascending ovals make the five-story building appear twice as tall as it really is. ■

LIBRARY OF CONGRESS

The world's largest library, the Library of Congress contains what many people regard as the most beautiful space in Washington: the Great Hall in the Thomas Jefferson Building. It dazzles with an abundance of murals, mosaics, sculptures, and architectural flourishes in Italian Renaissance style. The circular Main Reading Room with concentric rows of polished wood research desks is also splendid. Get the full dramatic effect from the elevated Visitors' Gallery.

The central desk is where books are requested for use in the Main Reading Room.

Library of Congress

- Map p. 51
- 1st St. & Independence Ave., S.E.
- 202-707-8000 or 202-707-5000
- Closed Sun. & major holidays
- Metro: Capitol South; Bus: 32–36, A11, Circulator

loc.gov

The Jefferson Building, which opened in 1897, is the main building of three on Capitol Hill that anchor the Library. The original Library, started in 1800 as a reference collection for Congress, was housed in the U.S. Capitol. After the British burned the Capitol in 1814, destroying the books, Thomas Jefferson sold his large and eclectic personal library—of 6,487 volumes—to Congress to reestablish the Library of Congress.

A second devastating blow came in 1851 when fire destroyed two-thirds of the Jefferson collection. The Library has searched worldwide for copies of the books; only 282 are yet to be replaced. Thomas Jefferson's library (re-created) now is on public display in the Jefferson Building.

Today the Library holds a mind-boggling array of items, totaling more than 162 million;

they take up 838 miles (1,349 km) of shelving! *(Access to the reading rooms requires a "reader card," available in the Madison Building.)* Besides books, the available items include manuscripts, maps, posters, photographs, sheet music, prints and drawings, films, and other audiovisual materials. An ever growing amount of the Library's collections can be accessed online. The Library also joined UNESCO's efforts to make available via the World Digital Library *(wdl.org)*, many of the world's greatest writing and art treasures held by national libraries and archives.

Among its many functions, the Library registers copyrights for published works and prepares legal research reports for Congress. The **Young Readers Center** in the Jefferson Building presents book information specifically targeted to families.

INSIDER TIP:

A stunning overview of the Jefferson Building's Main Reading Room is featured in the 1976 film *All the President's Men.*

—DIANA PARSELL
National Geographic writer

Touring the Library

You can take an organized tour of the **Jefferson Building** or pick up a self-guided tour brochure at the visitor desk, near the ground-level entrance. Touch-activated screens provide details on much of what you'll see.

Several galleries have exhibits on American history and culture. "Exploring the Early Americas," for example, displays the 1507 Waldseemüller World Map, the first to use the word "America." Other exhibits have showcased comedy

Miles of Books

Contrary to what many people believe, the Library of Congress does not have copies of every published book. That was the practice in the early years, when the flood of acquired materials included two copies of each copyrighted work in the country (which led to the need for construction of the Thomas Jefferson Building). Today the Library reviews and retains materials on an individual basis, adding about 11,000 items every day. It has several overseas offices to obtain foreign works deemed important to scholars; some 470 languages are represented in the collections.

materials from a Bob Hope collection, political cartoons, and artifacts of musical legends George and Ira Gershwin. Not to be missed on the entrance level: the Gutenberg Bible, the first book printed using movable metal type, and the Giant Bible of Mainz, both from the mid-1450s.

Proceed one level up to the **Great Hall,** reminiscent of a Mediterranean palazzo. Note the intricate mosaics and the overhead paintings honoring music, poetry, astronomy, and other disciplines. Stairs lead to a mezzanine with overhead views of the **Main Reading Room.** ∎

FOLGER SHAKESPEARE LIBRARY

A unique treasure, the library holds the world's largest collection of William Shakespeare's works. Originating from a gift by Henry Clay Folger, the library opened in 1932 and now houses 320,000 books and manuscripts, and 90,000 paintings, drawings, prints, and photographs—plus many musical instruments, costumes, and films.

Folger Shake-speare Library

- Map p. 51
- 201 E. Capitol St., S.E., bet. 2nd & 3rd Sts., S.E.
- 202-544-4600
- Metro: Capitol South, Union Station; Bus: 32–36, 96–97, Circulator

folger.edu

In 1879 a lecture on the Bard by Ralph Waldo Emerson fired the interest of Folger, then a 22-year-old student at Amherst College. A decade later, he bought his first Shakespeare folio. With money he made as president of the Standard Oil Company of New York, he went on to buy thousands of rare books, manuscripts, and paintings. In the early 1900s, he began casting about for a site to build a library; he chose one adjacent to the Library of Congress (see pp. 62–63). But just after the cornerstone was laid, in 1930, he died; his wife, Emily, saw the project to completion.

The bold lines of this art deco–inspired neoclassical marble building make it a fitting presence among its neighbors. Nine bas-reliefs on the north side depict scenes from the Bard's plays. On the east lawn lies an **Elizabethan flower and herb garden.**

For more details, take one of the daily tours, which start at the docent's desk. Or wander on your own through the wood-paneled 30-foot-high (9.1 m) **Great Hall,** which displays a copy of the Bard's first folio and changing exhibits from the collection. You may peer into the Tudor-style **Paster Reading Room** *(closed Sun.),* where a stained-glass window depicting the "Seven Ages of Man" *(As You Like It)* adorns the west end. A Shakespeare bust is on the east wall. The room is open to scholars and graduate students for research.

At the Folger's east end, the **Elizabethan Theatre** is an intimate spot for the Bard's plays. The oak columns and tiered balconies add to the atmosphere of a Renaissance courtyard.

A major multi-year renovation began in 2020, in which galleries will be reconfigured and expanded with a New Pavilion, to include the **Stuart and Mimi Rose Rare Book and Manuscript Exhibition Hall,** displaying such formative works as Caxton's Chaucer, John Donne letters, and documents of Elizabeth I. The **Shakespeare Exhibition Hall** is devoted to the Bard's life and works. ∎

■ The Folger's Reading Room evokes an Elizabethan great hall.

U.S. BOTANIC GARDEN

If you're surprised to suddenly find yourself in the thick of a tropical rain forest or surrounded by a soothing oasis in metropolitan Washington, D.C., then you've stumbled onto the U.S. Botanic Garden, an oasis of green in the shadow of the U.S. Capitol.

Congress established this garden in 1820 for the collection, growing, and distribution of important plants. The historic greenhouse, built in 1933, was renovated in 2001. Today, some 4,000 plants are on view at any one time in the glass-paneled **Conservatory,** with ten garden rooms. You can stroll through the various areas devoted to desert, tropical, and Hawaii flora, and explore exhibits on

■ For a good view of the Conservatory, head across Independence Avenue to the U.S. Botanic Garden's Bartholdi Park.

INSIDER TIP:

Inside, see carnivorous plants (thrilling for kids) from spring through fall, and an enthralling Christmas-season miniature train set.

—KEITH BELLOWS
National Geographic Traveler magazine editor in chief

medicinal and economically useful plants, primeval vegetation, and plant exploration, among others.

Don't miss climbing the stairs to the overhanging walkway in the large tropical atrium. In the orchid house, you can stroll through the outstanding collection of orchids and other unusual epiphytes.

The 3-acre (1.2 ha) **National Garden,** adjacent to the

Conservatory, has plants native to the mid-Atlantic region, as well as a butterfly garden, rose garden, and the First Ladies Water Garden.

Across Independence Avenue is the garden's beautifully planted pocket-size **Bartholdi Park,** a favorite of the locals. Frédéric-Auguste Bartholdi, who created the Statue of Liberty, sculpted the park's 30-foot-high (9 m) cast-iron fountain for the Centennial Exposition of 1876 in Philadelphia—the first world's fair. The sculpture's upper basin is borne by three upright sea nymphs, as water jets from the mouths of stylized fish and turtles. ■

U.S. Botanic Garden

🏛 Map p. 51

✉ 100 Maryland Ave., S.W.

☎ 202-225-8333

🚇 Metro: Federal Center SW; Bus: 32–36, A11, Circulator

usbg.gov

EASTERN MARKET & BARRACKS ROW

Farm stand, flea market, community center—historic Eastern Market is the heart and soul of Capitol Hill's residential area as well as a popular destination for residents from all across the city who love the ambience, and crab cakes at Market Lunch. Neighboring Barracks Row, Washington's oldest commercial corridor, is undergoing a revitalization that's attracting many new dining and retail establishments in recent years.

■ Eastern Market is where the locals go for food and flowers.

Eastern Market

- 🗺 Map p. 51
- ✉ 225 7th St., S.E.
- ☎ 202-698-5253
- 🕐 Closed Mon.
- 🚇 Metro: Eastern Market

easternmarket-dc.org

Barracks Row

- 🗺 Map p. 51
- ✉ 8th St., S.E.
- ☎ 202-544-3188
- 🚇 Metro: Eastern Market

barracksrow.org

The first **Eastern Market** was one of three public markets Pierre L'Enfant included in his design for the city. The present redbrick building opened in 1873. After it was heavily damaged by fire in 2007, the market was carefully restored and reopened in 2009.

Weekends draw crowds as patrons flood the South Hall food stalls for groceries or a bite to eat. At **Market Lunch,** in business for more than three decades, customers tolerate long lines for a taste of the renowned crab cakes and, on Saturday mornings,

blueberry buckwheat pancakes. A popular flea market fills the adjacent sidewalks.

The surrounding neighborhood buzzes with hip shops and bistros. On the market's south side, **Radici** (303 7th St., S.E., tel 202-758-0086, radici-market.com) serves authentic Italian fare. Pop into the charmingly cluttered **Capitol Hill Books** (657 C St., S.E., tel 202-544-1621, capitolhillbooks-dc. com) to find the perfect used biography, political treatise, or mystery novel to read while sipping a honey latte at **Peregrine Espresso** (660 Pennsylvania Ave., S.E., tel 202-629-4381, peregrineespresso.com).

Barracks Row gets its name from the U.S. Marine Corps Barracks that anchor one end of the corridor. Thomas Jefferson and other Episcopalians attended services at **Christ Church** (620 G St., S.E.), and composer John Philip Sousa took music lessons at a house on 8th Street. The area got a burst of cool with the opening of **The Fridge** (516 1/2 8th St., S.E., rear alley, tel 202-664-4151), an eclectic arts community that displays public street art, stages live performances from slam poetry to electronic music festivals, and hosts weekly art workshops. ■

NATIONALS PARK BASEBALL STADIUM

Four decades after the team called the Senators left town, professional baseball returned to Washington in 2005. Nationals Park, which opened in 2008 within sight of the U.S. Capitol, was located near the Anacostia River to spur area development. A full lineup of entertainment and beyond-the-usual food concessions (come hungry) has made a day at the park a popular local outing no matter how the Washington Nationals perform.

The look of the new ballpark was inspired by architect I. M. Pei's East Wing of the National Gallery of Art (see p. 86). An odd right-angled jog into the right center field was borrowed from the now demolished Griffith Stadium, where the Senators used to play. For many of the seats you can walk inside and take your place on the same level as the sidewalk; the field is 24 feet (7.3 m) below street level.

The design incorporates "green" elements such as high-efficiency lighting, recycled building materials, reflective roof materials, and a storm water management system that reduces runoff into the Anacostia. Tours are available on nongame days.

The favorite moment comes in the middle of the fourth inning, when a group of 10-foot-tall (3 m) giant-headed presidents—George Washington, Thomas Jefferson, Abraham Lincoln, Theodore Roosevelt, and William Howard Taft—run a clumsy, antics-filled race across center field to home plate.

Among the way-beyond-franks fare are falafel sandwiches, Jamaican BBQ, and a wide selection of microbrew beers. ■

Nationals Park

- ⛰ Map p. 195
- ✉ 1500 South Capitol St., S.E.
- ☎ 202-675-6287
- 🚇 Metro: Navy Yard-Ballpark; Bus: A9, P6, V7–V9, Circulator

mlb.com/nationals

EXPERIENCE: Catch a Game

Washingtonians love their sporting events. In 2020, many fiercely loyal fans plus NFL and team sponsors pressured the former Washington Redskins to drop the term "redskin" as (washingtonfootball.com) insensitive to Native Americans. The team rebranded temporarily as the Washington Football Team, with a permanent new name still to be chosen. The team plays at **FedEx Field** in Landover, Maryland, accessible by Metro and shuttle bus.

The streets around **Capitol One Arena** in Penn Quarter (see pp. 134–139) roar with energy on nights when the **Capitals** (nhl.com/capitals) meet another hockey team on the ice. Thanks to his thunderous style of play and his scoring exploits, spectators can't get enough of Russian import Alex Ovechkin, a three-time NHL Most Valuable Player.

In the decade since they arrived in town, the **Nationals** have become one of the most exciting teams in Major League Baseball. Superstar players and a new stadium make Nationals games a hot ticket.

Always popular, basketball gained an even bigger profile since basketball-playing President Obama was in office (2009–2017). Check out the **Washington Wizards** (nba.com/wizards) at Capitol One Arena.

More Places to Visit on Capitol Hill

Belmont-Paul Women's Equality National Monument

Robert Sewall built this two-story brick house in 1799–1800. In the 20th century, Alva Belmont helped purchase it for the National Woman's Party, founded by suffragette leader Alice Paul and headquartered here since 1929. Various collections document the movement to gain political rights for women. Midday tours are available Thursday through Saturday. *nps.gov/bepa* ⚑ Map p. 51 ✉ 144 Constitution Ave., N.E. ☎ 202-543-2240 ⊕ Closed Mon.–Tues. ⊠ Metro: Union Station, Capitol South

■ The Smithsonian National Postal Museum Exhibition

National Guard Memorial Museum

This small but engrossing museum at the National Guard Memorial uses memorabilia, light and sound effects, and narratives to chronicle the experiences of citizen soldiers who have served America at home and abroad for nearly four centuries. The displays and programs are especially poignant given the Guard's role in homeland security and war in the Middle East following the September 11, 2001, attacks. *ngef.org* ⚑ Map p. 51 ✉ 1 Massachusetts Ave., N.W. ☎ 202-789-0031 ⊕ Closed Sat.–Sun. ⊠ Metro: Union Station

National Postal Museum

The building that formerly housed the Washington City Post Office makes an elegant home for this interesting museum, near Union Station, which is part of the Smithsonian Institution complex. The galleries explore topics such as the history of mail delivery, stamp collecting, and the art of correspondence. Among the artifacts on display in the 90-foot-high (27 m) atrium are prop planes and a railway car, modes of mail conveyance in the past. Hour-long guided tours for groups are available by calling in advance. *postalmuseum.si.edu* ⚑ Map p. 51 ✉ 2 Massachusetts Ave., N.E. ☎ 202-633-5555 ⊠ Metro: Union Station; Bus: Circulator

---

INSIDER TIP:

With its grand space and elaborate architectural details, Union Station makes a case for the romance of rail travel.

—AMY ALIPIO
National Geographic Traveler magazine associate editor

Union Station

Completed in 1908 and beautifully restored in the 1980s, this grand beaux arts–style building is worth visiting just for its architecture. Faced in white Vermont granite, the station's huge Romanesque arches give way to a triumphal, echoing Main Hall where 36 larger-than-life Roman legionnaires preside on the gallery level. A barrel-vaulted ceiling with gold-leaf coffers soars 96 feet (29 m) above the station's bustle. Today there are shops and restaurants. *unionstationdc.com* ⚑ Map p. 51 ✉ 50 Massachusetts Ave., N.E. ☎ 202-289-1908 ⊠ Metro: Union Station

Must-see museums and monuments, to be sure, but also lots
of fun, games, picnicking, strolling, people-watching, and relaxing

NATIONAL MALL

Summer's annual Smithsonian
Folklife Festival on the Mall is all
about the energy of global cultures.

NATIONAL MALL

Lined and dotted with the most significant group of museums and monuments in the country, the National Mall is a long avenue of green grass edged by shade trees. You could spend a week (more, to tell you the truth) enjoying this world-famous tourist mecca.

One day hundreds of colorful kites fly near the Washington Monument, on another a crowd waves banners, and on yet another the Mall is just a peaceful stretch of green. From the U.S. Capitol to the Lincoln Memorial, America's grand promenade extends for more than 2 miles (3.2 km), sandwiched between Constitution and Independence

Avenues. Walkers, joggers, soccer players, and Frisbee throwers (and their dogs) regularly take to the inviting lawns.

Pierre-Charles L'Enfant's city plan of 1791 included a "vast esplanade" lined with grand residences. But by the end of the 1800s, the Mall was a place of coal piles, sheds, tracks, and a railroad station. In 1901 the MacMillan

Commission recommended reviving L'Enfant's plan. Tracks and debris were removed. With the addition of the Lincoln Memorial, the Mall stretched west to the Potomac River.

By the late 1980s, the Mall held nine Smithsonian museums and two National Gallery of Art buildings. In 2004 the National Museum of the American Indian and the World War II Memorial opened, and 2011 saw the openings of the Martin Luther King, Jr. Memorial, on the Tidal Basin, and the U.S. Institute of Peace, off the Mall's northwest corner. The National Museum of African American History & Culture, just northeast of the Washington Monument, opened in 2016. ∎

NOT TO BE MISSED:

James McNeill Whistler's Peacock Room in the Freer Gallery 72

The National Museum of Natural History's human origins exhibit 93

Julia Child's kitchen at the National Museum of American History 98

The wall of names at the Vietnam Veterans Memorial 101–102

Viewing the Mall from the steps of the Lincoln Memorial 102

NATIONAL MUSEUM OF ASIAN ART

The Smithsonian's National Museum of Asian Art combines two adjoining yet complementary art galleries, rebranded in December 2019 as a single entity acclaimed for housing the nation's foremost collection of Asian art. The mesmerizing collection spans more than 40,000 objects, from the fourth millennium B.C. to today and makes a comprehensive sweep, encompassing works from the Levant to Japan, Korea, and Southeast Asia.

■ Whistler painted the Freer's sumptuous Peacock Room as though it were a huge lacquer box.

National Museum of Asian Art

🏛 Map pp. 70–71

✉ 1050 Independence Ave.

☎ 202-633-1000

🚇 Metro: Smithsonian; Bus: 32–36, 52

asia.si.edu

Freer Gallery of Art

Opened in 1923, the Italian Renaissance–style Freer Gallery building has a pink granite exterior and polished white marble floors. Its galleries surround a hallway where large windows look out onto a refreshing inner courtyard. The lighting and exhibit space combine to lend a refined, contemplative atmosphere.

The collection was donated by Detroit businessman Charles Lang Freer (1856–1919). Of the 19 galleries, 16 are devoted to Asian art, including Indian sculpture, Japanese lacquerware, Chinese paintings, Korean and Vietnamese ceramics, and Islamic metalware. The Freer, which does not lend out its objects, rotates works from its vast and ever growing collection. In 2019, it

acquired 260 works of the Mary and Cheney Cowles Collection of Japanese painting and calligraphy.

The Asian collection is complemented by 19th- and 20th-century American pieces, including the world's largest collection of works by James McNeill Whistler (1834–1903). American treasures include the exquisite **Peacock Room,** which is a must-see. Whistler painted the room for a wealthy London shipowner. Recently restored to its original elegance, the room features antique gilded leather walls, a metal ceiling painted in a feather pattern, and a painting known as "The Princess in the Land of Porcelain." The opposite wall has a painting of two peacocks, a reference to a quarrel between Whistler and his patron over the fee. Freer bought the room intact from a London dealer and installed it in his Detroit home; it was moved to Washington in 1919.

Arthur M. Sackler Gallery

Immediately east of the Freer Gallery, and connected to it by a tunnel, the smaller Arthur M. Sackler Gallery is housed almost entirely belowground. Created in 1987, this gallery has at its core the Asian collection of research physician and medical publisher Arthur M. Sackler (1913-1987). Among its treasures are Chinese bronzes and jades, Persian manuscripts, ancient Iranian silver, and works from Tibet and Japan. The museum exhibits items from its growing permanent collection as well as from other collections in the United States and elsewhere.

The Sackler's **first level**—belowground—contains carefully curated works from a variety of cultures. Many rooms feature artfully arranged objects in plexiglass cases, with subtle lighting and just enough information to keep you interested but not overwhelmed. Recent exhibitions here have included "Empresses of the Forbidden City," "To Dye For: Ikats from Central Asia," and "Japanese Modern: Prints in the Age of Photography."

In the **Arts of China** galleries, also on the first level, the Ancient Chinese Art section displays 12th- to 13th-century B.C. jade knives crafted by artisans with meticulous care and great skill. Another section, the Arts of Six Dynasties and Tang in China, holds Tang dynasty tomb guardians adorned with brilliant horns and flames. The guardians look as fierce as they must have 13 centuries ago.

The **second level** of the gallery is composed mainly of administrative offices. Be sure to visit the third level of the Sackler, where a rotating ceramics gallery, most recently highlighting items from Vietnam and Thailand, is complimented by a small pool and bubbling fountains.

From the **third level,** visitors can make their way to the S. Dillon Ripley Center, which features temporary exhibits. ∎

The Smithsonian: All the Museums

African Art Museum
Air & Space Museum
Udvar-Hazy Center (Va.)
African American History & Culture Museum
American Art Museum and its Renwick Gallery
American History Museum
American Indian Museum
Anacostia Community Museum
Cooper-Hewitt (NYC)
National Museum of Asian Art
Hirshhorn Museum & Sculpture Garden
National Zoo
Natural History Museum
Portrait Gallery
Postal Museum
Smithsonian Institution Building, the Castle
Arts & Industries Building

NATIONAL MUSEUM OF AFRICAN ART

This museum, with more than 9,000 pieces, traces its roots to a town house on Capitol Hill once owned by Frederick Douglass, a former slave who became a noted abolitionist. In 1964 Warren M. Robbins founded the Museum of African Art there as a private educational institution that mainly displayed some Douglass memorabilia. But that was just the beginning.

National Museum of African Art

Map pp. 70–71

950 Independence Ave., S.W.

202-633-4600

Metro: Smithsonian, L'Enfant Plaza; Bus: 32–36, 52

africa.si.edu

The museum's early holdings also included a collection of 19th-century paintings by African-American artists, but for exhibitions of African works Robbins had to rely on loaned objects.

In 1979 the museum became part of the Smithsonian Institution. Three years later it was officially renamed the National Museum of African Art, and in 1987 the steadily growing institution moved to its present location on the Mall. Its permanent collection has grown to represent 900 cultures across the continent and a vast range of materials and art forms—textiles, sculpture, pottery, paintings, jewelry, masks, musical instruments, furniture, tools, and religious and household objects. Together they show the degree to which art permeates African culture. Changing exhibitions highlight treasures from the museum's collection along with pieces from public and private collections.

The displays are designed to illuminate the high aesthetic and technical craftsmanship in African art. They show, for example, how Africans often fashion all kinds of materials—from simple household utensils to ceremonial objects to monumental sculptures honoring the living and the dead—in ways meant to embody expressions of an "ideal" that reflects standards of beauty, moral behavior, leadership, intelligence, and fertility. Contemporary traditional ceramics show the dexterity and artistry of the continent's master potters—mainly women.

The ongoing **"Visionary: Viewpoints on Africa's Arts"** exhibition features highlights from the museum's permanent collection that reflect visionary ideas and styles spanning the African continent. Many of the items, which represent most of Africa's major artistic traditions, are unique and rare works from throughout sub-Saharan Africa.

The museum also houses the Warren M. Robbins Library and offers cultural programs. Its **Eliot Elisofon Photographic Archives,** named for the famous *Life* magazine photographer, has an expanding collection of some 350,000 items, ranging from photo prints and transparencies to slides and film footage. ■

An Attie peoples mask from Côte d'Ivoire

HIRSHHORN MUSEUM & SCULPTURE GARDEN

A striking touch of modernity on the Mall, the Hirshhorn houses the Smithsonian's pre-eminent works of international modern and contemporary art. The museum opened in 1974, after American entrepreneur and philanthropist Joseph H. Hirshhorn (1899–1981) donated his art collection to the Smithsonian. A drum-shaped building three stories high, this eye-catching landmark has a bi-level sculpture garden and plaza of nearly 4 acres (1.6 ha).

■ The Hirshhorn's circular courtyard often serves as a setting for receptions.

Architect Gordon Bunshaft designed the museum to have outdoor spaces that encourage intimate, contemplative viewing of the artworks. The Hirshhorn has a permanent collection of more than 12,000 works by leading artists from the late 19th century to the present. Paintings, mixed-media pieces, photography, works on paper, videos, and films are among the holdings, along with an outstanding modern sculpture collection that's regarded as one of the most comprehensive in the world. A piece that is hard to miss is Roy Lichtenstein's towering "Brushstroke" (1996), installed on the plaza. Among the 60 pieces in the sculpture garden are traditional figures by artists such as Auguste Rodin and Aristide Maillol, biomorphic figures by Henry Moore and Barbara Hepworth, and abstract

Hirshhorn Museum & Sculpture Garden

🗺 Map pp. 70–71

✉ Independence Ave. & 7th St., S.W.

☎ 202-633-1000

🚇 Metro: L'Enfant Plaza; Bus: 32–36, 52

hirshhorn.si.edu

and kinetic works by Alexander Calder and Mark di Suvero.

Other major artists represented in the museum's wide-ranging collection of paintings and sculpture include Willem de Kooning, Alberto Giacometti, Jackson Pollock, Pablo Picasso, Clyfford Still, Gerhard Richter, Ana Mendieta, Georgia O'Keeffe, Ernesto Neto, Hiroshi Sugimoto, Lorna Simpson, Robert Lazzarini, Ann Hamilton, Yoko Ono, and many others. The artworks on view change frequently, with the focus on ever changing exhibitions.

In an effort to continually expand its holdings and showcase modern works, the Hirshhorn works closely with today's artists. To present pieces from its col-

What Was Here Before?

Prior to the Hirshhorn, this piece of the Mall was occupied by the U.S. Army Medical Museum—now the National Museum of Health & Medicine (see p. 192)—from 1887 to 1968. The museum was established during the Civil War to help advance medical treatment. More than 25,000 specimens of diseased or wounded flesh and bones were kept here, and morbidly fascinated visitors could see preserved gunshot wounds, and disfigured and diseased organs. Over the years the tastes of the public changed, and the museum relocated to the Walter Reed Army Medical Center until its recent move to 2500 Linden Lane, Silver Spring, Maryland.

lection in fresh, new ways, the museum introduced an exhibition series, titled **"Ways of Seeing,"** in which working artists, filmmakers, and other creative thinkers were invited to organize exhibitions

INSIDER TIP:

Bringing life to the lawn right next to the Hirshhorn is sculptor Juan Muñoz's dazzling "Last Conversation Piece." The five figures suggest both whimsy and intensity.

—SHEILA BUCKMASTER
*National Geographic Traveler
magazine editor at large*

using objects from the museum's holdings. In one such installation, for example, artist John Baldessari incorporated paintings by Milton Avery, Philip Guston, and Thomas Eakins, photographs by Eakins, and sculpture by Emily Kaufman.

Other programs include "Meet the Artist" lectures, gallery talks, and themed "How to Look at Art" presentations that offer tips for thinking about and interpreting works of modern and contemporary art, plus art-related activities such as "STORYTIME" for children. Several times a year the Hirshhorn hosts "After Hours" events that offer inviting social environments in which to enjoy the exhibits.

In addition, a renowned film program—one of the first in the United States to focus on independent cinema—presents narrative and experimental features, documentaries, shorts, and presentations by directors and others in the museum's 272-seat auditorium. ■

NATIONAL AIR AND SPACE MUSEUM

The excitement of aeronautical and spaceflight technology has made the National Air and Space Museum one of the most visited museums on the planet. Every year millions of people roam its flagship building on the Mall, where the exhibits feature only 10 percent of the Smithsonian's aviation and space collection. Many of the remaining artifacts are on display at the Steven F. Udvar-Hazy Center annex in suburban Virginia (see pp. 222–223).

■ The 1903 "Wright Flyer"

The Smithsonian's involvement in air and space goes back to 1857, when it began using balloons to collect weather data. Later, during the Civil War, the first secretary of the Smithsonian, Joseph Henry, won President Abraham Lincoln's support for making military observations from balloons. The third secretary, Samuel Pierpont Langley (1887–1906), was an astronomer and airplane pioneer. He experimented successfully with large, powered model aircraft on the Potomac in the 1890s.

During the first half of the 20th century, the Smithsonian participated in and funded major rocket research and astrophysical observation projects. In 1971, Apollo astronaut Michael Collins was appointed director of the new National Air and Space Museum, which opened to the public in 1976.

In 2018, the Smithsonian began a complete $650 million renovation, to extend through 2025. Initial construction began on the west wing, with the first new galleries reopening in 2022;

National Air and Space Museum

⬛ Map pp. 70–71

✉ Independence Ave. & 7th St., S.W.

☎ 202-633-2214

🚇 Metro: L'Enfant Plaza; Bus: 32–36, 54, A9

airandspace.si.edu

thereafter the east wing will close for renovation. The visitor experience will be in flux as all 23 galleries are updated with new settings, or completely revamped with new themes. Check the website for updates.

Visiting

With so much to see at this museum, it's best to map out your visit, especially if you're with children or others who tire easily (see floor plan this page, showing the museum after renovation). Moving around can be a challenge during peak visiting times because of the huge crowds, so pace yourself—and agree on a place to meet others in your party if you get separated.

If you want to see any of the shows in the IMAX theater or the Planetarium, it's a good idea to purchase the tickets at the start of your visit, because tickets often sell out. Then tour the galleries that interest you until the show starts. At lunchtime, you can grab a bite to eat at the museum's large, airy cafeteria.

More than 1,400 new artifacts will be displayed, as well as scores of digital interactives. Almost all

the artifacts are the real thing: Labels indicate if it's a backup, test vehicle, or reproduction.

First Floor

In 2022, the Mall entrance will close through 2024 for a rebuild, with a new curved-wing overhang. During this time, visitors will enter from Independence Avenue. Take time to study the two impressive murals to either side. Robert T. McCall's 1976 "The Space Mural: A Cosmic View" traces space history from the Big Bang to lunar exploration and beyond. On the opposite

Einstein
Planetarium

IMAX exit

Modern Military
Aviation

Destination
Moon

Pioneers
of Flight

SECOND FLOOR

One World
Connected

WWI

Flight and the Arts

America
by Air

Lockheed Martin
IMAX Theater

WWII

Discovering
Our Universe

Museum
shop

Milestones
of Flight

Living
in Space

James Webb
Space Telescope

FIRST FLOOR

Wright
Brothers

We All Fly

South Lobby

Future of
Spaceflight

How
Things Fly

At Home
in Space

Cafeteria

Independence Avenue

wall, Eric Sloan's mural "Earth Flight Environment" (1976) shows a Western landscape beneath a sky filled with various weather systems pilots must fly through.

Proceeding to the left, you'll come to the museum's store. Opposite, the **Wright Brothers & the Invention of the Aerial Age** offers an eye-level view of the famous wood-and-fabric Wright Flyer that was flown at Kitty Hawk, North Carolina, in 1903, marking the dawn of modern aviation. Other exhibits and panels explain how the

brothers overcame the challenges to taking-off, staying aloft, and steering their flimsy craft.

Beyond that is the **America by Air** gallery, which explores the history of air transportation in the United States. Attractions include a giant nose cone section from a Boeing 747 and a cockpit simulation of an Airbus A320. Opposite, the new **We All Fly** gallery celebrates the breadth and depth of general aviation and explores how it impacts our lives.

Next to America by Air, the reimagined **Early Flight** gallery explores the time when flight was still a novelty. Among the featured artifacts are the world's first military plane, the 1909 Wright Military Flyer, and an 1894 Lilienthal glider with batlike ribbed wings. The new **Innovations** gallery, adjacent, will trace key moments that revolutionized flight, laying the groundwork for aerospace exploration. Included in this display is the infamous Messerschmitt Me 262, the first jet-powered fighter.

As you cross the hall to the east wing, passing the Mall entrance, the two-story **Mile-**

INSIDER TIP:

Charles Lindbergh's *Spirit of St. Louis* is an obvious Air and Space must-see; Amelia Earhart's bright red plane is a fine surprise.

—DANIEL R. WESTERGREN
National Geographic Traveler magazine director of photography

stones of Flight gallery hall (closed 2022–2024) hosts the Welcome Center and highlights aviation's "greatest hits," with such iconic artifacts suspended overhead as the *Spirit of St. Louis,* in which Charles Lindbergh made the first solo nonstop flight across the Atlantic in May 1927; the Bell X-1 in which "Chuck" Yeager first broke the sound barrier; and *SpaceShipOne,* the first private crewed vehicle to reach space. At ground level, you can peer into John Glenn's Mercury Friendship

7 capsule and admire an Apollo Lunar Module built for an unmanned Earth-orbit test flight and modified to look like Apollo 11's *Eagle.*

Immediately on your left is the **Lockheed Martin IMAX Theater** *($$–$$$).* Its 3-D films include the thrilling, long-running classic "To Fly!" projected onto a screen five stories high. Catercorner to the theater, and a favorite among children, the **How Things Fly** gallery has hands-on exhibits that explain principles such as lift, drag, air pressure, and wave action.

The other five galleries in this wing, all opening after 2022, are dedicated to space travel. Directly opposite the IMAX Theater, the immersive **Future of Spaceflight** gallery will explore the evolution of commercial spaceflight technologies in recent decades, and the future possibilities, including asteroid mining. Exhibits include the RocketMotorTwo engine from Virgin Galactic's VSS *Unity.* **At Home in Space** takes visitors inside the International Space Station and the experience of astronauts living in low Earth orbit. The **James Webb Space Telescope** exhibit profiles the largest, most powerful and complex space telescope ever built, launched in 2022 to replace the Hubble Space Telescope. **Discovering Our Universe** showcases many of the tools and space vehicles that have enhanced our knowledge of the solar system, the galaxies, and beyond. Finally, **Living in Space** offers a glimpse of the future of space travel and colonization of the planets, including human

EXPERIENCE: Joining the Revelry on the Mall

During the warm months of the year, there's bound to be something special happening on the National Mall just about any time you might be visiting. Some activities are targeted to particular groups—such as D.C. Yoga Week (April–May) and the Black Family Reunion (September)—but most cater to the general public and a wide range of interests.

Summer is the busiest time, and no Mall event has a bigger bang than the annual **Fourth of July** celebration (nps.gov/foju). The spectacular display of fireworks will have you "oohing" and "ahhing" at the colorful streamers of light bursting around the silhouetted monuments. Some spectators start arriving on the lawn as early as 10 a.m. to claim choice places (everyone must enter the grounds through a security checkpoint). Starting at midday, an Independence Day parade of fife and drum corps, drill teams, guest bands, and national dignitaries wends its way down Constitution Avenue, from 7th to 17th Streets.

Around the same time, the two-week-long **Smithsonian Folklife Festival** (late June–early July; festival.si.edu) also draws crowds. Each year the festival spotlights the cultural traditions of several nations, regions, ethnic groups, and occupations. The packed program of events includes presentations by musicians, artists, storytellers, and dancers, along with traditional foods and crafts.

A popular springtime event is the **Blossom Kite Festival,** when butterflies, dragons with long tails, and an array of colorful geometrical shapes dot the sky above the Mall. It's part of the month-long National Cherry Blossom Festival, mid-March to mid-April.

Many military memorials host special events in honor of America's armed forces and fallen heroes on **Memorial Day** (last Monday in May), and **Veterans Day** (November 11). The former includes the massive "Rolling to Remember" motorcycle rally.

If you are out for an evening stroll on the Mall, you may catch a free **military band concert** (schedules on websites of the military branches) held regularly Memorial Day through Labor Day. The Army, Navy, Air Force, and Marine Corps have traditional military bands and specialty groups such as jazz ensembles and string quartets; venues include the Lincoln Memorial and the U.S. Capitol lawn.

On the Fourth of July, the Mall crackles with pyrotechnic action.

physical, psychological, and cultural adaptations to an out-of-this-world lifestyle.

Second Floor

Escalators in the entrance lobby carry you to the museum's second floor, where you can visit the **Einstein Planetarium** ($$) and view multimedia presentations in the domed theater.

Across from the planetarium, **One World Connected** tells the story of how aviation and spaceflight have accelerated human interconnectivity of ideas, images, and people; and how human actions, enabled by space travel, are inseparable from Earth's well-being and fate.

Next comes **Destination Moon,** a new blockbuster exhibit that traces the challenges of the quest to put humans on the moon. Its fabulous collection of artifacts from the Mercury, Gemini, and Apollo missions includes Neil Armstrong's meticulously restored Apollo 11 spacesuit, plus the *Columbia* command module, housed in a custom-designed, climate-controlled case.

Then comes a redesigned gallery, **Exploring the Planets,** which regales the history and science of solar system exploration and profiles the diversity of the planets and their moons. Visitors can marvel at a full-scale model of a Mars rover.

Also in the west end of the second floor, the new **Nation of**

Celebrated Aviator Charles Lindbergh

Perhaps more than any other aviator, Charles Lindbergh (1902–1974) captured the public's heart. Son of a Minnesota congressman, he spent some early years in Washington, D.C. Later he attended a Wisconsin college but dropped out to enroll in a Nebraska flying school. For a few years he was a stunt flyer and an airmail pilot. Then he competed for a $25,000 prize offered to the first person to fly from New York to Paris nonstop.

On May 20, 1927, the aviator took off in the *Spirit of St. Louis*, named for the city where he received financial backing. Because the large fuel tank partially blocked his view, Lindbergh relied on a periscope or tilted the plane to see forward. He flew for 33.5 exhausting hours before landing at Le Bourget Field near Paris and receiving a warm welcome by a cheering crowd of 100,000.

Back in Washington, Lindbergh stayed a few days at the Patterson House on Dupont Circle with President Coolidge, who lived there while the White House was being renovated. Later that year the U.S. Congress awarded him a Medal of Honor. The following year he gave his plane to the Smithsonian, where it is prominently displayed.

In 1929, Lindbergh wed Anne Morrow, and together they made several flights to chart airline routes. When their son was kidnapped and killed in 1932, the unending publicity drove them abroad. Lindbergh's advocacy of neutrality in World War II led him to resign his commission in the U.S. Army Air Corps, and to criticism by President Roosevelt. Nonetheless, after Pearl Harbor, he flew as a civilian consultant on combat missions over the Pacific. He described his famous transatlantic flight in thrilling detail in *WE* (1927) and *The Spirit of St. Louis* (1953).

Speed gallery pursues the human desire to go ever faster on land, sea, air, and in space, including how the technological ingenuity to achieve greater speed has shaped contemporary culture. Iconic vehicles on display include Mario Andretti's Indy 500–winning race car and the Sharp Nemesis NXT Air Racer.

Once you leave this end of the second floor and head in the other direction, you'll come to the **Pioneers of Flight** gallery, devoted to individual feats in aviation history. Although transformed with a new layout, design, and presentations, it still focuses on such icons of the 1920s and '30s as Charles Lindbergh and Amelia Earhart.

Opening in 2025, the next two galleries focus on various aspects of aviation during the two **World Wars,** offering an unromanticized view of aerial combat during WWI and a focus on revolutions in technology and tactics in WWII. A P-51D Mustang and Messerschmitt Bf 109G are among the iconic fighter aircraft displayed.

The gallery across the hall in the far corner, **Modern Military Aviation,** will explore how air warfare has evolved since WWII. Finally, the **Flight and the Arts** gallery in the southeast corner will showcase works from the museum's huge flight-related art collection, which includes paintings by Francisco Goya, Norman Rockwell and Alexander Calder.

To view another of the museum's popular exhibits, return to the first floor and step outside, through the Mall entrance. There,

Neil Armstrong's Apollo 11 spacesuit

Voyage: A Journey Through Our Solar System depicts the solar system—at one ten-billionth of its actual size—in an arrangement that depicts the relative sizes of the planets and the vast distances between them. The planets are represented by porcelain balls mounted atop stainless steel posts; the sun is about the size of a large grapefruit; Earth is the size of the head of a pin. The installation runs for 647 yards (592 m) along the Mall, all the way from the Air and Space Museum to Pluto, far away near the Smithsonian Castle. ∎

NATIONAL MUSEUM OF THE AMERICAN INDIAN

Striking in its architecture, which was inspired by the rocky mesa cliffs of the American Southwest, the National Museum of the American Indian opened in September 2004 after 15 years of planning. It gives the nation a vibrant center for Native American events and educational programs as well as a showcase for outstanding Indian art and artifacts.

The museum got its start at the turn of the 20th century when a wealthy New York banker, George Gustav Heye, needed a place to house the objects he had obtained from North and South American native cultures in a buying frenzy from 1903 to 1954—an astonishing collection of almost a million pieces

■ The museum's undulating curves and deep window ledges suggest the work of wind and water.

spanning 10,000 years. He established a museum in what is now the restored Alexander Hamilton U.S. Custom House in lower Manhattan, New York.

In 1989, Heye's collection was transferred to the Smithsonian Institution. Among the artifacts were human remains that had to be repatriated and buried in native grounds. As the Smithsonian's Native American collection swelled to some 400,000 objects, a campaign began to build a major museum for Indian art and culture. The original location in New York City is now a branch of this 4.25-acre (1.7 ha) museum on the Mall, along with a 200,000-square-foot (18,580 sq m) Cultural Resources Center in Suitland, Maryland, where a large bulk of the collection is preserved.

The museum's collection of Native American artifacts is one of the most extensive in the world, with about 266,000 items that represent more than 12,000 years and more than 1,200 indigenous cultures throughout the Americas, from the Arctic to Tierra del Fuego. Plus, its Photographic Archive holds about 324,000 images dating from the 1860s to the present, while the 12,000-item Media Archive includes film and audiovisual collections ranging from phonograph discs to 35mm film and digital video.

Among the museum's treasures are intricate carvings and masks from Pacific Northwest coastal tribes; embellished hides and feather bonnets from North American Plains Indians; pottery and basketry from the Southwest; 18th-century pieces from the Great Lakes area; and early Navajo weavings. Artifacts from Mexico, Central and South America, and the Caribbean include Mayan carved jade, Colombian gold pieces, and Amazonian feather works.

Visiting

As you wander about the four-story museum, observe the many symbolic references to the cultures it honors. The curvy outside façade of Kasota limestone was made to appear like an ancient slab of stratified stone. Crystal prisms embedded in the south-facing wall create "light shows" when reflecting the midday sun, while the main doors bear native sun symbols.

Inside is a central space called the **Potomac,** a Piscataway word for a place "where the goods are brought in." The overhead dome, 120 feet high (36.5 m) and 120 feet wide, has an oculus offering views of the sky and celestial bodies. On the floor is a circle of red sandstone and rings of black and red granite that map the solstices and equinoxes. A wall of copper bands woven to suggest baskets and textiles encircles the room.

A theater on the ground floor features storytelling, music, and dance. The Potomac Atrium area spotlights changing artisan craft exhibits.

Take an elevator to the exhibition areas on the upper levels. The 120-seat **Lewali Theater** on the fourth floor offers an orientation program explaining the themes

---

INSIDER TIP:

Driving by the monuments at night is a D.C. delight. The Museum of the American Indian also makes for a fine nighttime spectacle.

—JUSTIN KAVANAGH
National Geographic Travel Books editor

---

and messages of the exhibits.

The museum has three ongoing exhibits. **Our Universes: Traditional Knowledge Shapes Our World** looks at the primary role of cosmology in the myths and lives of native peoples, and their reverence for the spiritual relationship between mankind and the natural world. The exhibit **Americans** examines how American Indian images, names, and stories infuse American contemporary life; displays include a 1948 Indian Chief motorcycle. **Return to a Native Place: Algonquian Peoples of the Chesapeake** features displays that highlight events affecting the Nanticoke, Powhatan, and Piscataway tribes. ■

National Museum of the American Indian

🗺 Map pp. 70–71

✉ 4th St. & Independence Ave., S.W.

☎ 202-633-1000

🕐 Closed Mon.– Tue.

🚇 Metro: L'Enfant Plaza; Bus: 30, 32–36

americanindian .si.edu

NATIONAL GALLERY OF ART

One of the country's top art museums, the National Gallery of Art holds a comprehensive collection of Western masterpieces, more than 150,000 pieces strong. The West Building exhibits European painting and sculpture from the 13th to 19th centuries; American art; and prints, drawings, photography, and decorative arts. The East Building contains modern and contemporary art. Both buildings also present temporary exhibits.

Rising between the East and West Buildings, tetrahedrons are skylights for the concourse below.

National Gallery of Art

- Map pp. 70–71
- Constitution Ave. bet. 3rd & 9th Sts., N.W.
- 202-737-4215
- Metro: Archives-Navy Memorial-Penn Quarter, Smithsonian; Bus: 32–36, 54, A9, V8

nga.gov

In the 1920s, financier and Secretary of the Treasury Andrew Mellon began planning to establish a museum in Washington. In 1931 he completed a purchase of 21 paintings from Russia's Hermitage Museum, including Raphael's "Alba Madonna." Mellon died in 1937, the same year that construction began for the new museum designed by John Russell Pope and funded by the A. W. Mellon Educational and Charitable Trust. In March 1941, President Roosevelt presided over a dedication ceremony attended by nearly 9,000 guests.

The holdings grew rapidly, thanks to many generous donations, and in the late 1960s, architect I. M. Pei was hired to create a plan for a new building to accommodate the collection. Opened in 1978, the glass-fronted East Building had to fit a trapezoidal site and mesh with the neoclassical West Building. An underground concourse connects the two buildings.

Under phased renovation plans, various galleries in the two buildings close temporarily and some works may be moved to different locations in the museum, so check the website before your visit if there's a particular masterpiece you want to see.

Also check for special exhibitions and new acquisitions. In recent years 22 new galleries were added on the ground floor of the West Building, featuring 900 works of art such as sculpture masterpieces from the Middle Ages, antique Roman coins, and porcelain vases from the Ming and Qing dynasties. The galleries for photographs and works on paper opened in 2004.

West Building

All entrances other than on the Mall put you on the **ground floor,** from where you can reach the East Building via a belowground concourse under 4th Street, N.W. The ground floor showcases sculptures, from ancient Roman and Etruscan pieces (Gallery 14) to an astounding ensemble of bronzes by Rodin and Degas, including the latter's famous "Little Dancer" series. Don't miss Rodin's iconic "The Thinker" and "The Kiss" in Gallery 2. Several

galleries also display decorative arts, from Renaissance furniture to helmets, plus an eclectic range of still-lifes and portraits, including by Manet, Renoir, and Toulouse-Lautrec.

One level up is the **main floor,** where European art from the 13th to 19th centuries and American painting and sculpture from colonial times to the early 20th century are displayed. The spectacular **Rotunda,** ringed by Tuscan marble pillars, rises to a high oculus above a central fountain graced by a statue of Mercury. The dome is strongly reminiscent of John Russell Pope's other great

Vermeer's Legacy of Light & Beauty

Art aficionados and experts alike are invariably struck by the paintings of the Dutch artist Johannes Vermeer (1632–1637), particularly his style and his gift of contrasting light and dark. The National Gallery has the honor to possess four of the world's 35 known Vermeer paintings.

"Girl with a Pearl Earring," held by the Mauritshuis gallery in the Hague, Netherlands, is regarded as Vermeer's ultimate masterpiece and lies at the heart of a fictionalized novel of the

same name written by Tracy Chevalier (later made into a movie directed by Peter Webber).

Of the canvases credited to Vermeer, the famous tear-shaped pearl was featured in eight of them, including "A Lady Writing" and "Girl with the Red Hat," both displayed at the National Gallery of Art. Was the same woman the model for multiple paintings? No one knows for sure, but it's a favorite topic of conversation.

West Garden Court
West Sculpture Hall
Rotunda
East Sculpture Hall
East Garden Court

Main Floor

Ground Floor

West Building

Washington structure, the Jefferson Memorial.

Extending from either side of the Rotunda, the **West Sculpture Hall** contains works in bronze, while the **East Sculpture Hall** has works in marble. Each hall ends in a garden court, where free concerts are often held. Several cafés and coffee bars throughout the National Gallery offer light fare.

The museum's hushed halls and courts are surrounded by galleries that are numbered 1 to 93 and generally proceed in chronological order, with nationalities grouped together.

Galleries 1–13 hold **13th- to 16th-century Italian paintings.** Representing the early Florentine and central Italian Renaissance, these works range from Byzantine iconography to the beginnings of the high Renaissance. Masterpieces include Giotto's "Madonna and Child" (ca 1320–1330); Leonardo da Vinci's "Ginevra de' Benci" (1474); and Botticelli's "Adoration of the Magi" (ca 1478).

You'll find **16th-century Italian, French, and Spanish works** in Galleries 17–28. Here is art from the northern Italian

West Building Galleries

Main Floor

13th- to 16th-century Italian paintings and scultures

16th-century Italian, French, and Spanish paintings, sculptures, and decorative arts

17th- and 18th-century Italian, French, and Spanish paintings

15th- to 16th-century Netherlands and German paintings and sculptures

18th- and early 19th-century French paintings and sculptures

18th- and 19th-century French and Spanish paintings

18th- and 19th-century French paintings and sculptures

British paintings and sculptures

American paintings and sculptures

19th-century French paintings

Ground Floor

19th- and 20th-century paintings and sculptures

Ancient, Medieval, Renaissance, and Baroque sculptures and decorative arts

17th- and 18th-century sculptures, decorative arts, and paintings

American decorative arts and paintings

National Gallery of Art

East Building

Renaissance, distinguished by allegorical and religious scenes within a colorful, sensual, pastoral setting. Especially outstanding are paintings by the Venetian master Tiziano Vecelli, or Titian, whose "Venus with a Mirror" (1555) is vibrant with life. Raphael's "Alba Madonna" (1510) hangs here, as do works by Tintoretto, one of the great Venetian painters. Gallery 28 has works by the Spanish painter El Greco.

Galleries 29–34 and 36–37 display **17th- and 18th-century Italian, Spanish, and French baroque paintings.** Among the artists are Canaletto, a Venetian

master known for his views of Venice, and Tiepelo, another Venetian, who painted in a colorful style. Look for Georges de la Tour's "The Repentant Magdalene" (1640).

In Galleries 35, 35A, and 38–41A, **15th- and 16th-century Netherlands and German** painters include Albrecht Dürer and Matthias Grunewald, whose few works, mostly religious, such as "The Crucifixion" (ca 1520), were enough to secure his reputation as one of the greats of his time.

Among the most popular areas of the museum, Galleries 42–51 feature **17th-century Flemish** and Dutch paintings. The large collection of Van Dyck portraits is among the finest in the world. Here also is Rubens's monumental "Daniel in the Lions' Den" (1614). Dutch realism can be found in portraits by Frans Hals, landscapes by Jacob van Ruisdael, and still lifes by Ambrosius Bosschaert. Great treasures on display include the luminous paintings of Johannes Vermeer (among them "Girl with the Red Hat") and the forceful images of Rembrandt van Rijn, including his brooding "Self-Portrait" of 1659 and "The Mill" (1645), with its chiaroscuro effects.

INSIDER TIP:

Leo Villareal's "Multiverse" (2008), installed along the concourse walkway between the East and West Buildings, is a hypnotic play of light and movement.

–KAREN CARMICHAEL
National Geographic writer

In the east side of the rotunda, Gallery 52 contains **18th- and 19th-century Spanish paintings,** notably by Francisco de Goya. **French art from the 18th and early 19th centuries** lines the walls of Galleries 53–56, much of it in a florid style depicting light-hearted sophistication in French society. Among the treasures are Antoine Watteau's "Italian Comedians" (1720), Boucher's "Madame Bergeret" (1746), and

Fragonard's "A Young Girl Reading" (1776).

British works fill Galleries 57–59 and 61. Represented here are Reynolds, Gainsborough, Constable, and Turner. The landscapes of Constable and the seascapes of Turner are well worth noting.

American paintings are on view in Galleries 60A–B and 62, 71. Gilbert Stuart's portraits of early U.S. presidents, George Catlin's portraits of Native Americans, and Augustus Saint-Gaudens' busts of "Black Soldiers" of the Union Army vie for attention with the big mid-19th-century landscapes of Bierstadt, Cole, and Church. Other works are by Homer, Whistler, Bellows, Cropsey, Ryder, and Sargent.

Impressionist and other 19th-century French painting is on exhibit in Galleries 80–93. These rooms are filled with the light and color of leading exponents, from Renoir to Toulouse-Lautrec, including the idiosyncratic styles of Cézanne and van Gogh. Among the great works are Cézanne's "The Harlequin" (1888), Degas' "The Dance Lesson" (1879) and Monet's "Woman with a Parasol—Madame Monet and her Son" (1875).

East Building

The walls and angles of the East Building, added in 1978, are marvels in themselves. The building itself consists of two triangular shapes, covered in some 16,200 pink marble panels. A five-year renovation completed in 2016 removed and reinstalled each panel with new supports and added 12,260 square feet (1,139 sq m) of art exhibition space on four levels atop the building's current footprint. The wing focuses on modern and contemporary art representing a Who's Who of international greats, from Modigliani, Mondrian, and Matisse to Picasso, Georgia O'Keeffe, Diego Rivera, and Mark Rothko. On the **ground floor** look for Modigliani's "Nude on a Blue Cushion" (1917), George Bellows' "Blue Morning" (1909), plus Walker Evans' photography and Henry Moore's travertine "Stone Memorial" (1961). A highlight on the **Mezzanine** is Picasso's "The Tragedy" (1903), while standouts on the **Upper Level** include Jean Miró's "The Farm" (1921) and Andy Warhol's "Green Marilyn" (1962). Above, the **Tower** displays many of Alexander Calder's iconic mobiles.

Sculpture Garden

Opened in 1999, the 6-acre (2.4 ha) sculpture garden is across 7th Street, N.W., from the West Building. Its 21 works include "Puellae" (1992), featuring 30 headless, shriveled, 3-foot-tall (1 m) girls—Polish-born sculptor Magdalena Abakanowicz's chilling depiction of a Holocaust story. You can't miss Louise Bourgeois's 9-foot-tall (2.7 m) "Spider" (1997), part of a series exploring childhood memory and loss. Another large piece, "Aurora" (1992–1993) by Mark Di Suvero, illustrates elegance and balance on a massive scale.

An attractive glass-sided café in the garden serves

■ **Sculpture and modern architecture in the East Building of the National Gallery of Art**

refreshments and offers free "Jazz in the Garden" concerts on Friday evenings from Memorial Day to Labor Day. Nearby is a fountain that becomes an ice-skating rink from November to March. ■

NATIONAL MUSEUM OF NATURAL HISTORY

Dinosaur fossils, sparkling gems, mammals, an insect zoo, and rare Native American artifacts—these are the kinds of things that make this such a popular museum. The Smithsonian's National Museum of Natural History explores in wondrous detail the natural world
and our place in it. Housed in a green-domed beaux arts building from 1910, this was the
third Smithsonian building, erected to hold the institution's bursting collection.

■ Millions of people have viewed the African elephant on display in the Rotunda since 1959.

**National Museum
of Natural History**

- Map pp. 70–71
- 10th St. &
  Constitution
  Ave., N.W.
- 202-633-1000
- Metro: Federal
  Triangle,
  Smithsonian;
  Bus: 32–36,
  52–54

mnh.si.edu

Fascination with the natural world
never goes out of style. More
than 90 percent of the Smithsonian's entire collection of artifacts,
specimens, and works of art
belongs to this museum alone.
That's more than 127 million individual specimens and artifacts.

Researchers from around the
world use the collection—much
of it stored off-site—to carry out
various systematic studies. Just
think of all the millions of beetles,
butterflies, mosquitoes, sponges,
mollusks, mineralogical samples,
birds' eggs, and microscopic

organisms stored in drawers and
on shelves.

Visiting

You can easily spend a day wandering through the museum, getting sidetracked from whatever it
was you had set out to see. If you
have only a few hours, pinpoint
a couple exhibits and plot your
route (maps are available at information desks at both entrances).

While the museum was closed
for 461 days during the COVID-19
pandemic, curators updated many
displays and wheelchair-friendly

walkways were added to the entrance from the Mall, now the sole entrance, although visitors may exit to Constitution Avenue.

First Floor

You'll step into the grand **Rotunda,** one of the city's great interior spaces. The eight-sided Rotunda rises to a dome 125 feet (38 m) from the floor; columned galleries offer splendid views of the space from above. Towering over the ticketing and information booths is **Henry, the African elephant.** Standing 13 feet 2 inches (4 m) at the shoulder, the bush elephant weighed 12 tons (10.8 tonnes) while alive. In 1959, it was donated by a Hungarian game hunter and has graced the rotunda ever since; in 2015, Henry's platform was redesigned as a marble plinth inset with educational panels.

More mammals await in the West Wing's **Kenneth E. Behring Family Hall of Mammals,** to the left of the Rotunda. The 25,000-square-foot (2,322 sq m) permanent exhibition, which tells the story of mammal evolution through adaptation to changing habitats, features 274 taxidermied specimens artfully posed in a variety of environments—from polar to desert, dry to humid. Interactive features enhance the displays by explaining aspects of the remarkable diversity of mammals. A short film traces 225 million years of mammal evolution.

Adjoining, **Unsettled Nature** examines how humans have shaped and are shaping the world in ways large and small. A complementary exhibit, the **Hall of Human Origins** tells the story of human evolution. Among the skulls and fossils is the only Neanderthal skeleton in the U.S. The exhibit, spanning six million years, includes forensically reconstructed faces of prehistoric relatives. Facing this hall in the East Wing, the **African Voices** exhibit offers perspectives on how the people of Africa have influenced global culture.

The Rotunda opens north to **Sant Ocean Hall,** the museum's largest exhibit. Extraordinary in scope, the hall presents 674 marine specimens and models, including replicas of a right whale, a giant squid, and a 52-foot-long

---

INSIDER TIP:

Well worth a visit is the Sant Ocean Hall, which stresses the importance of healthy seas to the future of humankind.

—KENNY LING
Mapmaker & National Geographic contributor

(15.9 m) megalodon—a fearsome prehistoric shark that once roamed the oceans between 23 and 2.6 million years ago. You can even take a selfie in the massive fossilized jaws of a real megalodon.

To the right of the Rotunda, the new **David H. Koch Hall of Fossils—Deep Time** opened in 2019 after a five-year renovation, with more than 31,000 square feet (2,880 sq m) of exhibition space showcasing the museum's unparalleled collection of 46 million fossils. Together, they trace the origins and evolution of life back 4.6 billion years to the Earth's formation. The center-pieces include a nearly complete 66.5-million-year-old *Tyrannosaurus rex* skeleton that was unearthed in Montana in 1990; a 90-foot-long (27 m) skeleton of the plant-eating *Diplodocus* sauropod; and an Ice Age wooly mammoth. More fossils await upstairs in the West Wing's **Bone Hall** (*download the "Skin & Bones" app off the website to view how the skeletons look live in the flesh*). The skeletons, many of which have been displayed since the museum opened in 1881, represent every major group of vertebrate animals, from snakes, mice, and chimpanzees to massive sea turtles and an even bigger gray whale overhead.

Second Floor

Opposite Bone Hall are real live critters in **O. Orkin Insect Zoo,** a storehouse of delights for any-one who appreciates the most abundant animals on Earth. Live exhibits, animated by buzzing and chirping sounds, give this display an edge. Watch live bees, water striders, darkling beetles, centi-pedes, tarantulas, and whip scorpi-ons go about their daily lives. Also at work are unfailingly industrious leaf-cutter ants, while you can stroll among live lepidoptera in the leafy **Butterfly Pavilion.**

Also tucked into the West Wing is the long-running **Eternal Life in Ancient Egypt,** focus-ing on Egyptian burial ritual and cosmology. Visitors can learn

A *Triceratops* fossil at the National Museum of Natural History

how scientists use computer scans to study mummies without unwrapping them, and view alabaster tomb vessels and a vivid blue beaded necklace that was wrapped around a mummy's neck.

Many people, however, head straight for the **Janet Annenberg Hooker Hall of Geology, Gems, and Minerals.** Here you can learn how a meteorite impact may have wiped out the dinosaurs, build a virtual volcano, watch a film on plate tectonics, and view gems of every shape, size, and color. A 45-foot-long (13.7 m) model of a salt crystal, enlarged nearly 1.5 billion times, is particularly mesmerizing. Outshining them all, however, is the 45.52-carat Hope Diamond, the largest blue diamond in the world. Other outstanding riches include a thousand-diamond diadem given by Napoleon I to his wife Empress Marie Louise; a pair of Marie Antoinette's earrings; the world's largest perfect quartz sphere, a magically clear 107-pound (48.5 kg) globe from China; and the Carmen Lúcia Ruby, a stunning 23.1-carat Burmese ruby set in a platinum ring with diamonds.

Opened in May 2018, the **Outbreak: Epidemics in a Connected World** exhibition seemed uncannily timely on the eve of the COVID-19 pandemic, especially as it was opened by the Center for Centers for Disease Control's Dr. Anthony Fauci. Interactive exhibits even let you team with other visitors to contain a deadly outbreak before it spreads further in a multi-player game.

James Smithson

The man who originally endowed the Smithsonian Institution and gave it his name, English scientist James Smithson (1765–1829), never actually visited the United States. Passionate about chemistry, mineralogy, and geology, he dedicated himself to the advancement of science, at times even risking his life while gathering observations. He directed that a large portion of his estate—$12 million in today's dollars—be used to create an "Establishment for the increase and diffusion of knowledge" in Washington. Why he left his fortune to the United States is a mystery. His remains are interred in a crypt in the Smithsonian Castle, thanks to Alexander Graham Bell, who had them brought here from Italy, where Smithson died.

Ground Floor

Downstairs, walk to the back of this floor, past the Atrium Café and Museum Shop, to the **Birds of D.C.** exhibit, flanking the **Baird Auditorium.** Many people miss this compendium of taxidermied eastern birds (native and migratory) on display since the 1920s. Along with bald and golden eagles, swans, and yellow warblers, the extinct Carolina parakeet and passenger pigeon are represented.

At the other end of the floor, by the Constitution Avenue exit, is the **Q?rius** (pronounced "curious") lab, designed for teens and tweens. In the interactive and experimental learning space, students can chat with scientists and interact with thousands of authentic specimens. The **Q?rius Jr. Discovery Room** lets kids nine and under get hands-on with real museum artifacts such as fossils, skulls, shells, and minerals. ■

NATIONAL MUSEUM OF AMERICAN HISTORY

The Smithsonian Institution, with 19 separate museums and galleries, has been called "the nation's attic," and the National Museum of American History is particularly rich in treasures that document American history and culture. At any one time, only about 3 to 5 percent of the three million artifacts in the museum's collection are on display.

■ A museum visitor takes to the podium and delivers an impromptu Inaugural Address.

National Museum of American History

Map pp. 70–71

14th St. & Constitution Ave., N.W.

202-633-1000

Metro: Federal Triangle, Smithsonian; Bus: 52, 13F–G, X1

americanhistory .si.edu

When it opened in 1964, the building was called the National Museum of History and Technology. That name was changed in 1980 to reflect the museum's changing focus.

In recent years, the museum has been redesigning its exhibits to present various artifacts in the context of broad themes relevant to U.S. life from colonial to modern times. The museum closed down in late 2006 for major renovations. It reopened in November 2008 with a new state-of-the-art

gallery at the center of the museum, safeguarding one of the country's most beloved artifacts: the original Star-Spangled Banner, which inspired the poem that became the national anthem.

The museum continues to transform, including a major five-year renovation project, completed in 2020, that renewed its 120,000-square-foot (11,150 sq m) west exhibition wing and incorporates a panoramic window with a sweeping view of the Washington Monument and the National Mall.

New third floor exhibitions on entertainment, culture, and the arts were also added. The three floors are themed to "Innovation" (first), "The Nation We Build Together" (second), and "American Culture" (third).

Some of the most popular artifacts at the museum are Dorothy's ruby slippers from *The Wizard of Oz;* President Lincoln's top hat; a compass used by Lewis and Clark during their journey across the Louisiana Territory; the Woolworth lunch counter from Greensboro, North Carolina, where four African-American students staged a nearly six-month-long sit-in to protest segregation (see sidebar right); Thomas Jefferson's Bible; and Kermit the Frog from *Sesame Street.*

Visiting

If you enter the museum from Constitution Avenue, you'll be on the first floor; the Mall entrance puts you on the second floor, where there's a **Welcome Center.** Maps and information are available at both entrances. The museum has stores on floors 1 and 2, and food services on the lower level.

First Floor

A large exhibition, **America on the Move,** anchors the Hall of Transportation and Technology. More than 300 vehicles and other artifacts are showcased in period settings that offer a chronological look at how transportation has shaped America. The journey takes you, for example, along 40 feet (12 m) of Route 66's pavement in Oklahoma and aboard a commuter car of a Chicago "L" train in the 1950s. Be sure to check the impressive **John Bull locomotive.** The oldest operable self-propelled locomotive and striking symbol of the industrial revolution, it was built in England and brought to America in 1831 for use on one of the first public U.S. railroads, which carried passengers from Philadelphia and New York City.

Historic Protest

On February 1, 1960, four male African-American college students sat down at the "whites only" lunch counter at F. W. Woolworth's in Greensboro, North Carolina, and politely asked for service. They were refused. When asked to leave they remained in their seats. Their peaceful sit-in ignited a movement: Hundreds of students, residents, civil rights organizers, and church members joined the protest.

In the two months that followed, sit-ins occurred in 54 cities in nine states. By late July 1960, the Woolworth's lunch counter had been desegregated. You can see part of the original counter on the second floor of the National Museum of American History's east wing.

"What So Proudly We Hail'd"

The 30-by-34-foot (9 x 10 m) flag known as the Star-Spangled Banner is fragile despite its size. Woven loosely to fly on a 90-foot (27 m) flagpole, its expected life span in 1813 was only two years. Flying over Fort McHenry, it incurred much damage. When the British attacked Baltimore in 1814, amateur poet Francis Scott Key was on a ship in the Chesapeake Bay. Moved by the sight of the enormous flag still flying in "the dawn's early light" after a 25-hour bombardment, he scribbled the words that became the lyrics for a popular patriotic song; Congress made it the national anthem in 1931. As part of conservation efforts, specialists at the Smithsonian recently removed a cloth backing (and 1.7 million stitches) added decades ago for support. Photo images documented the original flag's condition close up, guiding work to ensure the flag's survival for future generations.

On the Water traces the history of the country's maritime trade and transportation, which fueled national growth and the development of major cities by connecting people and places across the continent.

The star attraction of **Food: Transforming the American Table 1950–2000** is Julia Child's kitchen. Museum staff catalogued and packed 1,200 items from the late chef's custom-designed home kitchen in Cambridge, Massachusetts, where many of her TV shows were taped. They then reassembled everything in the museum.

A new exhibition for 2019, **Health & Medicine–Overview,** profiles how America has struggled to control and contain disease. And the **Spark!Lab** offers hands-on interactive history-related learning for kids. Also here is a five-story-tall miniature **Doll's House** with 23 rooms and 1,354 tiny items..

Second Floor

The **Star-Spangled Banner Gallery** preserves the museum's most stirring icon: the original Star-Spangled Banner (see sidebar above), laid out in a special environmentally-controlled chamber. Interactive displays let you investigate the flag in detail, and tell of how it was made, and its subsequent history.

An 18th-century colonial house from Ipswich, Massachusetts, is a highlight of **Within These Walls.** An examination of the everyday life of five families who occupied it from the mid- 1760s through 1945 includes American colonists working to spark a revolution, African Americans struggling for freedom, abolitionist activists and immigrants striving to build new lives, and a grandmother and her grandson serving on the home front during World War II. New in 2017, the **Hall of Democracy–American Democracy: A Great Leap of Faith** explores what makes the United States unique; **Many Voices, One Nation** maps the nation's cultural geography and how diverse peoples, from Native Americans through its many immigrants have shaped the United States.

Among the other special

artifacts on display on this floor are the **Greensboro lunch counter,** and a marble statue of George Washington, commissioned by the U.S. government in 1932 and sculpted by Horatio Greenough.

Third Floor

The East Wing of this floor is given to military history. **The Price of Freedom: Americans at War** surveys the entire span of U.S. military conflicts and looks at how they have been defining episodes in American history. The featured objects include a rare Revolutionary War uniform, a restored Huey helicopter that was used in the Vietnam War, and the uniform worn by Gen. Colin Powell during Operation Desert Storm.

A separate exhibit, **Gunboat Philadelphia,** illustrates events in October 1776 when American troops with only a ragtag collection of boats faced an advancing line of ships of the British Navy on Lake Champlain in New York. The Americans, under the command of Benedict Arnold, were forced to retreat, but not before they fought the British to a standstill. The American vessel *Philadelphia*, a small gunboat, sank during the battle, but was retrieved from the lake in 1935 and has been part of the museum's holdings since 1964.

The **First Ladies** exhibition has been moved to the Rose Gallery in the central section on the third floor profiles the contributions of presidents' wives. Displayed are more than two dozen original gowns worn to presidential inaugurations, including those worn by Jacqueline Kennedy and Michelle Obama.

The west wing has separate halls devoted to sports, music, and entertainment. ■

A portrait primer on U.S. presidents presents a time line of command.

WALK AROUND THE MONUMENTS

The western end of the Mall, where you'll find the city's most significant monuments and memorials, is a delightful place for walking. A 3-mile (4.8 km) loop taking you past a half dozen major memorials makes for a wonderful morning or afternoon; benches along the way offer rest stops. About two blocks from the start is the Smithsonian Metro station.

U.S. flags adorn the black granite wall of names at the Vietnam Veterans Memorial.

Begin at the **Washington Monument ❶** (nps. gov/wamo), off 15th Street between Constitution and Independence Avenues. Set on a slight rise, this 555-foot (169 m) marble obelisk is surrounded by flags from every state in the nation. Begun in 1848, the monument rose slowly but steadily for five years to 152 feet (46 m); then funding ran out and building ceased for almost 25 years. Look about a third of the way up to see where the work stopped: The more recent marble is darker.

From the Washington Monument grounds you can see the Lincoln Memorial to the west and the Jefferson Memorial across the Tidal Basin, but your next destination is hidden among the trees of **Constitution Gardens,** a memorial to the founders of this nation. Walk down the hill, cross 17th Street, and take the sinuous trail through lovely landscaping just north of the **Reflecting Pool.**

> **NOT TO BE MISSED:**
>
> **World War II Memorial • Vietnam Veterans Memorial • Lincoln Memorial • Jefferson Memorial**

On the pool's east end is the **National World War II Memorial ❷** (nps.gov/wwii). Thousands of veterans were on hand for the Memorial Day 2004 dedication of the $174 million, privately funded memorial. Around a fountain are two facing arcs of granite columns, each bearing two bronze wreaths; the 56 pillars represent U.S. states and territories during the war and the District of Columbia. The columns are anchored by a pair of 43-foot-high (13 m) arches—one for the war's Atlantic theater and one for the Pacific. Two dozen bronze panels depict scenes from the war, and a Freedom Wall with 4,000 gold stars honors the 400,000 Americans who were killed during World War II. Now follow the northern perimeter of Constitution Garden Pool. On **Signers Island,** a memorial honors the 56 signers of the Declaration of Independence.

Just west, architect Maya Lin's stunning **Vietnam Veterans Memorial** ❸ *(nps.gov/ vive)* presents a moving contrast to the classical-style monuments all about. A tremendous black-granite wedge, bermed into the earth instead of standing above it, is inscribed with the names of all the 58,209 Americans who

🗺 See also area map pp. 70–71
🅿 Washington Monument
🕐 2 hours
Ⓘ 3 miles (4.8 km)
🅿 Jefferson Memorial

Top of the Town

On August 23, 2011, Washington, D.C., was rocked by a 5.8-magnitude earthquake. The tremors damaged several city landmarks, including the Washington Monument. Closed for 32 months while more than 150 cracks in its structure were repaired, the monument finally reopened in May 2014.

Go early for free same-day admission and a trip to the top of the obelisk. The kiosk opens at 8:30 a.m. and tickets go fast. Or reserve in advance through the National Park Service's reservation page *(recreation.gov)*.

Inside, the elevator shoots to the 500-foot-high (152 m) viewing level in 70 seconds. On the leisurely ride down, you'll see the 195 commemorative stones inside the monument.

died or were missing in action in the Vietnam War. Polished to a reflective sheen, the walls of the wedge seem to project life as much as honor death. As you walk the path beside the memorial, the names of the dead increase dramatically as the walls reach their high point at 10.1 feet (3 m). The nearby bronze group of three soldiers, by Washington sculptor Frederick Hart, adds a dose of gritty realism. Dedicated in 1982, the memorial was supplemented in 1993 by another bronze group, the **Vietnam Women's Memorial.**

Continue on to the magnificent **Lincoln Memorial** ❹ *(nps.gov/linc),* built from 1914 to 1922 to honor Abraham Lincoln, president during the Civil War. The 36 Doric columns represent the number of states at the time of Lincoln's death. Inside, facing the Mall, the 19-foot-tall (5.7 m) statue of a seated Lincoln was carved from 28 blocks of white Georgia marble. The walls of the memorial are inscribed with words from the Gettysburg Address and Lincoln's second Inaugural Address.

Just to the southeast is the **Korean War Veterans Memorial** ❺ *(nps.gov/kowa).* Dedicated in 1995, it features 19 gray soldiers warily crossing a field of scrubby junipers. Next to this riveting stainless-steel group, a black-granite wall is etched with a mural of those who served, while another wall bears the simple message: "Freedom Is Not Free." Beside a "pool of remembrance" stands a stone carved with the war's toll—the numbers of killed, wounded, missing, and captured.

Walk east, to the **D.C. WWI Veterans Memorial,** a rotunda honoring the District's veterans of that war, then turn south in the direction of the Tidal Basin, and cross Independence Avenue S. at West Basin Drive.

A broad walk leads you through two towering hunks of granite, part of the **Martin Luther King, Jr. National Memorial** ❻ *(nps.gov/mlkm).* Dedicated in 2011, the memorial's centerpiece is a 30-foot-high (9 m) relief of King carved out of rock and gazing across the Tidal Basin. The design represents a line from his 1963 "I Have a Dream" speech: "Out of a mountain of despair, a stone of hope."

Farther along amid the trees of West Potomac Park on the basin's west side is the **Franklin Delano Roosevelt Memorial** ❼ *(nps.gov/frde),* honoring the 32nd president. Four unroofed, granite-walled alcoves—one for each of his four terms in office—spread along the water's edge, surrounded by landscaped plazas, statuary, and waterfalls.

On the south side of the Tidal Basin stands the **Jefferson Memorial** ❽ *(nps.gov/thje).* The view from here, across the Tidal Basin with its gulls and paddleboats and springtime cherry blossoms, is not to be missed. Dedicated to the author of the Declaration of Independence

Springtime Display: Cherry Blossoms as D.C. Icon

The first cherry tree near the Tidal Basin and Washington Monument was planted on March 27, 1912, by First Lady Helen Taft. But the idea had been put forward more than 25 years earlier. Washington resident Eliza Scidmore, who became a well-known travel writer, so admired groves of flowering cherries during a trip to Japan that she pitched a similar scheme to park officials in 1885. They showed no interest.

The idea gained support at the turn of the 20th century after a botanist at the U.S. Department of Agriculture, David Fairchild, tested flowering cherries at his estate and had several hundred planted in Chevy Chase, Maryland. Soon afterward, Mrs. Taft chose Japanese cherries to beautify a drab area along the Potomac. Things went awry when 2,000 of the trees, a gift from Japan, arrived full of pests and disease. They had to be burned. Japan graciously sent a new collection of carefully cultivated trees.

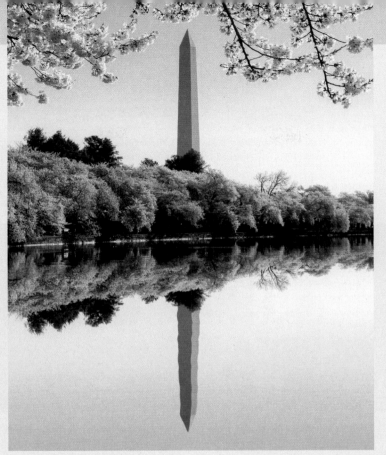

The Washington Monument appears to rise from a wreath of cherry blossoms.

and third president of the United States, the structure was designed by John Russell Pope in the style of the ancient Roman Pantheon and completed in 1943. Inside the airy colonnaded building a 19-foot (5.7 m) bronze of Jefferson stands beneath a towering dome. Among the quotes on the wall is one from a letter written in 1800: "I have sworn upon the altar of God eternal hostility against every form of tyranny over the mind of man."

Behind the monument on Ohio Drive is the **George Mason Memorial Garden.** In keeping with the quiet patriot's love of his gardens at Gunston Hall (see p. 228), across the river in Virginia and not far from Mount Vernon, the setting is a classical landscape designed as a peaceful, contemplative place.

The act of commemoration is a perennial work in progress. New memorials are being planned for the Mall and its immediate surrounds, with 20 candidate sites under consideration in 2021. Meanwhile, Arlington, Virginia, has two landmarks worth visiting: the **Air Force Memorial** (see p. 209), with three elegant stainless-steel spires visible from downtown D.C., and the **Pentagon Memorial** (see p. 209), honoring the 184 people who died when American Airlines Flight 77 was hijacked and flown into the Pentagon on September 11, 2001.

U.S. HOLOCAUST MEMORIAL MUSEUM

Opened in 1993, this museum serves as a memorial to the millions of people murdered during Nazi rule in Germany from 1933 to 1945. The architecture—windowless recesses, brickwork guard towers, and obscured windows—suggests some of the themes and images documented within. Inside, the skylit first-floor atrium is overshadowed by heavy steel trusses. A factory-like brick wall on one side is where visitors enter and ascend, via a cargo-style elevator, to see the permanent exhibition, starting on the fourth floor.

■ Despite the light, the Holocaust Museum's first floor sets a somber tone for a visit to the galleries.

U.S. Holocaust Memorial Museum

Map pp. 70–71

100 Raoul Wallenberg Pl. (15th St.) S.W., just S of Independence Ave.

202-488-0400

Metro: Smithsonian; Bus: 13F–G, V7–9, Circulator

ushmm.org

Visiting

Pick up timed passes at the museum on the day of your visit or visit the website for advance passes ($). The exhibition is self-guided and takes two to three hours. You begin on the fourth floor. There are several films, audio programs, and a lot of text on the three-floor exhibit; you may want to make a selective tour of this section. Most of the exhibits are not recommended for children under 11; it's also a good idea to prepare older children for what they will experience.

On the top floor, **"Nazi Assault—1933-1939,"** which covers the spread of Nazism, visitors are funneled through hallways from one exhibit area to the next. The dim, quiet halls reflect the museum's somber content. A theater, grim photographs, and monitors displaying silent footage bespeak the early years of the Third Reich and the start of its sanctioned violence toward Jews, Poles, Gypsies, homosexuals, political dissidents, the handicapped, and others.

The middle floor, **"Final Solution—1940-1945,"** is a walk-through tower lined with family photos from a shtetl, a Jewish village; you later learn that this entire village of 4,000 was destroyed in

1941, bringing 900 years of continuous history to an abrupt end. Perhaps most telling are the shelf loads of victims' belongings—rusty scissors, can openers, graters, razors, toothbrushes—and the huge piles of old shoes. There are bunks from Auschwitz and a scale model that shows how the gas chambers and crematoria worked.

Video monitors show unsettling images such as medical experiments, executions, and malnourished children. The monitors are shielded by walls so young children cannot see them; adults can elect not to watch.

Also on this floor, the years from 1940 to 1945 are examined in detail through displays on ghet-

The Big Picture

In addition to its powerful exhibits, the U.S. Holocaust Memorial Museum houses a study center and a vast archive of photos, film footage, eyewitness accounts, artifacts, and other materials that document Jewish history and events relating to the Holocaust. Many of the items here have been donated by families whose members were affected by the tragic events. The Steven Spielberg Film and Video Archive is among the hundreds of motion picture footage dating primarily from the 1920s to 1948 that can be viewed *(collections.ushmm. org/search/special-collections)*.

The museum's extensive online Holocaust Encyclopedia *(ushmm.org/learn)*, accessible in a dozen languages, offers the history of Nazi tyranny through articles, podcasts, lesson plans, and mapping tools.

INSIDER TIP:

Amid all the horror is redemption in those who tried to save Jews. The museum does a fine job highlighting these people.

—SHEILA BUCKMASTER
*National Geographic Traveler
magazine editor at large*

tos, deportations, slave labor, and extermination camps. Among the powerful exhibits are those on armed resistance in the Warsaw ghetto and the legacy of Anne Frank. And audio theater presents the testimony of Auschwitz survivors.

"Last Chapter," on the final floor of the permanent exhibition, focuses on the liberation of the Nazi camps and the aftermath of

the Holocaust, including survivors' attempts to build lives anew. The efforts of courageous non-Jews who worked to save Jews from the Nazis is given special prominence. In the **Hall of Remembrance,** an eternal flame honors victims of the Holocaust; visitors may light candles in their memory.

On the **first floor,** the exhibit **"Remember the Children: Daniel's Story"** is targeted to families, including children eight years and older. It recounts the Holocaust from a child's perspective. The **lower level** has the **Children's Tile Wall,** with more than 3,000 tiles painted by American schoolchildren in memory of the estimated 1.5 million children who died. Outside the museum, it's a relief to look across the Tidal Basin to the Jefferson and FDR Memorials and remember those who stood against tyranny. ■

More Places to Visit on the National Mall

Bureau of Engraving & Printing

The bureau is the place to see a lot of money—millions upon millions of dollars—being printed daily. To replace worn-out bills and follow the requests of the Federal Reserve Board, this facility and a similar one in Fort Worth, Texas, churn out billions of notes a year in denominations from $1 to $100. Each 50-foot-long (15 m) high-speed press can print 10,000 sheets per hour, turning out mainly $20 bills, which have a shelf life of 7.7 years. You can see 32-note currency sheets as they roll through production and 4,000-note "bricks" of bills being prepared for distribution to the 12 Federal Reserve Banks around the country. *money factory.gov* Map pp. 70–71 ✉ 14th & C Sts., S.W. ☎ 202-874-2330 🕐 Call for tour hours; get free tickets at booth on Raoul Wallenberg Pl. 🚇 Metro: Smithsonian

International Spy Museum

Fans of espionage will love this spot, which offers inside looks at how professionals track and nail their targets. It has a wide range of interactive exhibits highlighting tools and techniques of the trade, historically significant people and events, and an array of fascinating artifacts. The exhibits were developed with the guidance of real agents and spy-catchers such as CIA masters of disguise. The displays incorporate hundreds of objects ranging from James Bond's Aston Martin DB5 from the movie *Goldfinger* to spying devices such as a KGB pistol encased in a lipstick tube. You begin the self-guided tour by adopting an alias and role-playing through exhibits that test your skill at analyzing situations and maintaining your cover, as real agents must do. Other exhibits convey stories of notable spy rings and intelligence gathering through time. During weekends, holidays, and the peak tourist season, it's a good idea to reserve in advance. *spymuseum.org* 🗺 Map pp. 70–71 ✉ 700 L'Enfant Plaza, S.W. ☎ 202-393-7798 🚇 Metro: L'Enfant Plaza; Bus: 52, 74, Circulator

National Museum of African American History & Culture

Housed in a stunning four-level structure covered with bronze panels, this Smithsonian addition was opened in September 2016 by President Barack Obama, who features prominently in one of its exhibits. It covers every aspect of the African-American experience, from slavery and the Civil Rights Movement to athletics and the arts. *nmaahc.si.edu* 🗺 Map pp. 70–71 ✉ 1400 Constitution Ave., N.W. ☎ 202-633-10000 🚇 Metro: Federal Triangle, Smithsonian

■ The International Spy Museum holds the largest collection of international espionage artifacts.

Starring America's most famous home, 1600 Pennsylvania Avenue, with surrounding streets filled with places of cultural interest

WHITE HOUSE & AROUND

The south portico of the White House remains a Washington icon.

WHITE HOUSE & AROUND

The home of the Chief Executive is a living museum of the U.S. presidency in downtown Washington, and the surrounding streets have additional attractions that make this a rich and charming neighborhood to explore.

In 1791 a surveyor and an engineer picked the site for a presidential "palace." The surveyor was George Washington, the engineer was Pierre-Charles L'Enfant, and the site was a cornfield above a tidal marsh where hunters shot ducks and geese. Just a mile (1.6 km) from the site of the future Capitol, the manse they envisioned would be about four times the size of the current White House.

Thomas Jefferson, Secretary of State at the time, persuaded Washington to hold a competition for the design. Unimpressed by the mundane entries, Washington urged Irish-born architect James Hoban to have a go. Hoban's entry, selected in 1792, was an adaptation of the Duke of Leinster's palace near Dublin. Regrettably, Washington—then on the verge of his second term as president—would not live to see the structure completed.

By the turn of the 20th century, after more than a century's worth of growing pains, it was

clear that the White House—Theodore Roosevelt's designation for it—truly enshrined the American presidential legacy.

The presidential neighborhood grew in tandem with the White House. In the 1810s, St. John's Church, Decatur House, and other posh, federal-style residences were built around President's Park (renamed Lafayette Square in 1824). By 1900, the area was a thriving mix of government buildings, art galleries, hotels, and homes. Notable landmarks include the Treasury Building, Old Executive Office Building (now officially the Eisenhower Executive Office Building), Corcoran School of Art and Design, Renwick building, Blair House, and the Octagon architecture museum.

From west of 20th Street to the Potomac River, the Foggy Bottom neighborhood is a mix of 19th-century row houses, apartment buildings, and major institutions, among them the State Department, World Bank, Kennedy Center, and George Washington University.

The White House area maintains and inspires a timeless polished decorum. At the same time, this segment of Washington underscores just how much times have changed. Until World War II, you could walk to the front door of the White House and leave your calling card. Today, security concerns have made visits understandably restrictive. ∎

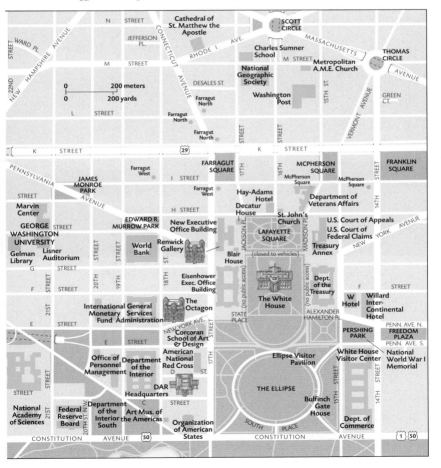

WHITE HOUSE

The oldest public building in the District of Columbia, the White House has been the home of every U.S. president except George Washington. In this most famous of residences, the president signs bills into law, meets with national and international leaders, entertains guests, and does his best to lead a private family life. Despite more than 200 years of expansions and renovations, the White House has kept its essential appearance and design.

The dignified north portico of the White House basks in the glow of early evening.

White House

- Map pp. 108–109
- 1600 Pennsylvania Ave., N.W.
- 202-456-1414
- Closed Sun.– Mon.
- Metro: Federal Triangle, McPherson Square, Metro Center; Bus: 32–36, Circulator

whitehouse.gov

Washington's designers intended the executive mansion to be one of two focal points of the new Federal City (the Capitol would be the other). Nine blueprints were submitted to a competitive design panel; among those rejected was a plan put forward anonymously by Thomas Jefferson.

The winning design—the work of Irish-born architect James

Hoban—honored the stately symmetries of Georgian manor houses in the British Isles. Not that the design lacked detractors: Benjamin Henry Latrobe, who worked on the White House in the early 1800s and is considered the country's first professional architect, assailed Hoban's concept as "a mutilated copy of a badly designed original near Dublin."

Nonetheless, the cornerstone

INSIDER TIP:

If you're near the White House and hear helicopters overhead, run to the South Lawn; you might just see the president boarding or deplaning *Marine One.*

—CAROLINE HICKEY
*National Geographic
Travel Books editor*

of the President's House (George Washington's preferred term for it) was laid in October 1792, a year before work began on the Capitol Building. The pale sandstone for the white-painted walls came from Aquia Creek, on the Virginia side of the Potomac. Eight years later, with President John Adams nearing the end of his term, the house was finally ready for occupation.

Jefferson, the third president, held the first Inaugural open house in 1805 and forged the tradition of throwing the house open to the public. The custom got out of hand in 1829, when some 20,000 well-wishers tromped through the White House, muddy boots and all; while President Jackson slipped away to a nearby hotel, his aides filled tubs with juice and whiskey and set them on the lawn to coax the crowds to remain outside. The Inaugural open houses continued until 1869, when Ulysses Grant replaced them with a parade, which he watched from the safety of a grandstand right in front of the White House.

During the War of 1812, the British retaliated for the American burning of public buildings in Canada by burning down the President's House and other city landmarks. When British soldiers arrived at the hastily vacated mansion on the night of August 24, 1814, they found Dolley Madison's dinner still on the table (a few of them sat down and polished it off). Shortly after midnight, soldiers threw flaming javelins into the mansion. By morning it was a smoldering shell. The house was rebuilt within its original walls over the next few years.

By the mid-20th century, the White House was suffering major structural problems: The walls and floors could no longer support the alterations and additions of previous decades. From 1948 to 1952,

Visiting the White House

The fact that you can step into the home of its president is one of the most endearingly democratic traditions of the United States. To go inside the White House you must schedule a tour. Requests must be submitted one to six months in advance through your member of Congress *(tel 202-224-3121, house.gov)* or your country's embassy in Washington, D.C. The free self-guided tours *(7:30 a.m.–11:30 a.m. Tues.–Thurs. & 7:30 a.m.–1:30 p.m. Fri.–Sat.)* are assigned on a first-come, first-served basis. Before your arrival, call the 24-hour line *(tel 202-456-7041);* tours are subject to cancellations. You can check security requirements and take a virtual tour online *(whitehouse.gov),* or stop by the White House Visitor Center *(1450 Pennsylvania Ave., N.W., open 11 a.m.–4 p.m. Wed.–Sat.)* for exhibits and a background video.

State Dining Room

West Wing

Red Room

South Portico

Inside: Diplomatic Reception Room

Blue Room

Green Room

China Room

White House

Harry and Bess Truman lived in Blair House across Pennsylvania Avenue, while the White House was gutted. Everything from furniture to paneling was taken out, a new basement dug, new foundations laid, and a steel framework installed. The basic house was still there, but it was now much safer. Since then, each first family has added its own decorative touches. The Kennedys, for example, redesigned the Rose Garden, while the Reagans contributed a new 4,730-piece set of Lenox china.

A Look Inside

If you have arranged a group tour in advance, enter the grounds from a visitor entrance around the corner from Pennsylvania Avenue on 15th Street, next to the Treasury building. When you arrive, take a minute to look through the gate to see a portion of the mansion's beautifully planted 18-acre (7.2 ha) grounds.

East Room

Library

East Wing

Visitor entrance

Vermeil Room

After being cleared by security, you enter a corridor on the ground floor that has photo displays on White House life and glass-walled views of the once beautiful **Jacqueline Kennedy Garden,** austerely remade by Melania Trump. Next, peer into the roped-off **Library,** filled with federal-style furniture. Across the hall, the **Vermeil Room** has portraits of recent first ladies and a collection of gilded silver.

The rooms you can actually walk through are up on the State

Floor. The first one you enter—the expansive **East Room**—is also the largest in the house: It hosts press conferences, award ceremonies, and concerts. Among the weddings held here were those of Nellie Grant, Alice Roosevelt, and Lynda Bird Johnson. The energetic children of Theodore Roosevelt are said to have roller-skated across the floor here.

Continue around to the **Green Room,** used by Jefferson as a dining room but now functioning as a reception parlor. The window affords a great view beyond the Ellipse (an open greensward just north of Constitution Avenue) to the Jefferson Memorial. Much of the Green Room's furniture came from the New York City workshop of Duncan Phyfe in the early 1800s. The green watered silk wall coverings were chosen by Jacqueline Kennedy.

The oval **Blue Room** contains several pieces of furniture bought by James Monroe, who refurbished the elegant room after the 1814 fire. Presidents still receive guests here in part because of the lovely view of the South Lawn. The Blue Room is the traditional location of the primary White House Christmas tree.

First ladies frequently entertain in the adjacent **Red Room,** furnished as an American Empire parlor of 1810 to 1830. It was the favorite sitting room of Mary Todd Lincoln.

Some 140 guests can be seated in the **State Dining Room,** which boasts painted oak paneling from a 1902 renovation. In the **Cross Hall** and **Entrance Hall** the floors are made out of Tennessee marble. The decorated concert grand piano was a 1938 gift from the Steinway company.

A carpeted marble staircase leads to the second and third floors, open only to the first family and their guests. Notable rooms there include the Queen's Bedroom, named for its many royal

The Red Room: A Favorite of First Ladies

Painted various shades of red since the 1840s, the small Red Room parlor had walls of yellow when legendary Washington hostess Dolley Madison used the room for bipartisan entertaining during a period of fierce political rivalry.

Eleanor Roosevelt launched her famous women-only press sessions here in response to the banning of women from presidential news conferences. Through the years, the room also has functioned as a living room, a music room, a venue for official photographs, and an intimate setting for small dinner parties.

But the space has seen sad moments, too. Mrs. Kennedy received foreign heads of state in the Red Room following President John F. Kennedy's state funeral.

President James Monroe chose Empire-style furnishings for the room when the White House was rebuilt after the British burned it in the War of 1812. The style changed many times, until the present American Empire decor was adopted during the Kennedy White House renovation. In 2000, the walls and upholstery were made deep carmine as more authentically reflective of the 19th century; they were refurbished in 2019.

■ **President Joe Biden talks in the Red Room of the White House.**

guests (including the queens of Great Britain, Norway, Greece, and the Netherlands), and the now famous Lincoln Bedroom.

In fact, the Lincoln Bedroom wasn't the 16th president's sleeping quarters but his office and Cabinet room. Under Mr. and Mrs. Theodore Roosevelt the space was converted to a guest suite known as the Blue Bedroom. It was President Harry Truman who decided to fill the room with Lincoln memorabilia. Scandal surrounded the historic chamber in the Clinton Administration when it was revealed that campaign donors were offered overnight stays here. Among the high-profile guests who spent the night were Steven Spielberg, Barbra Streisand, and Lee Iacocca.

The West Wing (*you can take a virtual tour of the wing at whitehouse .gov*) holds the Cabinet Room, numerous staff and reception rooms, and the president's Oval Office (built in 1909) and its adjoining Rose Garden. The White House also contains a jogging track, swimming pool, movie theater, and bowling lane. The total number of rooms in the White House: 132.

Your tour will exit the front door beneath a columned portico, then follow the walkway to the front gate. Photography inside the White House has been allowed since 2015, so don't forget to snap a few mementos before leaving. ■

A WHITE HOUSE AREA WALK

Strolling the streets around the White House will give you a concentrated taste of the capital's core. The tourists, security officers, and limousines that buzz around the executive mansion like drones around a queen bee are part of the picture, but so are restaurants, museums, art galleries, benches for idling, and, because local laws bar skyscrapers, long, green views across the Ellipse and the Mall.

Once you've viewed or visited the White House, you tend to forget it's there, as do the locals who go about their business in the area. The section of Pennsylvania Avenue on the north side of the **White House ❶** (see pp. 110–115) is closed to traffic, so it offers good photo opportunities if you aren't hampered at the time of your visit by security constraints and construction fences.

▪ **President Andrew Jackson sculpture in Lafayette Square**

> **NOT TO BE MISSED:**
>
> **White House • Lafayette Square • Octagon • Corcoran Gallery of Art**

The park just north of the White House, **Lafayette Square ❷,** is a perfect place to sit with a sandwich and people-watch. As a public park in full view of the White House, the square is strategically ideal for demonstrating for or against something. Activists for nuclear disarmament and other causes have mounted peaceful vigils here; in June 2020, President Trump had demonstrators brutally cleared so he could walk through the square. In the middle of the square is Clark Mills's statue of Andrew Jackson on a rearing horse. Statues of foreign-born Revolutionary War heroes occupy the four corners: Marquis de Lafayette, Baron Friedrich von Steuben, Thaddeus Kosciusko, and Comte de Rochambeau. Many of the federal-style row houses along the square are White House offices, saved from the wrecking ball by Jackie Kennedy's determination to preserve the historical character of the square.

Across H Street from the square stands the gold-domed **St. John's Church ❸** (see p. 130), known as the "Church of the Presidents." Diagonally across the corner from here, at Jackson Place and H Street, is **Decatur House ❹** (see p. 128), built in 1818 for naval hero Stephen Decatur.

Next, head south and turn right on Pennsylvania Avenue to see the 1810 white brick **Blair House,** the small building where foreign dignitaries often stay; Robert E. Lee was offered command of the Federal Army here in 1861. On November 1, 1950—about midway through the Trumans' four-year stay at Blair House while the White House was under renovation—a policeman was killed on the street defending the president from an assassination attempt.

In the same block, the **Renwick Gallery 5** (see p. 130), a Smithsonian museum, shows off its mansard roof and redbrick-and-sandstone exterior opposite the even more flamboyant **Eisenhower Executive Office Building.** A massive piece of architecture originally named the Old Executive Office Building, the EEOB is one of the country's finest Second Empire–style structures. Built from 1871 to 1888 (just after the Renwick), the granite pile shocked locals who had expected a neoclassical temple to house the State, War, and Navy Departments. It now holds offices of White House staff members, the Office of Management and

See also area map pp. 108–109

White House Visitor Center

3 hours

1.5 miles (2.4 km)

Corcoran Gallery of Art

Budget, and the Office of the Vice President.

Head south on 17th Street and turn right on New York Avenue. The historic **Octagon 6** (see p. 130) stands on the corner of 18th Street. The brilliant design of the three-story brick house exemplifies federal architecture. Go back to 17th and turn right; on your right is the **Corcoran School of Art & Design,** housed in an attractive beaux arts building. From here, walk east on E Street, between the South Lawn of the White House and the Ellipse. *Marine One,* the president's helicopter, lands on the South Lawn, site of the annual Easter Egg Roll. The National Christmas Tree, planted during the

The Willard InterContinental

While you're in the vicinity of the White House, drop into the Willard InterContinental (*1401 Pennsylvania Ave., N.W., tel 800-424-6835; see Travelwise p. 246*), a Washington landmark since the 1850s. Nathaniel Hawthorne called it the "center of Washington" for its role as the heart of political lobbying in the 19th century. The hotel has hosted presidents, heads of state, and a gaggle of household names, from Mark Twain to Mae West. Martin Luther King, Jr., penned part of his "I Have a Dream" speech here in August 1963.

In 1901, the venerable hostelry was rebuilt as a 12-story beaux arts hotel under the guidance of Henry Hardenbergh, architect of New York's famous Plaza Hotel. Closed in 1968 when much of Pennsylvania Avenue hit the skids, the Willard reopened in grand style in 1986.

The restored Willard boasts marble columns, polished wood paneling, glittering chandeliers, and other trappings of opulence. Shops, a bar, a café, and an elegant restaurant provide multiple opportunities to splurge.

Carter Administration, stands on the Ellipse near the Zero Milestone, the spot from which city distances are measured.

On the corner of E and 15th Streets, a bronze William Tecumseh Sherman sits astride a horse, its tail raised toward the South, on the spot where he reviewed victorious Union troops. Immediately east, in Pershing Park, is the **National World War I Memorial** 7 *(see p. 130)*, unveiled in April 2021. To the

north is the Greek Revival **Department of the Treasury** and its statue of Alexander Hamilton; sadly, the building blocks the view from the White House to the Capitol.

Cap the day with a drink at the trendy P.O.V. Roof Terrace bar of the **W Hotel** (see Travelwise p. 246). On clear days, this local favorite meeting place offers a great panoramic view of the White House, Mall, and abundant treetops of the city and neighboring Virginia.

The Willard Hotel is worth a peek for its grand historic style.

WHITE HOUSE VISITOR CENTER

Since September 11, 2001, the White House Visitor Center no longer serves as the starting point for visitors who've reserved a tour of the White House, yet it has been transformed into a thoroughly engaging alternative experience—or a complement to a tour—with its many exhibits from the president's iconic home.

White House Visitor Center exhibits

Operated by the National Park Service as an extension of President's Park, the White House Visitor Center was established in 1995 on the north side of the neoclassical Herbert C. Hoover Building (Department of Commerce), two blocks southeast of the White House. Originally, it served as a ticket center for White House tours. Following the 9/11 attacks, tickets became available solely through Congressional offices and embassies, and the center was transformed into an educational venue with static exhibits. In 2012, a $12.6 million expansion and update revitalized the visitor experience with museum-caliber interactive exhibits that provide a window into the "Executive Mansion."

Six permanent exhibits are themed to "Ceremonies and Celebrations," "First Families," "Symbols and Images," "White House Architecture," "White House Interiors," and "Working White House." Plus, there's a large-scale model of the White House. An interactive touchscreen lets you tour the White House. And other interpretive panels and looping videos of archival footage are interspersed with approximately 100 artifacts from the White House collection, including President Franklin D. Roosevelt's desk and a late 19th-century gold eagle finial from atop the White House flagpole. Other exhibits change throughout the year.

Don't miss the 14-minute film, "White House: Reflections from Within," featuring personal stories and reflections by presidents, first ladies, and other first-family members through the years. And be sure to browse the excellent bookstore operated by the White House Historical Association. ■

White House Visitor Center

⛰ Map pp. 108–109

✉ 1450 Pennsylvania Ave, N.W.

☎ 202-208-1631

🕐 Closed Sun.– Tue.

🚇 Metro: McPherson Square, Metro Center; Bus: Circulator

nps.gov/whho/ planyourvisit

whitehousehistory. org

DAR HEADQUARTERS

This robust beaux arts building was built between 1905 and 1929 to serve as the headquarters of the Daughters of the American Revolution (female descendants of American Revolution patriots). Encompassing an entire city block, it is one of the largest buildings in the world exclusively owned and maintained by women.

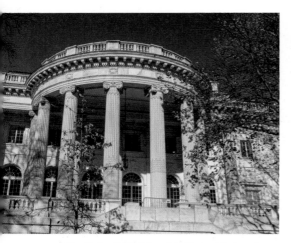

■ **Constitution Hall building of the National Society of Daughters of the American Revolution (DAR)**

DAR Headquarters

🅰 Map pp. 108–109

✉ 1776 D St., N.W.

☎ 202-628-1776 or 202-628-4780 (Constitution Hall event info)

🚇 Metro: Farragut West

dar.org

dolls from the late 18th to the early 20th centuries. A museum displays exhibits drawn from the DAR's collection of textiles, silver, glass, and furniture.

Built in the 1920s on the building's west side, **Constitution Hall** is a 3,702-seat auditorium designed by John Russell Pope (the architect behind the National Gallery of Art's West Building and the Jefferson

---

INSIDER TIP:

Before your visit, take the online virtual 360-degree tour of DAR Headquarters—especially useful for choosing seats for a show in Constitution Hall.

—JUSTIN KAVANAGH
National Geographic Travel Books editor

The oldest part of the DAR Headquarters, neoclassical **Memorial Continental Hall,** was designed by architect Edward Pearce Casey (1864–1940), who also designed the interior of the Library of Congress. Inside, visitors can tour more than 30 period rooms, each outfitted by a different state organization of the DAR. The California room recreates an 1860s parlor of the oldest adobe house in Monterey; the Michigan room presents a 1920s library with red bookshelves and blue-glazed earthenware; and the New Hampshire room is a playful children's attic with toys and

Memorial). All kinds of concerts and lectures are held here, but Constitution Hall is best (or most notoriously) known for the one that never took place: After the DAR's 1939 refusal to let black contralto Marian Anderson perform, Eleanor Roosevelt stepped in, and Anderson sang at the Lincoln Memorial. ■

NATIONAL GEOGRAPHIC SOCIETY

Robert Peary, Jacques Cousteau, and Jane Goodall are among the explorers and scientists who have been supported by the National Geographic Society, founded in Washington, D.C., in 1888. At the headquarters of the Society—one of the world's largest nonprofit scientific and educational institutions—visitors find exhibits at the National Geographic Museum and a wealth of cultural programs.

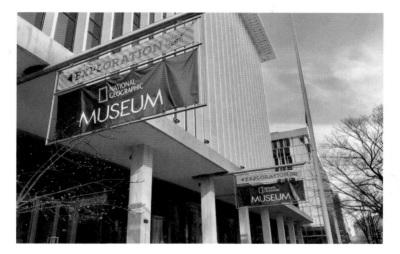

■ Home base: National Geographic's explorers, writers, and photographers have traveled the Earth, sharing its amazing stories with each new generation. A rich sampling of discoveries awaits visitors.

The National Geographic Society's magazines, books and guidebooks (including this one), maps, websites, TV programs, and classroom materials—all aimed at "the increase and diffusion of geographic knowledge" and to "inspire people to care about the planet"—are produced here at the headquarters.

National Geographic Museum, formerly Explorers Hall, showcases the greatest hits of National Geographic photographers, researchers, and explorers. Artifacts include the camera Robert Peary used at the North Pole. Videos include Jane Goodall's chimpanzee research camp, and the discovery of the *Titanic* and Machu Picchu. Recent temporary exhibitions have included "Becoming Jane: The Evolution of Jane Goodall" and "Queens of Egypt."

National Geographic *Live!* presents live talks by National Geographic explorers in the auditorium.

The National Geographic Society sells a wide array of educational, entertainment, and decorative items from around the world. ■

National Geographic Society

- Map pp. 108–109
- 17th & M Sts., N.W.
- 202-857-7700
- Metro: Farragut North, Farragut West

nationalgeographic .com
nationalgeographic.org (museum)

IT'S A SPOOKY LITTLE TOWN

Intrigue. Mystery. Romance. Spies have captured the imagination of moviegoers for decades, but in Washington—home of the CIA, the FBI, and the Pentagon—such cinematic fare is real, with city streets alive with secret agents seeking or supplying classified information. Every now and then an agent is nabbed, exposing a world in which backyard barbecuers such as Aldrich Ames or Robert Hanssen turn out to have led lives of deceit.

Spying caught on in Washington during the Civil War, when amateur agents on both sides of the Mason-Dixon Line scoured the capital city for war-related information. Thomas Nelson Conrad, a former Georgetown College headmaster, sat in Lafayette Park across from the White House for hours, meticulously noting President Lincoln's comings and goings. Conrad hoped to kidnap the president, then exchange him for prisoners of war. The Confederacy rejected his plan as infeasible.

The most romantic figure in Washington's espionage history may be the Rebel Rose. Intelligent, beautiful, and duplicitous, Rose O'Neal Greenhow (1815–1864) haunted Washington's loftiest social circles before the Civil War, befriending presidents, senators, and tycoons. When war broke out and men left for battle, spying became women's work. None was more deft than Greenhow. Inside her modest Northwest house at 398 16th Street (it's no longer standing), she plied unsuspecting targets with oysters, wild turkey, and champagne, pumping them for information all the while.

At one dinner party, Greenhow learned that the Federals were planning to move into Virginia. By quickly passing a coded message to Confederate Gen. Pierre G. T. Beauregard inside a woman's hair bun, she enabled him to reposition some of his troops—and, ultimately, to win the First Battle of Bull Run.

Soviet KGB colonel Vitaly Yurchenko made world headlines when he strolled into the U.S. Embassy in Rome in August 1985 and stated he wished to defect. Among the tidbits he had to share: NSA analyst Ronald Pelton had served as a double agent since 1980 and CIA officer Edward Lee Howard since 1984.

But Yurchenko was not a happy decamper. His ex-girlfriend, who married a Russian diplomat stationed in Montreal, had no plans to leave her husband. Worse, the good colonel was relegated to a prisonlike existence in the United States, where his CIA case officers insisted on escorting him everywhere.

EXPERIENCE: Tracing the Routes of Espionage

Why is there a tunnel under the Russian Embassy? What does the National Cathedral have to do with spying? Learn the answers to questions like these in spy walking tours led by Rosanna Minchew, a retired CIA operative and cyber intelligence expert (airbnb.com/experiences/1122478, $$). Various tours focus on tales of intrigue that unfolded inside chic homes of

Georgetown, around the White House during the Civil War, in embassies, apartments, and restaurants of upper Northwest D.C.

To try your hand at intelligence activities, check out Operation Spy ($$) at the International Spy Museum (see p. 106). You'll decrypt secret conversations and arrange video surveillance of clandestine meetings.

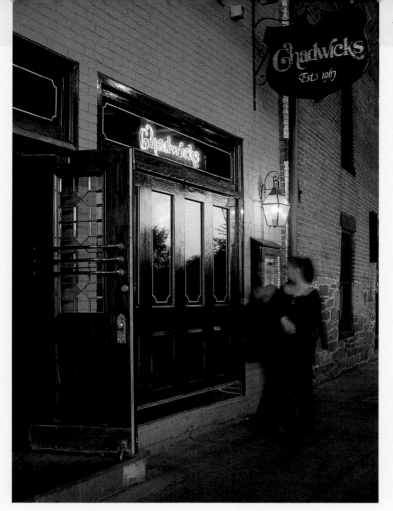

At this K Street spot, traitorous Aldrich Ames spilled critically important beans to Russian agents.

On November 2, 1985, Yurchenko and his CIA handler repaired to a popular neighborhood restaurant in Georgetown that is now defunct. At some point Yurchenko stepped out for a breath of fresh air—and grabbed a cab to the Soviet Embassy, where he rescinded his defection. Four days later he was on a plane to the Soviet Union, leaving the intelligence community to debate whether he had been a legitimate defector or a KGB plant.

Following in the forked footsteps of Greenhow and Yurchenko came career CIA officer Aldrich Ames, who in 1994 was accused of exposing U.S. intelligence assets inside the former Soviet Union. The info swap occurred at Chadwicks, at 3205 K Street in Georgetown; Ames chalk-marked a blue mailbox on R Street at 37th Street as a dead-drop signal. For his tip-offs, Ames received more than $2.7 million from the Soviets—and from the Americans, a lifelong prison sentence.

WATERGATE COMPLEX

Perhaps the third most famous building in Washington, after the Capitol and the White House, "The Watergate" is synonymous with the famous burglary that ultimately led to the downfall of President Nixon. The complex of six buildings is also a modernist architectural icon that draws a steady stream of curious visitors.

■ Built between 1963 and 1971, the Watergate Complex covers a total of 10 acres (4 ha).

Watergate Complex

🗺 Map pp. 108–109

✉ West end of Virginia Ave., N.W.

🚇 Metro: Foggy Bottom; Bus: 31, 32, 38B, 80, Circulator

Located on the banks of the Potomac, this luxury apartment and office complex was conceived in 1961 as an urban redevelopment project to replace an industrial gas works. Designed by Italian architect Luigi Moretti as one of the first architectural projects employing computer-aided design, it was completed in 1971 with six swirling concrete structures offering expansive views over the river. It soon became one of the most desirable addresses in Washington: Illustrious tenants included Plácido Domingo, Mstislav Rostropovich, Elizabeth Taylor, and an A-list of politicians, from Robert McNamara to Bob Dole.

The Democratic National Committee headquarters was also here, and the name "Watergate" became synonymous with the bungled burglary of their offices by Republican cronies during the presidential campaign of 1972. The subsequent cover-up and investigation of the break-in resulted in Nixon's resignation, while lending the "-gate" suffix to scores of subsequent scandals.

One building is today the **Watergate Hotel** (*thewatergate hotel.com*), where the "Scandal Room" is open to view: Used in the 1972 Watergate break-in, it is furnished with a reel-to-reel tape recorder and other accouterments of the times. *The Watergate: Inside America's Most Infamous Address* by Joseph Rodota provides a wealth of fascinating detail about what *The Washington Post* called the "glittering Potomac Titanic." ■

Bird's-eye Views

The **Washington Monument** (see sidebar p. 101) isn't the only place with a panoramic perspective. Though few people know it, the **Old Post Office Tower** (see pp. 145–146) offers one of the best views of the Mall. For decades the open-air roof deck of the old Hotel Washington was a favorite hideaway for its treetop views of the White House; today it's part of the **W Hotel** (see p. 118) and still a great place for cocktails. The **National Cathedral** (see pp. 189–191) sits on one of the highest points in the city. From the observation gallery you can see for miles across the Potomac and into Virginia. And from the rooftop terrace bar of the **Watergate Hotel** (*2650 Virginia Ave., N.W., thewatergatehotel.com*), you get a 360-degree vista over Washington.

ORGANIZATION OF AMERICAN STATES & ART MUSEUM

Blending classical and Spanish colonial elements, this striking white building is the head-quarters of the Organization of American States, a regional alliance of 35 nations promoting peace and economic cooperation among its member countries from the Americas and the Caribbean. It's art museum is world class.

■ Removed from typical city energy, the OAS courtyard offers a relaxing sense of the tropics.

Dedicated in 1910, the grand building with its marble facade and monumental bronze gates was the work of architects Paul Cret, designer of the Folger Shakespeare Library (see p. 64), and Albert Kelsey. Just inside the elaborate triple-arched entry, a lush villa-like courtyard boasts an octagonal Aztec-style fountain and overflows with tropical plants. Upstairs, the large **Hall of the Americas** auditorium is graced by Tiffany stained-glass windows, massive Corinthian columns, and a vaulted ceiling.

In the back, a walkway through an Aztec garden leads to the **Art Museum of the Americas,** roofed in red tile (the museum must be entered from 201 18th St.). Several attractive galleries host exhibits from the museum's permanent collection, plus traveling shows of Latin American and Caribbean art and photography.

After your visit, head for the triangular park across 18th Street to view the raised-sword equestrian statue of Simón Bolívar the Liberator, a gift to the United States in 1958 from Venezuela. ■

Organization of American States & Art Museum

🗺 Map pp. 108–109

✉ 17th St. & Constitution Ave., N.W.

☎ 202-370-0147

🕐 Museum closed Mon.

🚇 Metro: Farragut West; Bus: 80, H1, L1, S1

oas.org
museum.oas.org

JOHN F. KENNEDY CENTER FOR THE PERFORMING ARTS

Once maligned as an unsightly pillbox along the Potomac, the modernist Kennedy Center, immediately south of the Watergate Complex, has since earned the affection of Washingtonians. Its 1971 opening elevated the city from a cultural backwater to a leader in the live arts. The world's foremost singers, pianists, jazz musicians, classical artists, dancers, and actors have performed on Kennedy Center stages. Based here, the National Symphony Orchestra and Washington National Opera have achieved international respect.

■ The Kennedy Center, Washington's premier bastion of culture, stretches along the Potomac River.

John F. Kennedy Center for the Performing Arts

🗺 Map pp. 108–109

✉ 2700 F St., N.W.

☎ 202-467-4600

🚇 Metro: Foggy Bottom–GWU; Bus: Shuttle from Metro

kennedy-center.org

The Kennedy Center is the "national living memorial" to a fallen president, John F. Kennedy. A presidentially appointed board of trustees oversees the operation of the center, which is supported both by ticket sales and by private donations.

Visiting

Free guided tours are offered daily; call for times. You may also wander about on your own, but some theaters are closed to the public during rehearsals. Tickets (purchase at box office or call 202-467-4600 or 800-444-1324) are necessary for most performances.

The Kennedy Center is at its best at night, when floodlights envelop its white Carrara marble in a vibrant glow. The north entrance opens into the **Hall of States**, its soaring ceiling lined with state flags; at the south entrance the **Hall of Nations** contains the flags of countries with diplomatic ties to the United States. Both halls lead to the **Grand Foyer**—at 630 feet (192 m) one of the longest rooms in the world. This royal, red-carpeted space is outfitted with floor-to-ceiling mirrors and 16 crystal chandeliers donated by Sweden. Halfway down the hall you'll find Robert Berks's big, emotive bronze bust of John F. Kennedy.

Attending a performance is the reason to come here—and the best way to take in the auditoriums. The 2,465-seat **Concert Hall,** renovated in 1997, is home to the National

Symphony; the 1,164-seat **Eisenhower Theater** is named for the president who signed legislation for a National Cultural Center; and the spectacular 2,362-seat **Opera House** completes the trio of fine performance spaces. Just inside the north entrance, off the Hall of States, the 324-seat **Family Theater** presents performances for young audiences.

On the Roof Terrace level, the 513-seat **Terrace Theater** is a delightful venue for jazz, solo recitals, chamber music, and drama. You can also take in an experimental or family show at the 399-seat **Theater Lab.** The 200-seat **Jazz Club** swings on this level, too. On the Roof Terrace, walk onto the patio for views of the memorials, the Potomac, Arlington high-rises across the river, and the distant hilltop Washington National Cathedral as you stroll around the building.

The center got a major boost with the opening in September 2019 of the $250 million **REACH,**

with three new performance pavilions that double the center's outdoor space and include significant works of art. Of particular note is Deborah Butterfield's iconic "Milk Rive" (2019), a life-size horse assembled from driftwood. And an 1823 copper engraving of the The Declaration of Independence hangs on Level A in the Justice Forum. The REACH's family-friendly outdoor **Vintura Park** food and wine garden at the River Pavilion makes a lovely place for a snack. ∎

EXPERIENCE: Tuning in to Free Concerts in D.C.

Numerous groups offer no-charge music performances, but the most ambitious lineup is the Kennedy Center's **Millennium Stage** concerts at 6 p.m. every day in the Grand Foyer. Marimba, show tunes, classical works, jazz—programs run the gamut. No tickets needed. The Harman Center for the Arts (see p. 138), in Penn Quarter, offers free hour-long performances Thursday evenings as part of its **Happenings at the Harman** program; reservations are advised. Performers include many local arts groups. And each summer Shakespeare Theatre Company offers two weeks of free performances of a Shakespeare classic; it's so popular that you must enter a lottery to score tickets (see *shakespearetheatre.org/events/free-for-all* for details).

The Church of the Epiphany *(epiphanydc.org)* downtown hosts free midday concerts every Tuesday with its **Tuesday Concert Series.** Less well known is the excellent concert series sponsored by the Library of Congress (see pp. 62–63). View the program schedule and reserve free tickets online *(loc.gov/concert)*. The **Friday Morning Music Club** *(fmmc.org)* has arranged free concerts in the Washington area for 120 years as a public service under its mission of promoting classical music. Performances are now held throughout the week.

More Places to Visit Around the White House

Cathedral of St. Matthew the Apostle

This redbrick 1890s cathedral, with its ribbed copper dome, is where the funeral Mass of President John F. Kennedy was held in 1963. The cavernous interior, embellished with mosaics, a skylit dome, flickering votive candles, and paintings and statues, is a haven for prayer. *stmatthewscathedral.org* Map pp. 108–109 ✉ 1725 Rhode Island Ave., N.W. ☎ 202-347-3215 🚇 Metro: Dupont Circle, Farragut North

Charles Sumner School

This building was opened in 1872 as a school for African-American children and named for the abolitionist senator from Massachusetts. It is now an archive and a D.C. public schools conference center and museum. The Sumner School also hosts concerts, lectures, films, and art exhibitions. 🗺 Map pp. 108–109 ✉ 1201 17th St., N.W. ☎ 202-730-0478 🕐 Closed Sat.–Sun. 🚇 Metro: Farragut North, Dupont Circle

Decatur House

For his triumphs in the War of 1812, Commodore Stephen Decatur earned enough to build this federal-style town house on Lafayette Square. Benjamin Henry Latrobe designed the house, completed in 1818, but Decatur never really got to enjoy it: He was killed in a duel with a fellow officer 14 months after moving in. His wife rented the house to the likes of Henry Clay. In 1829, Charlotte Dupuy, a woman enslaved by Clay, then the Secretary of State, sued him for her freedom while living at Decatur House. In January 2010, the National Center for White House History was established here for research and events. *decaturhouse.org* 🗺 Map pp. 108–109 ✉ 1610 H St., N.W. 🕐 Guided tours Mon. 11 a.m., 12:30 p.m., & 2 p.m. 🚇 Metro: Farragut West

Department of the Interior Museum

This small, quiet museum chronicles the Interior Department's 1930s origins, when it comprised the National Park Service, U.S. Fish and Wildlife Service, U.S. Geological Survey, and the Bureaus of Mines, Indian Affairs, Reclamation, and Land Management. Paintings, Native American artifacts and crafts, handmade maps, tools, and videos tell the story of the country's settlement, natural beauty, and conservation. Adults must present photo ID to enter. *doi.gov/interiormuseum* 🗺 Map pp. 108–109 ✉ 1849 C St., N.W. ☎ 202-208-4743 🕐 Closed Sat.–Sun. & federal holidays 🚇 Metro: Farragut West, Foggy Bottom–GWU

■ A bronze Albert Einstein sits in thought at the National Academy of Sciences (see opposite).

Department of State

On the eighth floor of the imposing State Department building you will find the elegant suite of **Diplomatic Reception Rooms** decorated with one of the country's finest collections of early American furnishings. Take the 45-minute tour and you will discover such surprises as George Washington's Chinese porcelain *(reservations required, often months ahead)*. The rooms on the south side—among them the State Dining Room—offer views of the Mall and its monuments. *receptiontours.state.gov* Map pp. 108–109 23rd & C Sts., N.W. 202-647-3241 Closed Sat.–Sun. & federal holidays Metro: Foggy Bottom–GWU

INSIDER TIP:

Schedule an hour-long tour of the 1941–1942 murals by New Deal artists plus photographer Ansel Adams at the Department of the Interior. For details, contact the DOI [tel 202-208-4743].

—CAROLINE HICKEY
National Geographic Travel Books editor

Hay-Adams Hotel

The elegant Italian Renaissance–style Hay-Adams, one of Washington's finest small hotels, fronts Lafayette Park, with a good view of the White House. Built in the 1920s, it occupies the site of residences owned by statesman John Hay and historian Henry Adams. Stop in for fine dining at the hotel's Lafayette Restaurant or sip cocktails at its cozy bar Off the Record. *hayadams.com* Map pp. 108–109 16th & H Sts., N.W.

Teatime

Whether you take it with honey and milk or prefer to sip green-leaf varieties, there are plenty of spots in Washington to enjoy afternoon tea. Two of the poshest locales are elegant Peacock Alley (take a peek at the mosaic floor) at the historic Willard InterContinental (see sidebar p. 118) and the radiantly skylit Greenhouse atrium in the renovated Jefferson Hotel (1200 16th St., N.W., tel 202-448-2300, jeffersondc.com). For an authentic Asian atmosphere, try Teaism (teaism.com), with several locations around town. For a garden-style setting, head to Hillwood Estate (see pp. 187–188).

202-638-6600 Metro: Farragut West, Farragut North, McPherson Square

National Academy of Sciences

Housed here are committees representing foremost U.S. experts in science, medicine, and engineering. Outside is a bronze of Albert Einstein (see opposite) by Robert Berks, who sculpted the Kennedy Center's JFK bust. The NAS offers lectures and other events and activities that explore the intersections of science and culture. *nasonline.org* Map pp. 108–109 2101 Constitution Ave., N.W. 202-334-2000 Metro: Foggy Bottom–GWU

National World War I Memorial

Unveiled in April 2021 and taking up the entirety of a remodeled Pershing Park, the National World War I Memorial honors those who gave their lives in the "Great War." Designed by architect Joseph Weishaar, it features a Peace Fountain and a statue of Gen. John J. Pershing, commander of the American Expeditionary Forces. The central feature is "A Soldier's Journey," a 58-foot-long (17.7 m) bas-relief wall of remembrance by Sabin Howard showing 38 figures of a single American soldier and representing the larger American experience of World War I. *worlwar1 centennial.org.* 🗺 Map pp. 108–109 ✉ Pennsylvania Ave., N.W., & 15th, N.W. 🚇 Metro: Metro Center, Federal Triangle

---

INSIDER TIP:

Breakfast at the Hay-Adams Hotel might be a splurge, but it sometimes comes with paparazzi-worthy sightings of household-name folks in the worlds of politics and entertainment. You never know.

—AMY ALIPIO
*National Geographic Traveler
magazine associate editor*

Octagon Museum

A gem of early Washington history, the redbrick Octagon was the neighborhood's first private residence. Its designer, William Thornton, was also the first architect of the Capitol. The house was completed in 1801 for entrepreneur John Tayloe III. When the British burned the President's House in 1814, the Madisons took shelter here. President Madison signed the war-ending Treaty of Ghent in an upstairs parlor.

The American Institute of Architects bought it in 1902. It now houses a museum operated by the American Architectural Foundation. Despite its name, the Octagon house only has six sides. *architectsfoundation. org* 🗺 Map pp. 108–109 ✉ 1799 New York Ave., N.W. ☎ 202-626-7439 🕐 Open Thurs.–Sat. 1–4 p.m.; call for guided tours 🚇 Metro: Farragut West, Farragut North

Renwick Gallery

The architecturally distinctive Renwick Gallery has housed the Smithsonian American Art Museum's contemporary craft program since 1972. Designed in 1858 by James Renwick, Jr., architect of the Smithsonian's Castle, the striking Second Empire–style building features sandstone pilasters and garlands gracing the redbrick and decorative ironwork crowning the tripartite mansard roof. In addition to crafts, it also displays decorative arts and hosts eclectic exhibitions that have in recent years spanned "The Automobile and American Art" to "¡Printing the Revolution! The Rise and Impact of Chicano Graphics." *americanart. si.edu/renwick* 🗺 Map pp. 108–109 ✉ 17th St. & Pennsylvania Ave., N.W. ☎ 202-633-7970 🕐 Closed Mon.–Tue. 🚇 Metro: Farragut West; Bus: 32, 36, Circulator

St. John's Church

Presidents since James Madison have worshipped at this Episcopal church on occasion. A brass plate marks the president's pew, No. 54, and the kneelers are covered in needlepoint. A national historic landmark, the gold-domed yellow stucco church, completed in 1815, has daily services, as well as concerts and community events. *stjohns-dc.org* 🗺 Map pp. 108–109 ✉ 1525 H St., N.W. ☎ 202-347-8766 🚇 Metro: Farragut West, McPherson Square

St. Mary's Episcopal Church

Called St. Mary's Church for Colored People when it opened in 1887, this was Washington's first house of worship for African-American Episcopalians. The altar triptych depicts two saints of African descent; the center window is Tiffany stained glass. *stmarysfoggybottom.org* 🗺 Map pp. 108–109 ✉ 728 23rd St., N.W. ☎ 202-333-3985 🕐 Closed Fri.–Sat. 🚇 Metro: Foggy Bottom–GWU

A metropolitan mélange of historic structures, entertainment spots, museums, office buildings, shops, hotels, and a slew of restaurants

DOWNTOWN

An imposing figure adorns the National Building Museum.

DOWNTOWN

Just north of the Mall since the city's founding in 1791, downtown D.C. sprung from the intersection of Pennsylvania Avenue (the city's main street) and 7th Street (the main northern thoroughfare). The area now sprawls to 14th Street and Louisiana and Massachusetts Avenues. Booming with new vitality, downtown buzzes with restaurants, shops, theaters, and galleries, as well as several long-established museums.

Throughout the 1800s, boutiques, hotels, and theaters thrived downtown, catering to the area's residents. The turn of the 20th century, however, brought the exodus of affluent merchants and residents to the suburbs, thereby opening up the downtown area to successive groups of lower income citizens. Then came the assassination of Martin Luther King, Jr., in 1968, instigating riots and the large-scale abandonment of commercial ventures. As buildings fell into miserable disrepair and the crime rate exploded, the area became one to avoid.

That outlook soon changed. In 1972, Congress created the Pennsylvania Avenue

■ **Downtown Washington D.C. Historic Architecture**

Development Corporation (PADC) to plan the revitalization of Pennsylvania Avenue—the neglected streetscape was unbefitting what many consider to be America's Main Street.

Initially, the PADC focused on renovating Pennsylvania Avenue's historic buildings: the Old Post Office, the Willard Hotel, and the National and Warner Theatres. Each successful venture encouraged the next, as city planners and developers saw the exciting possibility of reviving downtown.

Coupled with renovation, new construction brought Market Square (1989; *N of the Archives*), with offices and apartments; the Lansburgh (1992; *8th & E Sts.*), a residential/retail/cultural arts complex; and in 2003 the new convention center (*N of Mt. Vernon Sq.*). In the last two decades, billions of dollars have been invested in the area's development, including many new restaurants. A popular attraction is the Harman Center for the Arts.

The arrival of the MCI Center in 1997 (now the Capitol One Arena) has been important to development, drawing large numbers of visitors to basketball and hockey games, concerts, and other special events.

All this new life complements several museums often overshadowed by those on the nearby Mall. Highlights include the Smithsonian American Art Museum, National Portrait Gallery, National Museum of Women in the Arts, and National Building Museum. The National Law Enforcement Museum is the newest addition.

Amid the modernization, tiny Chinatown clings to its heritage. Clustered on the north side of Pennsylvania Avenue in the 1880s, the enclave established its distinctive appearance after moving to the H Street area in the 1930s, where it remains today, with Cantonese, Szechuan, and Hunan restaurants, as well as traditional Chinese pharmacies. ■

NOT TO BE MISSED:

"The FBI Experience" at the J. Edgar Hoover FBI Building 137–138

Creative stagings of Shakespeare at the Lansburgh or Harman 139

Seeing the theater box where President Lincoln was shot 140

The Charters of Freedom at the National Archives 142–143

The Great Hall of the National Building Museum 144

The Bell Tower in the Old Post Office 145–146

PENNSYLVANIA QUARTER

The shining star of downtown's revitalization, the Pennsylvania Quarter neighborhood—
also called the 7th Street corridor—has become a hip hangout. With an explosion of luxury
apartment complexes, trendy restaurants, theaters, and galleries joining a panoply of established and new museums, the once neglected area now teems with life both day and night.

■ The Friendship Archway spans H Street in the heart of Chinatown.

Pennsylvania Quarter

Map pp. 132–133

5th to 9th & E to I Sts., N.W.

Metro: Gallery Place–Chinatown; Bus: 70, 79, Circulator

The real success story of the Pennsylvania Quarter begins with the abandoned Lansburgh department store. In 1992 this imposing building was rehabilitated into a mixed-use complex housing several hundred residential units, retail space, and a cultural arts venue. The Lansburgh's reigning tenant, the nationally renowned **Shakespeare Theatre** (see p. 139) moved to 7th Street from Capitol Hill in 1992. Devoted to presenting the Bard's works—as well as those of his contemporaries and of the playwrights he influenced—the theater is considered one of the nation's

most prestigious. It expanded dramatically in October 2007, when the new **Harman Center for the Arts** opened. The center's **Sidney Harman Hall** added 774 seats and a second venue to the theater's performance capacity.

The well-established repertory **Woolly Mammoth Theatre** (641 D St., N.W, tel 202-393-3939, woolly mammoth.net) is located nearby.

Another major contributor to revitalization was the colossal Verizon Center, now **Capitol One Arena** (601 F St., N.W, tel 202-628-3200, capitalonearena.com), which draws thousands of visitors on any given day. Opened in 1997, the

INSIDER TIP:

There's a vibrant theater scene on 14th Street, N.W., a quick cab ride or long walk from Penn Quarter. Before you head in to see the show, have Thai food at Rice [1608 14th Street, N.W.].

—M. J. JACOBSEN
*National Geographic
vice president of communications*

20,000-seat arena hosts circuses, ice-skating performances, concerts, and other special events. It's also home to the Washington Wizards and Mystics professional basketball teams (men and women, respectively), the Georgetown Hoyas college basketball team, and the Washington Capitals hockey team.

An even bigger addition to downtown is the **Washington Convention Center** (*801 Mount Vernon Pl., eventsdc.com*), which opened in 2003. With 2.3 million square feet (more than 214,000 sq m) of space—covering six city blocks on 17 acres (6.8 ha)—the behemoth boasts state-of-the-art facilities and a $4 million art collection.

Keeping in step with the quarter's new face, many of its museums—including the **National Portrait Gallery** (see pp. 136–137) and the **Smithsonian American Art Museum** (see this page)—have been renovated.

Increasing the area's appeal are several museums added in recent years, including the National Law Enforcement Museum (see p. 138). The most dynamic was the imposing Newseum, dedicated to all aspects of journalism. Located on Pennsylvania Avenue, mid-way between the White House and the U.S. Capitol, it made a powerful statement about First Amendment freedom of expression. Opened in 2011, it closed in 2019. Also nearby is an outpost of **Madame Tussauds wax museum** (*1001 F St., N.W., madametussauds.com/washington*). Several blocks away, the **Washington Historical Society** (*8th & K Sts., N.W., washmohistorical.org*) occupies a beaux arts building, the former Carnegie Library.

Sandwiched amid all this growth is Washington's small but distinctive **Chinatown** (*6th to 8th Sts. & G to H Sts., N.W.*), which has thrived since it was established here in the 1930s.

Smithsonian American Art Museum

Housed in a historic landmark that Walt Whitman called the "noblest of Washington buildings" is the nation's first collection of American art. Here and at its Renwick Gallery (see p. 130) are works in every medium—all by American artists and spanning more than three centuries. The National Portrait Gallery shares the impressive building, which reopened in 2006 after a major overhaul.

One of the finest examples of Greek Revival public architecture in the United States, this stunning building has porticos modeled on

Smithsonian American Art Museum

🗺 Map pp. 132–133

✉ 8th & F Sts., N.W.

☎ 202-633-7970

🕐 Closed Mon.–Tue.

Ⓜ Metro: Gallery Place–Chinatown; Bus: 42, 70, 79, D3–D6, Circulator

americanart.si.edu

National Portrait Gallery

⚐ Map pp. 132–133

✉ 8th & F Sts., N.W.

☎ 202-633-8300

⏱ Closed Mon.–Tue.

🚇 Metro: Gallery Place–Chinatown; Bus: 42, 70, 79, D3–D6, Circulator

npg.si.edu

the Parthenon in Athens, a curving double staircase, colonnades, and vaulted galleries. Construction began in 1836 under the direction of Robert Mills, then architect of public buildings. The building was used as a hospital and barracks during the Civil War, and President Abraham Lincoln held his second Inaugural Ball here in 1865.

More than 7,000 artists are represented in the Smithsonian American Art Museum's

African-American art, Latino art, and folk art.

Highlights include Depression-era Works Progress Administration art in the Level One **Experience America** gallery; more than 400 paintings of Plains Indian tribes by George Catlin in the **Indians Gallery;** works by hallmark early-20th-century painters Winslow Homer, John Singer Sargent, and James McNeill Whistler in the **Gilded Age** gallery, on Level Two; plus Roy Lichtenstein's "pop-art" pieces, and David Hockney's "Snails Space with Vari-Lites, 'Painting as Performance'" on Level Three.

Among the several public spaces are a courtyard with café, as well as a conservation center where visitors can observe restoration and repair of important works of art.

National Portrait Gallery

Recognizing the nation's heroes, intellects, and rogues, the National Portrait Gallery reveals America's history through portraiture and sculpture. The idea of a national portrait gallery dates back to 1857, when Congress commissioned George P. A. Healy to paint official portraits of all the presidents for the White House. After World War I, a national portrait gallery was proposed, yet this gallery didn't open until 1968.

The collection consists of more than 20,000 objects in a wide range of media, including marble, oil on canvas, drawing, and photography. Among the formal portraits of all the presidents on Level Two is Gilbert Stuart's famous

■ **A painted portrait of former President Barack Obama by artist Kehinde Wiley hangs at the National Portrait Gallery.**

400,000-piece collection, which features colonial portraits, 19th-century landscapes, American Impressionism, 20th-century realism and abstraction, sculpture, photography, prints and drawings,

"Lansdowne" portrait of George Washington (1796). The museum's most popular portraits are those of President Barack Obama (by Kehinde Wiley) and Michelle Obama (by Amy Sherald); unveiled in February 2018, they became instant icons. This floor also hosts a revolving set of special exhibits, plus **The Struggle for Justice,** dedicated to Americans who have fought for civil rights equality throughout the years.

Opening onto the magnificent third-floor Great Hall are four galleries that feature 20th-century Americans who were significant in politics, culture, and science. **"Champions"** salutes figures whose impact has extended beyond their achievement in American sports. **"Bravo!"** showcases composers and performers from the beginning of the 20th century to the present, with video clips of performances by such legends as P. T. Barnum, John Wayne, Katharine Hepburn, Leonard Bernstein, and Aaron Copland.

Other notable personalities appear in the exhibit **"American Origins,"** from the first meeting of Native Americans and European explorers through the onset of the gilded age. The Civil War galleries have selections from the museum's outstanding daguerreotypes. Caricatures by Al Hirschfeld, *Time* magazine portrait covers, and sculptor Jo Davidson's bronze and terra-cotta portraits of famous Americans such as Franklin D. Roosevelt, Gertrude Stein, and Gertrude Vanderbilt Whitney all round out the museum experience.

J. Edgar Hoover FBI Building

Completed in 1974 as the Federal Bureau of Investigation headquarters, the "brutalist" FBI Building of poured concrete contrasts sharply with the elegant neoclassical granite and marble government buildings that surround it. Its 2,800,876 square feet (260,210 sq m) house more than 7,000 FBI agents and other employees. Although the building is otherwise off-limits, the **Education Center** offers a fascinating self-guided tour—**"The FBI Experience"**—that teaches about the agency's role in protecting the nation.

Check out the desk of J. Edgar Hoover, the infamous FBI Director for whom the building is named; and the case with ephemera from the World Trade Center debris following the terrorist attacks of 9/11. And try to spot the surveillance camera hidden in a painting (hint: Look closely at the period in the artist's signature). You can even watch FBI agents blasting away on the firing range!

Note the ten American flags

J. Edgar Hoover FBI Building

- Map pp. 132–133
- 935 Pennsylvania Ave., N.W.
- Closed Sat.– Sun.
- Metro: Federal Triangle, Archives—Navy Memorial—Penn Quarter; Bus: 32, Circulator

fbi.gov

Sightseeing With a Twist

If walking from one big monument to another feels ho-hum, add something different to your day. Follow a guide as you glide past the sites on a motorized Segway or explore on an electric-bike with **Fat Tire Tours** (*fattiretours.com*) or **Bike and Roll** (*bikeandrolldc.com*). They'll even deck you in reflective gear for an evening tour of the monuments. **Monuments by Moonlight** (*historictours.com*) offers trolley tours that feature major sites after dark, as well as by day.

■ The National Law Enforcement Officers Memorial

National Law Enforcement Museum

🅰 Map pp. 132–133

✉ 444 E St., N.W.

☎ 202-737-3400

💲 $$$$$

🚇 Metro: Judiciary Square; Bus: 80, D3, X2

lawenforcement museum.org

flying from the façade on Pennsylvania Ave: Each is different, with the earliest being the "Continental Colors" first raised on January 1, 1776. All visitors must be U.S. citizens or permanent residents, and visits must be scheduled through your congressional representative's office no later than four weeks in advance.

National Law Enforcement Museum

Twin entrance pavilions fronting the D.C. Court of Appeals provide access to this underground museum extending beneath **Judiciary Square,** with its **National Law Enforcement Officers Memorial**—the nation's monument to law enforcement officers killed in the line of duty. A plaque inset in the center of the square is cusped by 304-foot-long (93.7 m) blue-gray marble walls engraved with the names of more than 21,000 officers who have died in

the line of duty since 1786. New names are added each May during National Police Week.

The National Law Enforcement Museum opened belowground in October 2018. It displays an arresting assemblage of more than 20,000 artifacts, from a Colt M1849 Revolver issued to the Baltimore, MD, Police Department in 1857, and Al Capone's bulletproof vest, to the U.S. Park Police Eagle One helicopter used to rescue airplane crash survivors from the Potomac River on January 13, 1982.

The museum's interactive exhibitions provide a captivating "walk in their shoes" immersive experience of American law enforcement. Be a 911 telephone operator in the interactive 9-1-1 Emergency Ops Dispatch Experience. Learn the forensic techniques that detectives use to solve crimes. And, gun in hand, hone your split-second decision making in the video Training Simulator.

Shakespeare Theatre & Harman Center for the Arts

Since its founding in 1985, Washington's Shakespeare Theatre has become one of the city's most beloved cultural institutions. Under artistic director Michael Kahn and, since 2019, Simon Godwin, the company has won wide acclaim for its highly imaginative modern interpretations of classical plays that in some cases make them more comprehensible and relevant to 21st-century audiences. In 1992 the Shakespeare Theatre helped spearhead a renaissance of the downtown area near Pennsylvania Avenue by moving from its Capitol Hill quarters to the converted Lansburgh department store on 7th Street. Steady audience growth led the company to expand in 2007 to additional space around the corner in a handsome new $89 million glass-fronted building.

Today, the existing 451-seat **Lansburgh Theatre** and the 774-seat **Sidney Harman Hall**—together known as the Harman Center for the Arts–provide multiple spaces for staging a broad range of works.

Besides presenting familiar plays like *Hamlet, Romeo and Juliet, The Tempest,* and *A Midsummer Night's Dream,* the Shakespeare Theatre has undertaken ambitious productions of rarely produced works such as *Coriolanus, King John, Troilus and Cressida,* and *Pericles.* Modern masterpieces by George Bernard Shaw, Oscar Wilde, Eugene O'Neill, Henrik Ibsen, and others also are represented.

EXPERIENCE:
Sample Undercover Cocktails

Many an FBI agent has bent an elbow undercover at watering holes once used by foreign spies. After visiting FBI headquarters (see pp. 137–138) and International Spy Museum (see p. 106), see if you can suss out any secret agents at **The Exchange Saloon** *(1719 G St., N.W.).* In the 1970s, this sports bar was a wife-swapping club where husband-and-wife Czech spies Karl and Hana Koecher gleaned intel while canoodling with libertine military and CIA officers. Be sure to ask for your martini shaken, not stirred, at the **Annual International Spy Gala** *(spydc.com),* at the Washington Plaza Hotel. And with the right connections, you can even tipple mojitos by invitation-only at **Hemingway's** bar in the Cuban Embassy *(2630 16th St., N.W.).*

In its more than three decades, the Shakespeare repertory company has received numerous Helen Hayes awards for excellence in its theatrical presentations. They often include renowned guest artists, such as Stacy Keach playing King Lear. In 2010, a Harman performance of *Phèdre,* produced by the National Theatre of Great Britain and starring Helen Mirren, sold out within five hours after tickets went on sale.

As part of its commitment to make classical theater more widely accessible, the Shakespeare Theatre offers a Free for All performance every summer. It also organizes educational programs for students, and partners with many groups to provide concerts, ballet, and other arts performances. ∎

Shakespeare Theatre & Harman Center for the Arts

🅰 Map pp. 132–133

✉ Lansburgh Theatre: 450 7th St., N.W. Sidney Harman Hall: 610 F St., N.W.

☎ 202-547-1122

🚇 Metro: Archives–Navy Memorial–Penn Quarter, Gallery Place–Chinatown, Judiciary Square; Bus: 70, 74, D3–D6, Circulator

shakespearetheatre .org

FORD'S THEATRE NATIONAL HISTORIC SITE

A working theater and a museum dedicated to one of the nation's most tragic dramas, Ford's Theatre has a morbidly compelling quality. John Wilkes Booth shot President Abraham Lincoln here on April 14, 1865, five days after Lee's surrender at Appomattox. Lincoln's untimely death pushed to legendary heights the historical greatness he had achieved by keeping the Union from falling apart.

Ford's Theatre National Historic Site

- 🗺 Map pp. 132–133
- ✉ 511 10th St., N.W.
- ☎ 202-347-4833
- 💲 $
- 🚇 Metro: Metro Center; Bus: 42, 79, D3–D6

fordstheatre.org

Serving as a government office building and then a storage facility, the small 10th Street edifice was acquired by the National Park Service in 1933, restored to its original 1865 splendor in the 1960s, and renovated again in 2008. The theater now hosts a full program of contemporary American plays, musicals, and other entertainment.

The ornate interior boasts the authentically re-created

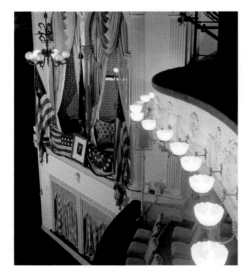

■ The Presidential Box is on permanent display at Ford's.

Presidential Box with American flags, lace curtains, red velvet wallpaper, plush seats, and the original settee. The museum downstairs contains various historic artifacts.

When the theater is not in use, Park Service officials offer short informative talks on the night's events. Booth, a disgruntled actor and Confederate sympathizer, shot Lincoln in the head and then jumped down to the stage, breaking a bone in his leg. He hobbled off and fled on horseback through the southern Maryland countryside, only to be caught 12 days later and shot dead.

Continue following the night's events across the street at the **Petersen House** *(516 10th St., N.W.)*, where Lincoln was taken after the shooting. Never regaining consciousness, the president died the next day. Peek into the parlor where Mary Todd Lincoln waited through the night, the back parlor where Lincoln's secretary of war began investigating the murder, and the period-furnished bedroom in which Lincoln died. Pick up tickets *($)* to enter the museum and house at the box office, or visit the website. Occasional walking tours *($$$)* are led by costumed actors. ■

NATIONAL MUSEUM OF WOMEN IN THE ARTS

This museum focuses solely on the work of women artists. Founder and art collector Wilhelmina Cole Holladay opened it in 1987 to correct the historical lack of exposure of female artists by showcasing the talent of women artists around the world, from the Renaissance to the present. Although it closed in September 2021 for a two-year restoration, collections will be on view in special exhibitions at institutions throughout Washington, D.C.

Notable in itself, the majestic, trapezoidal Renaissance Revival building began as a Masonic temple in 1907, served as a movie theater in the 1960s, and was rescued from demolition when purchased by Holladay in 1983. Restored to its former glory, the façade retains Masonic symbols (ironically, the Masons did not admit women), while the **Great Hall** shines with polished marble floors and decorative plasterwork. The latest restoration will completely transform the interior for a more visitor-friendly experience, with new and enlarged gallery space featuring innovative state-of-the-art technology.

New **outdoor sculptures** will engage visitors before they enter the building, where an **orientation gallery** chronicles women's artistic achievements from the 16th century through to modern times. Select works in the permanent collection of more than 5,500 pieces are on view on three levels.

Look for "Portrait of a Noblewoman" (1580) by Lavinia Fontana, the first widely known woman to sustain a career as an artist. Other treasures include "Highland Raid" (1860) by Rosa Bonheur (1822–1899), and "The Bath" (1891) by American Impressionist Mary Cassatt (1844–1926). Georgia O'Keeffe, Helen Frankenthaler, Alma Woodsey Thomas, Chakaia Booker, Jaune Quick-to-See Smith, and Hung Liu are among the artists represented.

INSIDER TIP:

The elegant National Museum of Women in the Arts occupies a gorgeously impressive building. Try the café on the mezzanine level for a snack or lunch.

—SUSAN STRAIGHT
National Geographic Travel Books editor

This museum is the only place in Washington where you can see work by Mexican painter Frida Kahlo. Her "Self-Portrait–Dedicated to Leon Trotsky" (1937), also known as "Between the Curtains," was donated by journalist, playwright, and ambassador Clare Boothe Luce and is part of the permanent collection.

The fourth floor has an 18,500-volume **library, research center,** plus new **education studio.** ∎

National Museum of Women in the Arts

- Map pp. 132–133
- 1250 New York Ave., N.W.
- 202-783-5000
- $$
- Metro: Metro Center; Bus: 80, D1–D6, S2–S4, X2, Circulator

nmwa.org

NATIONAL ARCHIVES

Serving as the nation's memory bank, the National Archives contains 12 billion pages of documents, including the original parchment copies of the Declaration of Independence, the U.S. Constitution, and the Bill of Rights. John Russell Pope, architect of the Jefferson Memorial, designed the 1935 building expressly to house these manifestos, although today the majority of documents are in various other buildings of the National Archives.

The National Archives Building

National Archives Building

- Map pp. 132–133
- 701 Constitution Ave. bet. 7th & 9th Sts., N.W.
- 202-357-5000 or 866-272-6272
- Metro: Archives–Navy Memorial–Penn Quarter; Bus: 30–36, A42–A48, P1–P4

archives.gov/dc
museum.archives. gov/visit

Ringed with 72 massive Corinthian columns, Pope's grand neoclassical edifice takes up a whole city block. Bas-reliefs decorate the pediments atop the north and south porticos. The 39 limestone steps that front the south portico on Constitution Avenue represent the 39 signers of the Constitution. The foot-thick (0.3 m) bronze doors at the top of the stairs soar 40 feet (12 m) high.

Inside, the echoing **Rotunda** rises to a 75-foot-high (23 m) dome. New York artist Barry Faulkner painted the two 1930s murals. "The Constitution" depicts James Madison presenting the document to George Washington. "The Declaration of Independence" shows Thomas Jefferson submitting the proclamation to John Hancock, presiding officer of the Continental Congress.

The low-lit Rotunda is where you can view the United States' most important documents: the **Charters of Freedom.** The Declaration of Independence, the U.S. Constitution, and the Bill of Rights lie in state-of-the-art cases that fiercely protect the them from air and moisture. The cases allow all four pages of the Constitution to be shown at the same time.

In cases flanking the Charters of Freedom are documents related to the exhibit "The Charters of Freedom: Our Nation's Founding Documents."

The interactive exhibit **"Public Vaults"** presents stories of how records in the National Archives "stacks"—documents, maps, photos, and films—are used by the federal government, organizations, and individual citizens to clarify historical events, investigate mysteries, make documentaries, and pursue family history. The exhibits include Abraham Lincoln's telegrams to his generals and audio recordings from the Oval Office.

Every few months, the Archives presents fresh exhibits in the **Lawrence F. O'Brien Gallery.** The focus ranges from photographic displays to selected holdings from the presidential libraries and other museums. The **McGowan Theater** shows a short film about the Archives between 11 a.m. and 12 p.m. and 1 p.m. and 2 p.m., and screens documentary films at night. The **Boeing Learning Center** (closed Sat.–Sun. & federal holidays) offers a variety of programs for children and adults that detail the methods of document-based research.

A Rich Repository

The Archives preserves more than 12 million maps, charts, and architectural drawings; 25 million photos; hundreds of thousands of films, videos, and sound recordings; and more. The National Archives and Records Administration, established in 1934 to oversee what to save,

deems about 3 percent of federal records generated annually to be worthy of permanent storage.

Representing more than 200 years of history, the repository is creating a rich paper trail. Among the original treasures are the Louisiana Purchase Treaty, the Emancipation Proclamation, Mathew Brady's Civil War photographs, Robert Peary's polar expedition journals, Dust Bowl photographs, Indian treaties,

Family Traces

People seeking genealogical history are heavy users of the National Archives. Every one of its twelve billion documents helps tell the story of some person or event. But putting it all together isn't straightforward. There's no master index, so you have to search individual collections; raw records are stored in boxes arranged by agency and program. A few records collections are available online, such as those on census data, military service, naturalization, and land claims. For more complex searches, you might need to visit other Archives branches around the country. The National Archives website (archives .gov) offers tips on getting started.

recordings of FDR's fireside chats, captured German records and Japanese surrender documents from World War II, and Richard Nixon's letter of resignation.

The Archives is popular among scholars, historians, and researchers, who use the research facilities here and in College Park, Maryland. Opened in 1994, the Maryland branch is the largest archival facility in the world. ■

NATIONAL BUILDING MUSEUM

The huge redbrick Pension Building designed by Gen. Montgomery C. Meigs is one of Washington's architectural treasures. The 1887 structure, however, modeled on the 18th-century Palazzo Farnese in Rome, was called Meig's Old Barn by critics. Though it had deteriorated by the 1960s, a study highlighted its potential as a museum. And so it was spared the wrecking ball.

Arcaded galleries and marbleized columns define the Great Hall.

National Building Museum

- Map pp. 132–133
- 401 F St., N.W.
- 202-272-2448
- $$
- Metro: Judiciary Square; Bus: D3–D6, Circulator

nbm.org

Congress called for the building's restoration in 1980 for an architecture, urban planning, and design museum. Girding the entire building, the most striking exterior feature is the 3-foot-high (0.9 m) terra-cotta frieze designed by sculptor Caspar Buberl (1834–1899). Depicting a procession of Civil War infantry, artillery, cavalry, and other units, it is emblematic of the building's original purpose: serving the needs of Union veterans.

Inside, the **Great Hall** will take your breath away. Standing in the middle of this immense, light-filled space bordered on all sides with four tiers of arcades and high clerestory windows, you feel as if you've stepped into an Italian gallery. Eight Corinthian columns, made of brick but plastered and painted to resemble marble, rise 75 feet high (23 m) on either side of a central fountain. Meigs modeled aspects of this room after several classical and Renaissance palaces and churches.

The museum galleries, featuring changing exhibits on the building arts, are on the Great Hall's first two levels. The long-term exhibit **"House and Home"** artfully arranges photographs, objects, models, and films to explore how ideas about American domestic life have changed due to the evolution of technology and consumer culture. The seven galleries feature touchable walls of materials used in residential construction and commissioned scale models of 14 iconic American homes.

The museum offers lectures, films, area building tours, a café, and an excellent gift shop. ∎

More Places to Visit Downtown

Carnegie Library

In 1899, Andrew Carnegie donated $682,000 to build this main library and three additional branches in Washington. This classic white marble beaux arts–style structure was completed in 1903 and served as the city's central library until 1972. Today, the Historical Society of Washington, D.C., operates a research library here and sponsors activities that include workshops, author readings and lectures, and the Urban Photography series that documents D.C.'s neighborhoods. *dchistory.org* 🗺 Map pp. 132–133 ✉ 801 K St., N.W. at Mount Vernon Square ☎ 202-516-1363 🚇 Metro: Mt. Vernon Square 7th Street–Convention Center, Gallery Place–Chinatown

Freedom Plaza

This granite plaza is anchored by an equestrian statue of Casimir Pulaski, the Polish nobleman who fought for America in the Revolutionary War and was mortally wounded at the siege of Savannah. The plaza, which was named in 1988 in honor of Dr. Martin Luther King, Jr., offers a sweeping view down Pennsylvania Avenue to the U.S. Capitol. Inlaid in bronze on the ground are depictions of L'Enfant's 1791 city plan, along with floorplans for the Congress House (Capitol) and President's Palace (White House). 🗺 Map pp. 132–133 ✉ Pennsylvania Ave. bet. 13th & 14th Sts., N.W. 🚇 Metro: Metro Center, Federal Triangle

Mary McLeod Bethune Council House

A national historic site, the former home of educator and civil rights champion Bethune (1875–1955), who founded Bethune-Cookman College in Daytona Beach, Florida, and the National Council of Negro Women, stores and displays artifacts pertaining to African-American women's history. The house museum is decorated with Bethune's original furnishings and photographs. *nps.gov/mamc* 🗺 Map pp. 132–133 ✉ 1318 Vermont Ave., N.W. ☎ 202-673-2402 🚇 Metro: McPherson Square

National Theatre

The sixth theater erected on this site since 1835, the National Theatre can claim to be Washington's oldest continuously operating theater. The sumptuous decor includes dazzling chandeliers. Unlike most modern theaters, the mezzanine and balcony are close to the stage, lending an intimate feel for theatergoers. Lavish Broadway and pre-Broadway shows and other presentations are staged here, many with well-known performers from stage, screen, and concert hall. *thenationaldc.org* 🗺 Map pp. 132–133 ✉ 1321 Pennsylvania Ave., N.W. ☎ 202-628-6161 🚇 Metro: Federal Triangle, Metro Center

INSIDER TIP:

L'Enfant's plan of the city, inlaid on the ground in Freedom Plaza, is the ultimate interactive map. In seconds you can get a feel for the city's layout without having to rely on a map, aerial photograph, or satellite image.

—JUAN JOSÉ VALDÉS
*National Geographic
Maps editorial & research*

Old Post Office

This castlelike edifice was built in Romanesque style in the 1890s as headquarters for the U.S. Post Office. Its 315-foot (96 m) bell tower, the third tallest structure in

Around the world in 80-plus steps: The 100-foot-diameter (30.5 m) map at the Navy Memorial plaza

Washington, D.C., contains the Bells of Congress, donated by England during the U.S. Bicentennial. It was added to the National Register of Historic Places in 1993. Although it has served as the Trump International Hotel Washington, D.C., since October 2016, the National Park Service retains control of the clock tower and observation deck and offers ranger-led tours. *nps.gov/opot* ⛰ Map pp. 132–133 ✉ Pennsylvania Ave. & 12th St., N.W. ☎ 202-426-6841 🚇 Metro: Federal Triangle

Planet Word Museum

On June 3, 1880, Alexander Graham Bell sent the first wireless voice transmission from atop the roof of the Franklin School. Fittingly, this renovated historic landmark today hosts the Planet Word Museum, which opened in May 2020 as the world's first voice-activated language arts museum, where interactive galleries and exhibits bring words and language alive in fun ways. *planetwordmuseum.org* ⛰ Map pp. 108–109 ✉ 925 13th St., N.W. ☎ 202-931-3139 🕐 Closed Mon.–Wed. 🚇 Metro: Farragut North, Metro Center

U.S. Navy Memorial & Naval Heritage Center

Situated directly behind the National Archives (see pp. 142–143), this heritage center contains artifacts and changing exhibits that highlight U.S. naval history. A small theater screens films on historic maritime figures and events, and offers free noontime lectures. Outside on the plaza, the circular memorial features a 7-foot-tall (2.1 m) bronze statue of "The Lone Sailor" and a correctly oriented granite map of the world. Bronze relief sculptures depicting events in naval history ring the memorial's perimeter. *navymemorial.org* ⛰ Map pp. 132–133 ✉ 701 Pennsylvania Ave., N.W. ☎ 202-380-0710 🚇 Metro: Archives–Navy Memorial–Penn Quarter

Warner Theatre

A block east of the National Theatre, the Warner Theatre started life in 1924 as a silent-movie palace and vaudeville stage. From the mid-1940s to the late 1960s, it only presented movies. Thereafter it functioned mainly as a rock concert venue until being shut down completely. The Warner Theatre reopened in 1992, after being refurbished with dazzling crystal, red velvet, and gold leaf. The Warner now hosts theater and dance performances as well as entertainers from Eddie Izzard to the Ramsey Lewis trio. In December there are performances of *The Nutcracker* presented by the Washington Ballet. *warnertheatredc.com* ⛰ Map pp. 132–133 ✉ 13th & E Sts., N.W. ☎ 202-783-4000 🚇 Metro: Federal Triangle, Metro Center

Hip and historic: old row houses, shops brimming with hot fashions and furnishings, mule-drawn canal boats, a trendy after-dark scene

GEORGETOWN

If only these worn-smooth Georgetown cobblestones could talk ...

GEORGETOWN

Washington's poshest square mile is a high-octane cocktail of cultural refinement and giddy nightlife. While side streets exhibit elegant federal and Victorian architecture, Wisconsin Avenue and M Street inject excitement with boutiques, bars, and restaurants.

■ **The Georgetown skyline on the Potomac River**

Georgetown began life as a tobacco inspection and shipment port at the confluence of Rock Creek and the Potomac, the highest navigable point on the river, on a 795-acre (322 ha) tract acquired by Scottish immigrant Ninian Beall in 1703. The Maryland Assembly established a town there in the 1750s and named it for George II. After independence, when the country was planning its federal city, Georgetown had become a thriving trade center, with lordly merchants' houses rising on the hill and artisans' houses and warehouses dotting the riverside. The new city proved a boon to Georgetown's silversmiths, cabinetmakers, and other craftspeople, who did a brisk business fitting the White House and other federal buildings. During the Civil War, Georgetown's significant black community made it an important Underground Railroad stop.

In 1871 the city of Washington annexed Georgetown. By then the little town needed the capital more than the reverse. The advent of the railroad and steam power had greatly diminished the importance of the C & O Canal

NOT TO BE MISSED:

Wandering brick streets lined with historic town houses 150–154

A walk, run, or bike ride along the C & O Canal 151

Shopping along Wisconsin Avenue and M Street 152

A relaxing drink or snack at Washington Harbour 152

A stroll through the formal gardens of Dumbarton Oaks 155–156

Lunch or dinner at historic Martin's Tavern 162

and thus Georgetown at its eastern end. In the first half of the 20th century, Georgetown lost its cachet and functioned primarily as industrial muscle for Washington, its foundry and mills supplying iron, paper, and coal. During Roosevelt's administration, white-collar workers began moving back; then, in 1950, Congress declared it a national historic district, speeding its restoration and return to fashion.

Rock Creek and the Potomac River form Georgetown's eastern and southern borders; to the west lies Georgetown University and north the hill on which Dumbarton Oaks sits. In these blocks have lived members of such clans as the Washingtons, Lees, and Kennedys. Today diplomats, politicians, journalists, and socialites walk shady brick sidewalks and party in book- and art-filled houses. ■

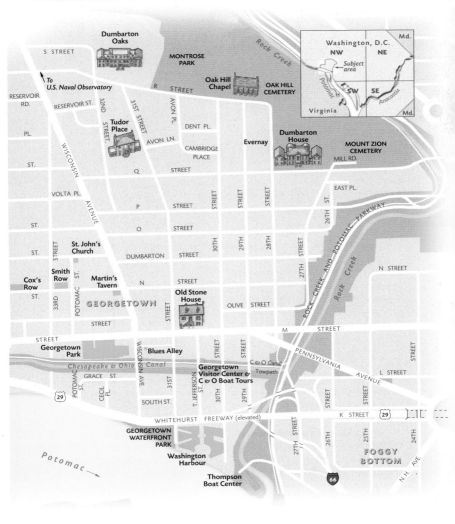

A BRICK SIDEWALK TOUR

With its venerable tree-lined streets and historic architecture, Georgetown was made for the leisurely stroller. You can try seeing the city's oldest neighborhood by car, but traffic moves slowly on the narrow streets, some of which are still cobbled and veined with trolley tracks. Better to leave the car behind and lace up your walking shoes.

Chesapeake and Ohio Canal National Historical Park in Georgetown

If you choose to drive, you can find street parking, but it may take a while, especially on the weekends. The network of streets north of M Street is your best bet for parking, though you should pay attention to the signs—most streets are zoned for two-hour parking from 7 a.m. to 9 p.m. (except Sunday). There are parking lots along M Street and below the canal. Metro buses service M Street and Wisconsin Avenue. You can also walk from the Foggy Bottom–GWU Metro station, just over a half mile (0.8 km) to the eastern edge of Georgetown.

If you do start from the Metro, you'll head west on Pennsylvania Avenue. Across the bridge, Pennsylvania feeds into M Street, Georgetown's main avenue for shopping, dining, and partying. Spring and summer evenings,

NOT TO BE MISSED:

Old Stone House • Washington Harbour • Cox's Row

the ten-block stretch from here to the Francis Scott Key Bridge is a steady parade of the chic, the casual, and the grungy. While the shops tend to be upscale, the bars, dance floors, and some restaurants cater to a young crowd, liberally supplied by Georgetown and George Washington Universities. A long-standing favorite restaurant for Sunday brunch, **Seasons ❶** (*2800 Pennsylvania Ave., N.W.*, see Travelwise p. 249), at the Four Seasons Hotel, features traditional and innovative cuisine, including organic dishes plus a renowned brunch.

Continue west on M to the **Old Stone House** ❷ *(3051 M St., N.W., tel 202-895-6000, nps.gov/rocr, closed Mon.–Tues.)*, the oldest house in the city. A craftsman named Christopher Layman built the first floor of the three-story house of local fieldstones in 1765, probably as both home and shop. A legend, later disproved, that George Washington had a headquarters here helped preserve the house. In 1953, the National Park Service acquired the property, restored it, and opened it to the public in 1960. The ground floor has a shop with replicas of 18th-century tools and a kitchen with cast-iron stove. On the second floor, built by the next owner, you'll find an oak-paneled dining room, a parlor, and bedrooms.

Cross M Street and head downhill on Thomas Jefferson Street to the eastern terminus of the **C & O Canal** ❸, a muddy-bottomed, shallow waterway, bordered by a towpath, that served as a key shipping link in the 19th century. Originally slated to stretch some 460 miles (740 km) to Pittsburgh and connect with the Ohio River, the Chesapeake and Ohio Canal, begun in 1828, made it only

Along the C & O Canal

A 184.5-mile (297 km) towpath parallels the C & O Canal *(nps.gov/choh)*, and the stretch of the path that runs through Georgetown invites cycling, strolling, or jogging. The **Georgetown Visitor Center** *(1057 Thomas Jefferson St., N.W., tel 202-653-5190)* has a good map. The towpath can be entered below M Street, at Thomas Jefferson Street. April through October, there are scenic rides on a replica 19th-century canal boat. You can also explore parts of the canal by canoe. Rent equipment at **Fletcher's Boathouse** *(4940 Canal Rd., N.W., tel 202-244-0461, boatingindc.com)*, about 3 miles (4.8 km) beyond Georgetown. A multi-year renovation of the canal began in 2019; check the website for construction updates.

🗺 See also area map pp. 148–149
🅿 M & 29th Sts., N.W. (Metro: Foggy Bottom–GWU)
🕑 2 hours
ⓘ 2 miles (3.2 km)
🅿 St. John's Church

INSIDER TIP:

Washington Harbour is a little bit of a Las Vegas experience with its oversize buildings, luxurious interiors, and restaurants. But instead of gambling, you have the Potomac River.

—KARIN KINNEY
National Geographic Books contributor

185 miles (298 km) up the Potomac to Cumberland, Maryland, where work stopped in 1850. Don't miss the small brick row houses that run along the canal just off Thomas Jefferson Street; they were built after the Civil War as homes for laborers. A few are now Asian takeout restaurants.

Go from the old to the new at the bottom of the hill by crossing K Street under the Whitehurst Freeway; in front of you spreads **Washington Harbour** ❹, a 1980s complex of offices, apartments, shops, and restaurants. A grand fountain in the center becomes a seasonal ice rink. The Harbour offers views of the Potomac, Roosevelt Island, the Kennedy Center, Watergate, and the high-rises of Rosslyn, Virginia, across the river.

The sleek glass box neighboring the Harbour to the east is the **House of Sweden** *(2900 K St., N.W., tours available).* It houses Sweden's embassy and business interests.

Next head up 31st Street. On your left you'll pass an alleyway that leads to **Blues Alley** *(1073 Wisconsin Ave., N.W., tel 202-337-4141, bluesalley.com),* which may look like a dive outside but is actually Washington's swankiest jazz joint. On nights when a big name is in town, you might see 50 people lined up just hoping for no-shows on the reservation list. Definitely arrive early, and expect to pay a hefty amount—well worth it for the intimate setting.

Turn right from the alley onto Wisconsin Avenue and walk up to old-world neighborhood haunt **Martin's Tavern** ❺ (see p. 162), then backtrack to M Street. This intersection is the area's busiest; the gold dome on the ornate old Farmers and Mechanics Branch of the PNC Bank serves as a landmark. Turn right heading west on M to the nearly block-long multi-level mall called **Georgetown Park** *(3222 M St., N.W.).*

Step into **Olivia Macaron** *(oliviamacaron. com),* where you can pick up delectable coconut or salted caramel *macarons* for a sweet treat. Erected in 1865, the building sits on a site that also held markets in the 18th century. A little

Shopping & More Shopping in Georgetown

The trendy shops of Georgetown line M Street and Wisconsin Avenue, some tucked into side streets and alcoves. Along with the big name purveyors (think Kate Spade, Puma, Hugo Boss) are independent boutiques with selections that will urge you to splurge. **Hu's Wear** *(2906 M St., N.W., tel 202-342-2020)* carries edgy designer finds handpicked by the owner, while **Anthropologie** *(3222 M St., N.W., tel 202-337-1363)* boasts women's apparel, accessories, and intimates. **Ledbury's** *(3319 Cady's Alley, tel 202-796-2626)* caters to the sartorial male.

Browse furniture stores—traditional and cutting edge—in Georgetown's design district, Cady's Alley. Shops include **Design Within Reach** *(3338 M St., N.W., tel 202-339-9480),* **Thos. Moser** *(3334 Cady's Alley, tel 202-793-2606),* and **Waterworks** *(3314 M St., N.W. , tel 202-333-7207).* While there, also visit **Relish** *(3312 Cady's Alley, N.W.)* for perfect-fit jeans.

The Lantern *(3241 P St., N.W., tel 202-333-3222)* is a trove of books, maps, and compact disks. And stop into **Wines & Spirits** *(2701 P St., N.W. , tel 202-338-5500)* to pick up a bottle of fine wine.

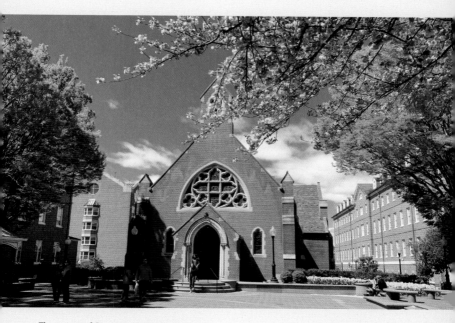

■ The campus of Georgetown University

farther down the street, you'll come to **Cady's Alley** ❻, the neighborhood's design district hub. Keep going down M Street and just before Key Bridge you'll see the 1788 **Forrest-Marbury House** ❼ (now the Embassy of Ukraine). Here George Washington met with local landowners in 1791 to work out the agreement on the sale of their land to create the new federal city. General Uriah Forrest owned the house then; in 1800–1835 it belonged to William Marbury of the landmark *Marbury v. Madison* case, in which the Supreme Court established the doctrine of judicial review.

For a small detour into cinematic history, cross to the north side of M Street and walk west a short distance. Tucked away near a gas station, an eerily familiar 75-step stone stairway stretches upward. Known as the **Exorcist Steps,** the stairs played a prominent role in the 1973 horror classic *The Exorcist.*

Prospect Street has some of Georgetown's most impressive 18th-century houses. For an easier ascent to Prospect, go back east on M and turn left onto 34th Street. At the corner of 34th and Prospect stands the classic Georgian-style **Halcyon House,** built by Benjamin Stoddert, the first secretary of the Navy. A few buildings away is **Worthington House** (*3425 Prospect St., N.W.*), built by prominent lawyer John Thomson Mason. Note the 24-paned windows lining both main floors. Just past 35th Street look for **Prospect House** (*3508 Prospect St., N.W.*), another imposing Georgian, home of a 19th-century shipping merchant. Much of its structure and impressive gardens lie hidden behind a brick wall.

Prospect Street continues past 37th Street, the eastern edge of **Georgetown University** ❽. The Gothic-spired private university is best known for its schools of medicine, law, and foreign service, and its basketball team, the Georgetown Hoyas.

From 37th Street, turn back east on N; across 34th Street is a line of five stately brick town houses known as **Cox's Row ⑨**, built in 1805 by John Cox, Mayor of Georgetown. Down the block, in 1957–1961, Senator John F. Kennedy and his wife, Jacqueline, lived at 3307 N Street, a three-story house with black shutters. On the corner of Potomac and O Streets, Anglican services are still held at **St. John's Church ⑩**, opened in 1804, and designed by William Thornton, first architect of the Capitol.

East of Wisconsin Avenue lie several more blocks of elegant 19th-century houses. Bare brick alternates with stucco facades painted in muted shades. Victorian bay windows and turrets are much in evidence. At the corner of Dumbarton and 31st Streets look for **Berry House,** built in 1810, when the street level was several feet higher. The front door stands unusually far above the street.

Walk one block south to N Street and turn left to see a noteworthy block. On your right is a large brick town house (3038 N St., N.W.), built in 1805 and the longtime home of statesman Averell Harriman and his wife, Pamela. The residence has a lovely arched doorway and odd, shingled dormers.

In a house across the street (3017 N St., N.W.), Jackie Kennedy lived for several months after the assassination of President Kennedy. Almost directly facing it stands the 40-room Colonial revival **Laird-Dunlop House** (3014 N St., N.W.), built in 1799. Robert Todd Lincoln, who was the only son of Abraham and Mary Todd Lincoln to survive into adulthood, lived here from 1918 to 1926. Especially notable is the building's raised fanlight doorway.

If you stroll on to 28th and Olive Streets, you'll come upon one of Georgetown's oldest—and smallest—houses. The tiny wooden cottage at No. 1222 was built sometime before the Revolution, though exactly when is uncertain. A veritable tribute to the past, very little has changed in the building's basic structure.

EXPERIENCE: Find Foodie Hot Spots in Georgetown

Before Adams Morgan and U Street became hip, anyone seeking delectable good times went to Georgetown. Though options have expanded to locations across the city and into the suburbs, Georgetown still reigns supreme as serve-it-up central. If you've a mind to join the fun, be aware that the revelry can be excessive at times, particularly on Halloween. Traffic woes —Key Bridge, the main feeder from Virginia, is a solid jam on weekend evenings— and parking woes don't deter the crowds dining along M Street. Cabbing here makes sense; the fare for two from downtown costs about as much as a movie ticket.

There are food and fun options of all sorts from which to choose. Long-standing favorites include **Fiola Mare** (3050 K St., N.W., tel 202-525-1402), for fine Italian fare; **Clyde's of Georgetown** (3236 M St., N.W., tel 202-333-9180), featuring vintage decor and afternoon appetizers; and, for pizza, **The Tombs** (1226 36th St., N.W., tel 202-337-6668), near Georgetown University. Located above the Tombs, **1789** (1226 36th St., N.W., tel 202-965-1789) presents elegant formal dinners in a federal-period house decorated with American antiques and Limoges china.

Kafe Leopold (3315 M St., N.W., tel 202-965-6005) serves its Austrian meals à la carte.

Sushi addicts can find a fix at **Susheria** (3101 K St., N.W., tel 202-906-9417), while those with a sweet tooth should visit **Georgetown Cupcake** (3301 M St., N.W., tel 202-333-8448), **Patisserie Poupon** (1645 Wisconsin Ave., N.W., tel 202-342-3248), or, for crepes and coffee, **Lutèce by Bonaparte** (1522 Wisconsin Ave., N.W., tel 202-333-8830).

DUMBARTON OAKS

An antique Provençal fountain, a miniature Roman amphitheater, and a 16th-century French-style arbor are among the many treasures awaiting you in Dumbarton Oaks's terraced gardens. Spring to fall, the grounds offer an ever changing display that includes early blooming dogwoods, magnolia blossoms, and cherries, peonies and roses, day lilies and chrysanthemums.

In addition to the floral landscape designs at Dumbarton Oaks, a Pebble Garden offers surprise.

Presiding over the gardens is a federal-style house acquired in 1920 by Mildred and Robert Woods Bliss, step siblings and antiquities collectors who married and traveled widely in the Foreign Service. They hired the architectural firm McKim, Mead and White to renovate and enlarge the house for their extensive library and collection of Byzantine and pre-Columbian art. In 1940 they conveyed the property and museum to Harvard University, though they remained actively involved in Dumbarton Oaks until their deaths (Robert in 1962, Mildred in 1969). In 1944 a series of informal conferences held at Dumbarton Oaks laid the foundation for the establishment of the United Nations.

Today the main part of the house functions as Harvard's research institute for Byzantine, pre-Columbian, and garden landscape studies and is not open to the public. Visitors are allowed into the gardens, which have only afternoon hours. The museum,

Dumbarton Oaks

- Map pp. 148–149
- Garden entrance: 31st & R Sts., N.W.; museum: 32nd St. bet. R & S Sts., N.W.
- 202-339-6400
- Closed Mon., federal holidays, & in inclement weather
- Gardens: $$ March–Oct., free in winter
- Metro: Dupont Circle, Foggy Bottom–GWU; Bus: 31–36, Circulator

doaks.org

music room, and museum shop are usually open to the public. Check the website for updates.

Visiting

Use the entrance on 32nd Street. Ten-acre (4 ha) formal gardens, designed by landscape architect Beatrix Farrand, spread across a gentle hill and down to a wooded valley. Ornate ironwork and stonework adorn the grounds. Brick paths lined by boxwoods and perennial borders lead from one garden to the next, and little trellised bowers offer places to sit and admire the birdsong, scents, and garden aesthetics.

A self-guided tour brochure, available at the entrance, highlights the gardens and plantings.

INSIDER TIP:

How is it that fall's yellows, reds, and oranges seem to blaze so bright on (and off) the exquisite trees in Dumbarton Oaks Park?

—SHEILA BUCKMASTER
National Geographic Traveler magazine editor at large

Inside the gates to the right stands an old katsura tree, its limbs almost touching the ground. Head up the path to the early 19th-century **Orangery;** a pre–Civil War fig tree climbs its walls. Through here you access the main gardens, including the **Rose Garden,** planted with nearly a thousand varieties of roses. Just below are gardens

with fountains and a wisteria-draped arbor based on a 16th-century French design.

At the property's edge, a winding walkway skirts the reflecting pool of Lovers' Lane and its small amphitheater. Farther north the garden becomes less formal, with flowering cherry trees, a hillside of golden forsythia, and views of Dumbarton Oaks Park, given by the Blisses to the National Park Service and now part of Rock Creek Park.

Head back uphill to the **Ellipse,** an oval formed by a double ring of hornbeams, enclosing a Provençal fountain. Up the steps lies the **Pebble Garden,** which is composed of rounded stones embedded on edge to create a terrace of varying textures; espaliered magnolias and wisteria vines bedeck the walls.

Filled with natural light, the **museum galleries** display Byzantine and pre-Columbian art objects. The Byzantine collection includes 6th-century ecclesiastical silver and beautiful 14th-century mosaic icons. Byzantine and Andean textiles are a highlight of the **Textile Gallery,** which includes a Byzantine mosaic floor. The Renaissance-style **Music Room** features 16th-century Italian marble arches and a French chimneypiece and is adorned with antique furnishings, plus tapestries, sculptures, and European paintings, while a **Rare Book Gallery** features changing exhibitions of the collection's rare books, manuscripts, and drawings focused on landscape architecture, garden design, and garden history. ∎

DUMBARTON HOUSE

Dumbarton House, originally called Cedar Hill, was built on a hill high above Rock Creek in the first years of the 19th century, when only a few large houses dotted the port of Georgetown. In 1991, the home was meticulously restored and updated with climate and safety features.

■ Inside the large Dumbarton House, furnishings date primarily from the federal period.

The federal-style brick house's second owner, Charles Carroll, changed its name in 1813 to Belle Vue; he sheltered Dolley Madison here the following year, after she fled the burning White House. In 1915, to make way for the extension of Q Street into Georgetown, the house had to be put on rollers and moved about 100 feet (30.5 m) north.

In 1928, the National Society of the Colonial Dames of America (NSCDA) bought the house, which would become its headquarters, and renamed it Dumbarton House after the Rock of Dumbarton, the tract that once encompassed much of present-day Georgetown. Name aside, the house has absolutely no connection to Dumbarton Oaks (see pp. 155–156), several blocks away.

With great attention to detail, NSCDA restored the house to its early 1800s appearance. The guided 45-minute tour here covers the parlor, dining room, library, breakfast room, and two bedrooms, with such items as a maple sewing work table, silver, ceramics, textiles (including a cloak belonging to Martha Washington's granddaughter), and paintings by artists such as Charles Willson Peale. The rooms are furnished and laid out to reflect the home life of its first resident, Joseph Nourse, first register of the United States Treasury. ■

Dumbarton House

🅰 Map pp. 148–149

✉ 2715 Q St., N.W.

☎ 202-337-2288

🕐 Closed Mon. –Thurs. & federal holidays

💲 $

🚇 Metro: Dupont Circle, Foggy Bottom–GWU; Bus: D1–D6

dumbartonhouse.org

TUDOR PLACE HISTORIC HOUSE & GARDEN

Six generations of the Peter family, relatives to George Washington and Robert E. Lee, lived in this handsome neoclassical house. During those years (1805–1983), the country passed through many wars, two of them waged just outside the Peters' door.

Tudor Place

- Map pp. 148–149
- 1644 31st St., N.W.
- 202-965-0400
- Closed Mon.–Fri.
- Metro: Dupont Circle, Foggy Bottom–GWU; Bus: 31–36, D1–D6, Circulator

tudorplace.org

Martha Custis, daughter of George Washington's stepdaughter, married Thomas Peter, son of Georgetown's first mayor. In 1805 the Peters purchased an 8.5-acre (3.4 ha) city block in Georgetown Heights; to design a home there, they hired William Thornton, architect of the Capitol—the building Martha would watch burn from a window of the house in 1814. The Peters' daughter Britannia inherited Tudor Place in 1854. A Southern sympathizer during the Civil War, she allowed Union officers to board at the house to prevent its becoming a hospital. In 1984 the house was transferred to the Tudor Place Foundation.

The one-hour guided house tour of Tudor Place begins with a look at Thornton's design. On the south lawn, a domed "temple" portico projects from the two-story stuccoed main building, while one-story hyphens connect the two wings, lending symmetry. All the furniture, silver, porcelain, and decorative objects, including weaponry, are original, some pieces acquired from an auction at Mount Vernon in the early 19th century. The belongings reflect 180 years of family continuity. The restored Pierce-Arrow automobile out in the garage, for example, was maintained by Armistead Peter III from 1919 until his death in 1983. Some exhibits focus on the domestic servants, among 153 slaves owned by the family.

The 5.5 acres (1.6 ha) of gardens include a sweeping south lawn, woodlands, and a formal federal-style garden on the house's north side. Among highlights are trees and roses planted in the early 19th century, and an old-fashioned "flower knot" pattern of English boxwoods and pathways. ∎

■ Tudor Palace with its beautiful gardens

OAK HILL CEMETERY

Occupying some of the city's finest real estate, this 1849 cemetery rambles over a hill above Rock Creek Park. William Wilson Corcoran, founder of the Corcoran Gallery, bought 15 acres (6 ha) from George Corbin Washington, a great-nephew of the first president, who gave the parcel to the congressionally established cemetery company. James Renwick, architect of the Smithsonian Castle, designed the iron entrance gates and the small English Gothic–style chapel.

■ The green trees set the mood for a visit to Georgetown's Oak Hill Cemetery.

At the attractive brick and sandstone gatehouse, you can get a map showing the locations of 68 graves and mausoleums, including those of W. W. Corcoran, Jefferson Davis, Edwin Stanton (Lincoln's secretary of war), Dean Acheson (Truman's secretary of state), and members of the Peter family from nearby Tudor Place (see page opposite). Also buried at Oak Hill is Philip Graham, publisher of the *Washington Post,* as is his widow Katharine, his successor at the *Post* until her death in 2001.

A murky overcast day makes a good time for wandering through this crowded village of the dead, with its elaborate Victorian monuments and obelisks. Winding paths circle knolls that offer views of adjoining Montrose Park, Rock Creek, and the parkway. Springtime sees a rush of bright flowers.

Hiding behind tall trees and high walls, the property at the corner of 28th and R Streets is another Georgetown mansion with a significant past: Evermay was built in the 1790s by Scotsman Samuel Davidson with funds acquired from selling some of his extensive property to the new federal city. Family members lie buried in Oak Hill. ■

Oak Hill Cemetery

🗺 Map pp. 148–149

✉ 3001 R St., N.W.

☎ 202-337-2835

🕐 Closed funerals, holidays, & in inclement weather

🚇 Metro: Dupont Circle, Foggy Bottom–GWU; Bus: D1–D6

oakhillcemetery dc.org

FAMOUS DENIZENS OF GEORGETOWN

By day, the power of government is exercised in places clustered around Washington's Mall and at both ends of Pennsylvania Avenue. But through the decades, Georgetown has been the residence of choice for political leaders, media heavies, diplomats, legal minds, writers, and society doyennes. In elegant 19th-century houses, a bill that seemed doomed by day may be quietly revived at a dinner party where wine and talk are equally savored.

Washington Post owner Katharine Graham called this house home from 1947 until her death in 2001.

Even Hollywood celebrities have found their way to Georgetown, though at times reluctantly. Elizabeth Taylor, married briefly to Virginia Senator John Warner, has said she thought the couple would live on his hunt country estate in Virginia. Instead, she found herself living in Warner's Georgetown house at 3240 S Street.

As a bachelor, Senator John F. Kennedy was peripatetic and lived in Victorian town houses at 1528 31st Street (1947–1950), 1400 34th Street (1950), and 3260 N Street (1951–53), today occupied by *New York Times* columnist Maureen Dowd. In fact, John and Jackie first met at a Georgetown dinner party in 1951. After their marriage on September 12, 1953, he and his bride moved to 3271 P Street. President-elect Kennedy purchased the three-story brick town house at 3307 N Street in 1957, while Jackie was in the hospital giving birth to their first child, Caroline. Tastefully austere, the 1811 house sits on an especially handsome street.

After her husband's death, Jackie Kennedy and her children moved temporarily to 3038 N Street, at the invitation of statesman W. Averell Harriman. (His widow, Pamela, a celebrated hostess and Democratic party activist, later became President Clinton's Ambassador to France.) The former first lady soon bought the house across the street at 3017 N Street, but departed for New York after only a few months to escape the busloads of gawkers.

At 3014 N stands another grand federal-style mansion with a presidential link. Built in 1799, it was the 40-room home of Robert Todd Lincoln, the 16th president's oldest son, a railroad lawyer who served as secretary of war and minister to Great Britain.

The top ranks of government have always been well represented in Georgetown. Dean Acheson, President Truman's secretary of state, lived in the Georgian town house at 2805 P Street. Here Acheson hosted a farewell luncheon for the president on his last day in office. A four-story town house at 3018 Dumbarton Street has been home to former secretaries of state Henry Kissinger and Cyrus Vance, while John Kerry and his wife, Teresa Heinz, live in the Bodisco House at 3322 O Street, and Madeleine Albright lives at 1318 34th Street.

Washington Post owner Katharine Graham, once called "the most powerful woman in America," lived in the mansion at 2920 R Street. Bob Woodward, the *Post's* most prominent journalist, lives around the corner at 3027 Q Street.

Other writers have found Georgetown congenial. In 1922, Sinclair Lewis moved to D.C. from his Minnesota hometown, calling it the perfect place to write, "with neither the

■ **Riggs-Riley House on 3038 N Street**

country nor lake tempting one out to play, as in Minnesota, nor the noise and phone calls of New York." As soon as he made his fortune with *Main Street,* which later won him the Nobel Prize in literature, he moved to a stately house at 3028 Q Street.

EXPERIENCE: Going Out to Brunch Around Town

Leisurely weekend brunch is a local institution, so it's a good idea to reserve ahead. In Georgetown, neighborhood blue bloods and Europeans gravitate to the eclectic **Peacock Café** *(3251 Prospect St., N.W., tel 202-625-2740)*. High on the list of favorites is the cozy **Tabard Inn** *(1739 N St., N.W., tel 202-785-1277)* on a pretty street in the heart of Dupont Circle. It's noted for exotic takes on regional U.S. foods. A brunch specialty: homemade donuts. In the West End area, a dazzling à la carte menu in the Juniper Restaurant draws many to brunches at the **Fairmont Hotel** *(2401 M St., N.W., tel 202-457-*

5020). **Ted's Bulletin** *(1818 14th St., N.W., tel 202-265-8337)* on trendy 14th Street has won over Washingtonians with classic American brunch fare with a twist, such as huevos rancheros, hash, and crab benedict. Another downtown option is **Brasserie Beck** *(1101 K St., N.W., tel 202-408-1717)*. **Perry's** *(tel 1811 Columbia Rd., N.W., tel 202-234-6218)*, in bohemian Adams Morgan, has delighted diners for 25 years with a fusion of Asian and cutting-edge American cuisine. More reasons to go: killer views from the rooftop deck and drag queen entertainment on Sunday morning.

More Places to Visit in Georgetown

The Kreeger Museum

Designed by Philip Johnson and Richard Foster and completed in 1967, the modernist travertine house of late philanthropist David Lloyd Kreeger and his wife, Carmen, opened in 1994 as an art museum showcasing the Kreegers' collection of 19th- and 20th-century paintings and sculptures. A chairman of Geico insurance company, Kreeger was famous for his contributions to the city's cultural life, at various times serving as president of the National Symphony, the Washington Opera, and the Corcoran Gallery of Art.

The art collection, which the Kreegers began acquiring in 1959, includes more than 180 works by artists such as Monet, Cézanne, van Gogh, Rodin, Picasso, Miró, Munch, Kandinsky, and Chagall; among Washington artists represented are Gene Davis, Sam Gilliam, and Thomas Downing. Also on display are pieces of traditional African and Asian art, as well as Mayan and Roman pieces, plus there's a Sculpture Garden. The building's spectacular **Great Hall,** with its 25-foot-high (7.6 m) domed ceiling, was often the scene of concerts; an avid amateur violinist, Kreeger played his Stradi-

---

INSIDER TIP:

There's no Metro station in Georgetown, but the Circulator bus *[dccirculator.com]* makes several stops here.

—LUBA VANGELOVA
National Geographic writer

---

varius with such greats as Pablo Casals, Isaac Stern, and Pinchas Zukerman. *kreegermuseum. org* 🅰 Map pp. 148–149 ✉ 2401 Foxhall Rd., N.W., 1.5 miles (2.4 km) NW of Georgetown ☎ 202-337-3050 🕐 Closed Sun.–Mon. & Aug.; by appointment tours Tues.–Thurs.; open visits Fri.–Sat. 💲 $$

Martin's Tavern

Opened by William G. Martin, a Georgetown University sports star who also played professional baseball in the early part of the 20th century, Martin's Tavern has been operating at the southwest corner of N Street and Wisconsin Avenue, N.W., since 1933. Four generations of Martins have managed the restaurant, and many of the staff have been here for years. Stop in for a draft or a meal and imbibe this Georgetown tradition. Wood floors, dark paneling, and a friendly bar create the ambience of a European pub. Souvenir cards list some of the politicos and celebrities that have visited or been regulars, including former Secretary of State Madeleine Albright, Elizabeth Taylor, and the Kennedys. Martin's serves lunch and dinner Monday through Friday and brunch on weekends at moderate prices. *martinstavern.com* 🅰 Map pp. 148–149 ✉ 1264 Wisconsin Ave., N.W. ☎ 202-333-7370 🚇 Metro: Foggy Bottom–GWU or Rosslyn, then bus

Mount Zion Cemetery

When Mount Zion Methodist Episcopal Church fathers realized in 1879 that they needed a place to bury members, they leased a parcel of land on the edge of Oak Hill Cemetery (see p. 159), where generations of slaves and freed blacks had been buried. The resulting Mount Zion Cemetery, with its crumbling gravestones, is D.C.'s oldest African-American burial ground. The last burial took place in the 1950s. In 1975 it was designated a national historic landmark. At the back is a brick vault where slaves escaping to the North via the Underground Railroad are said to have hidden. *mtzion-fubs. org* 🅰 Map pp. 148–149 ✉ 2501 Mill Rd., N.W. (27th St.) ☎ 202-596-6474 🚇 Foggy Bottom–GWU or Dupont Circle, then bus

An enjoyable melting pot of cultures, cuisines, embassies, and museums beyond hyperkinetic downtown D.C.

DUPONT CIRCLE & BEYOND

The figures on Dupont Circle's fountain symbolize the wind, sea, and stars.

DUPONT CIRCLE & BEYOND

At the intersection of three major thoroughfares, the Dupont Circle area is a true Washington gathering place. The energy of the neighborhoods, replete with row houses, cafés, bookstores, restaurants, and galleries spills out to the streets.

Well-situated Dupont Circle, north of the White House, marks a key interface between business and residential Washington. The circle, centered on a marble fountain, is in constant motion, with pedestrians passing through and traffic circling around. Yet it is also a place for casual picnics, jackets-off meetings, people-watching, and general loafing. Bicycle messengers form little impromptu gatherings, chess players study their next moves, joggers pound through. In 15 minutes the scene has changed, and a new series of small dramas has begun to unfold.

Starting in the 1870s, the area, then called Pacific Circle, began developing into the most elite neighborhood in Washington. New millionaires with fortunes from mining, steel, railroads, and shipping started putting up ornate beaux arts mansions and attending receptions and musicals in one another's houses, every hostess seemingly intent on outdoing her neighbors. This belle epoque lasted only until the 1930s, when the stock market crash and Depression forced many of the wealthy to scale back.

Some mansions were razed, though many were sold to private clubs, organizations, and embassies; surrounding row houses became boarding establishments and apartments. In the 1960s, the area was a haven for counterculturalists, and the circle became a focal point for marches and rallies. Development threatened many of the area's old "palaces" in the 1970s, but the efforts of preservation groups to save the neighborhood resulted in its designation as a historic district. Over the ensuing years Dupont Circle became the core of Washington's gay community. Today the bars, restaurants, shops, and museums attract a stimulating heterogeny of intellectuals, café-society sorts, and experimentalists of all stripes.

A residential zone of about ten blocks lies between the Dupont Circle neighborhood and the Latino enclave to the north, Adams Morgan, a magnet for immigrants, artists, and young professionals. To the northwest, "Embassy Row" leads to Kalorama—Washington, D.C.'s Beverly Hills, with grandiose mansions in spacious, leafy grounds. Running eastward from Adams Morgan into the Shaw neighborhood is the U Street corridor, where the black community was drawn beginning in the 1880s. This area possesses a rich legacy of music and culture—Pearl Bailey, Duke Ellington, and other greats once performed at its various theaters and clubs. Deteriorated after the 1968 riots, U Street has in recent years made a compelling comeback, with restored theaters and new clubs, restaurants, and shops. ∎

NOT TO BE MISSED:

The Phillips Collection and Renoir's "The Luncheon of the Boating Party" 166–169

Hanging out near the Dupont Circle fountain and peering over the shoulders of chess players 168

The historic mansions of Kalorama and Embassy Row 170–172

Exploring the universe of small shops in Adams Morgan 173–175

Sampling ethnic restaurants along 18th Street 175

Ben's Chili Bowl and black history landmarks on U Street 177

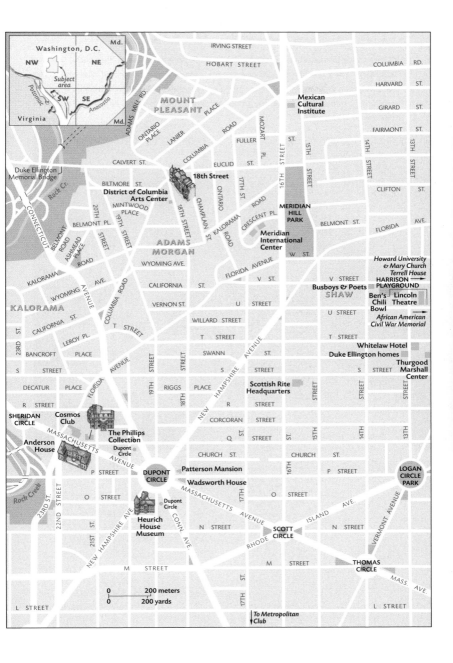

THE PHILLIPS COLLECTION

Visit the well-located Phillips, near Dupont Circle, and you'll see why it's the favorite museum of many Washingtonians and regarded as one of the best small museums in the world. It has an outstanding collection of works by masters of Impressionism and American and European modern art and carries out a stellar program of cultural and educational activities.

■ Renoir's "The Luncheon of the Boating Party" (1880–1881) is a highlight of the Phillips Collection.

Begun in the 1920s by founder Duncan Phillips (1886–1966), the Phillips Collection was the first modern art museum in the United States. Its permanent holdings include almost 6,000 carefully chosen pieces of art from the late 19th century to the present.

One of the most charming things about The Phillips

Collection is the feeling you get of touring a private home as you walk around the museum, which is still located in Phillips's 1897 Georgian Revival brownstone and has been expanded by compatibly scaled additions. The house gives off a comfortable, informal aura, and that effect is exactly what Phillips had in mind when, in a memorial to his recently deceased brother (James Laughlin Phillips) and father (Maj. D. Clinch Phillips), he opened up two rooms of his home in 1921 so that other art lovers could enjoy the works he and his brother had collected. After Phillips—himself an heir to the Jones and Laughlin steel fortune—married artist Marjorie Acker that same year, the couple began assembling an outstanding collection of Impressionist, Post-impressionist, and Cubist art.

In 1930, Phillips and his family moved to a new home on Foxhall Road and opened up their entire former home to the expanding collection. A new wing was added in 1960, and in the late 1980s it was renovated again. In 2006, the museum completed a major expansion that added galleries and other amenities. Two-thirds of the new space is belowground, thereby preserving the character of the neighborhood.

The museum's best known pieces are Pierre-Auguste Renoir's dazzling work of impressionism, "The Luncheon of the Boating Party," which features a mix of Renoir's friends, and Pablo Picasso's "The Blue Room," of a woman bathing in a basin.

The permanent collection also includes works by Paul Cézanne, Edgar Degas, Paul Klee, Henri Matisse, Claude Monet, Pablo Picasso, Georges Braque, Vincent van Gogh, Jacob Lawrence, Mark Rothko, Elizabeth Murray, Alexander Calder, and Sean Scully, as well as a strong portfolio of photography, including by such icons as Henri Cartier-Bresson and John Rawlings.

Dupont Circle
Visitor Information
Dupont Circle Business Improvement District
✉ 1601 Connecticut Ave., N.W.
☎ 202-525-4687
🚇 Metro: Dupont Circle; Bus: D1–D6, N2–N6, L1

dupontcirclebid.org

The Phillips Collection
🗺 Map p. 165
✉ 1600 21st St., N.W. (corner of 21st & Q Sts., N.W.)
☎ 202-387-2151
🕐 Closed Mon. & federal holidays
💲 Admission to permanent collection included in fee for special exhibits ($$$) but by donation on weekdays
🚇 Metro: Dupont Circle; Bus: D1–D6, N2–N6, L1

phillipscollection.org

EXPERIENCE: Pursuing Art for Sale

If the Phillips stirs your desire for an original painting of your own, Dupont Circle, with more than two dozen galleries, is the place to shop. In recent years one gallery offered a Toulouse-Lautrec lithograph for $70,000, a Picasso painting for a mere $16,000, and a piece by Miró for less than $5,000. Stop in **Geoffrey Dinner Gallery** *(1730 21st St., N.W., tel 202-904-5005, dinergallery.com),* renowned for its collectible decorative arts and fine art, from Caldwell and Lichtenstein to Nakashima and Warhol. Or check out **Studio Gallery** *(2108 R St., N.W., tel 202-232-8734, studiogallerydc.com),* showcasing contemporary art in a wide variety of media. Some of the galleries specialize in African art, Inuit sculpture, and English and American crafts. To find your way around, pick up a free gallery guide, available in any of the galleries. A consortium of some 25 galleries in the area holds opening receptions on the first Friday most months from 5 to 7:30 p.m.

URBAN PLAYGROUND—DUPONT CIRCLE HAPPENINGS

Named in honor of Rear Adm. Samuel Francis du Pont, a Civil War naval hero, Dupont Circle is a neighborhood that fans out from a beloved little park of the same name. The circle itself sits where three major avenues intersect, a calm amid the city's fast pace. It's a popular spot for an alfresco lunch, chess games, and a farmers market.

Land that served as a brickyard and slaughterhouse after the Civil War is now a magnet for relaxation, fun, and the occasional protest rally. The National Park Service maintains the Dupont Circle park with its benches, grass, and art deco fountain.

A mix of nightclubs and restaurants, embassies and office buildings, museums and historic row houses, shops and cafés gives the area a lively diversity that's reflected in the crowds that gravitate here. You'll find people of all ages and nationalities picnicking in the park, walking their dogs, or just hanging out. This area is also the center of the city's gay and lesbian community. The **Dupont Circle High Heel race,** an annual event since 1985, is the 9 p.m. climax of a drag queen parade along 17th Street, N.W. It takes place on the Tuesday before Halloween.

It's Your Move at Dupont Circle

After ten concrete chess tables were installed in Dupont Circle in 1968, players of every skill level and from all walks of life began coming here to challenge one other. Over the years, a sort of Chess University sprung up, with a number of skilled players giving lessons. Former homeless transient Tom Murphy became a legend before he moved on to Chicago. Even if you've just stopped by to observe, you may find yourself expected to pay a couple of bucks; some of the regulars are also experts at hustling. Checkers, anyone?

Market Central

On Sunday mornings check out the popular Dupont Circle **farmers market,** in a parking lot at Massachusetts Avenue and 20th Street, N.W. Operating year-round, rain or shine, it's been named one of the best of its kind in the country by the *Wall Street Journal,* the *Financial Times of London,* and others. During the peak season, more than 40 vendors sell a variety of things fresh, from bread to flowers, pies to pasta, as well as herbal products and artisan soap.

A Magnet for All Sorts of Occasions

When the city got hit with crippling back-to-back blizzards in February 2010—an event dubbed **Snowmageddon—**more than 2,000 bundled-up people converged at the circle for a massive snowball fight organized by a pair of neighborhood 30-something friends. "A whole bunch of people had a whole lot of fun," the *Washington Post* reported.

A few months later folks gathered at Dupont Circle for a **Green Rush** team scavenger hunt to celebrate the 40th anniversary of Earth Day. Speakers, entertainment, and exhibitors turned the circle into a green-for-a-day environment.

During the 2014 World Cup, giant television screens set up in the park drew hordes of soccer fans to outdoor viewing and cheering of the U.S. vs. Germany game.

Look for events, including musical performances, online at *washington.org/dc-neighborhoods/dupont-circle.*

A strong patron of emerging artists, Phillips collected works of many artists who had not yet become widely recognized, including Georgia O'Keeffe, Arthur Dove, John Marin, and Milton Avery. The **Rothko Room,** opened in 1960, was designed in accordance with both Mark Rothko's and Phillips's aesthetic preferences and represents a rare bond between artist and patron.

Phillips felt that artists were strongly influenced by their predecessors, and he sought to illustrate that in the museum's collection. A key link between Impressionism and expressionism, he believed, was Pierre Bonnard, and today the museum has one of the largest collections of works by this artist. Phillips also acquired pieces by such 18th-century masters as El Greco, Francisco Goya, and Jean-Baptiste-Simeon Chardin to show how they affected later painters of modern art.

In 2006, the museum launched the Phillips Collection Center for the Study of Modern Art, which brings together scholars from across academic fields to engage in discussion, research, and publishing of modern art. Intersections is a series of thought-provoking contemporary art projects that explore the intersections between old and new traditions.

Visiting

Some of the museum's galleries offer special exhibitions that change regularly, but selections

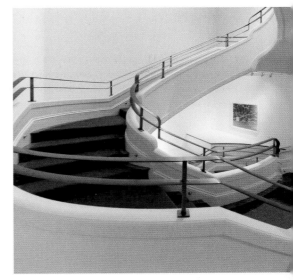

■ **Staircase at the Phillips Collection**

from the permanent collection are always on display. On the first floor, take time to visit the **Music Room,** a perennial favorite, with its dark oak paneling, decorative ceiling, and carved stone and wood mantelpiece. Since 1941, Sunday afternoon concerts *(Oct.– May, $$$$)* here have been a Washington favorite.

A café and museum shop are located on the main level near the entrance. Behind the café is an **outdoor courtyard,** which features a sculpture by Barbara Hepworth and a specially commissioned work by Ellsworth Kelly. The museum has extended hours on Thursday evenings, and on the first Thursday of the month it hosts Phillips After 5, a lively mix of art, music, and other entertainment. ■

A WALK THROUGH EMBASSY ROW & KALORAMA

This approximately 1-mile (1.6 km) stroll offers an impressive glimpse of early 20th-century Washington's affluence and its evolution. Many of the area's grand residences of the wealthy were sold to foreign delegations—for embassies—after the Great Depression, but many of the world's wealthiest people also now live here.

Heurich House Museum, a fine example of Richardsonian Romanesque residential architecture

The triangle formed by Massachusetts and Connecticut Avenues and Rock Creek holds more than 50 embassies (about one-third of the city's total) plus many other architectural treasures that reflect the glamour of the early 1900s, when this was a fashionable neighborhood for Washington tycoons. Today Kalorama, with its posh mansions in an eclectic compendium of styles, is the zip code of choice for a more eclectic ensemble. In 2018, for example, Barack and Michele Obama paid $8.1 million for an eight-bedroom, French Chateaux–style home *(2446 Belmont Rd., N.W.)*. Their neighbors include Jeff Bezos, plus Ivanka Trump and Jared Kushner.

On the northeast corner of 18th Street and Massachusetts Avenue stands the **Andrew Mellon Building ❶**, a beaux arts palace originally built in 1915 as the McCormick apartment

> ### NOT TO BE MISSED:
> **Andrew Mellon Building • Heurich House Museum • Islamic Center**

building. The building's first floor contained two apartments, while five floors above each held an 11,000-square-foot (1,020 sq m) apartment with six bedrooms and 14.5-foot (4.4 m) ceilings. Long the headquarters of the National Trust for Historic Preservation (now located in the Watergate complex), it is today home of the American Enterprise Institute.

Now head west toward Dupont Circle, where you can see examples of turn-of-the-20th-century mansions that never became embassies. Housing the Sulgrave Club *(private),* a sorority of socially prominent Washington ladies, the circa 1900 **Wadsworth House** *(1801 Massachusetts Ave., N.W., sulgraveclub.org)* was the winter residence of landowners Herbert and Martha Wadsworth of upstate New York. It shows how a large building could be designed to fit a triangular lot on the circle. Taking a different approach to the same problem, the Wadsworth's neighbor to the north, the ornate **Patterson Mansion** *(pattersonmansion.com),* fits into its wedge at 15 Dupont Circle with symmetrical wings and a concave front. Formerly a women's social club and now an event center, the 1903 house was designed by Stanford White for Robert W. Patterson, publisher of the *Chicago Tribune.*

In **Dupont Circle ❷** (see p. 168) you can see a striking example of how L'Enfant's city plan works, with grand avenues vectoring out from the central green. In the middle of the circle is a marble fountain designed in 1921 by Daniel Chester French, who is also known for

the giant statue of Lincoln in the Lincoln Memorial. Spilling into a large pool, an upper basin is supported by a central column that is surrounded by three allegorical figures representing the sea, wind, and stars. A block southwest at 1307 New Hampshire Avenue, the **Heurich House Museum ❸** (see p. 178) is one of the country's best examples of Richardsonian Romanesque residential architecture.

Now head north 1.5 blocks to the **Blaine Mansion** at 2000 Massachusetts Avenue. This brick Victorian mansion was built in 1881 for presidential candidate James Blaine, who lost in 1884 to Grover Cleveland. The curving sweep of the **Indonesian Embassy ❹** *(2020 Massachusetts Ave., N.W., embassyofindonesia.org)* has

---

🅰 See also area map p. 165
🅿 Andrew Mellon Building
🕐 3–4 hours
ⓘ 1 mile (1.6 km)
🅿 The Phillips Collection

marble columns, arched windows, and a red-tile mansard roof. It was built at the turn of the 20th century by Irishman Tom Walsh, who struck gold in a Colorado mine. He moved to Washington, built his dream house, and became part of the new moneyed class. His daughter, prominent hostess Evalyn Walsh McLean, was the last private owner of the Hope Diamond (now on display in the National Museum of Natural His-

---

INSIDER TIP:

Many embassies regularly host cultural open houses and international concerts. Check *washington. org* for upcoming events.

—KAREN CARMICHAEL
National Geographic writer

---

tory; see p. 95); in 1951 she sold the mansion to the Republic of Indonesia.

At 2100 Massachusetts Avenue, the building housing the **Fairfax at Embassy Row,** (see Travelwise p. 251) exudes the flair of a European-style hotel. Al Gore lived here when his father was a U. S. senator. The double-winged mansion at 2118 Massachusetts Avenue is the **Anderson House ❺** (see p. 178), headquarters of the Society of the Cincinnati (*societyofthecincinnati.org*). At 2121 Massachusetts Avenue stands the exclusive **Cosmos Club** (*private, cosmosclub.org*), completed in 1902 as the home of Richard Townsend, president of the Erie & Pittsburgh Railroad. The fabulous limestone mansion was sold in 1950 to the club.

A number of embassies edge **Sheridan Circle,** named for Union general Philip H. Sheridan; the 1908 equestrian bronze in the center is by Gutzon Borglum, sculptor of Mount Rushmore. Among the impressive buildings nearby is the **Turkish Ambassador's residence** (*1606 23rd St., N.W., turkishembassy.org*), built in the 1910s for industrialist Edward Everett and today fronted by a bronze statue of Kemal Atatürk. A block south, the 1914 **Dumbarton**

Bridge—often called the Buffalo Bridge for its bronze bison—carries Q Street over Rock Creek into Georgetown.

Back on Massachusetts is the **Barney Studio House** (*No. 2306*). The one-time home of philanthropist and socialite Alice Pike Barney, this Spanish mission–style building completed in 1902 was the first house built on the circle. It now houses the **Latvian Embassy.** At the corner of 24th Street you'll see the **Embassy of Croatia** (*2343 Massachusetts Ave., N.W., us.mfa.hr*). In front of the embassy is an avant-garde bronze statue of St. Jerome the Priest, sculpted by Croatian artist Ivan Meštrović. Several blocks farther is the **Islamic Center** (*2551 Massachusetts Ave., N.W., tel 202-332-8343, theislamiccenter.us*), a mosque richly embellished with tilework, arches, and pillars. In the carpeted sanctuary, shoes and shorts are not allowed and women must cover their heads. The network of streets to the east is the prestigious Kalorama neighborhood, with several embassies and many stately mansions.

Turn up 24th Street, then go east on S Street. The **Woodrow Wilson House ❻** (*2340 S St., N.W., tel 202-387-4062, woodrow wilsonhouse.org, closed Mon., $$*), designed in 1915 by Waddy B. Wood, stands out for its arched Palladian windows. The president spent the last three years of his life in this Georgian Revival brick town house after leaving the White House in 1921; his wife stayed until her death in 1961. It is maintained by National Trust for Historic Preservation as it was in 1924.

Continue along S Street to 22nd Street and turn right. Washington's version of Rome's Spanish Steps offers a shortcut to **Decatur Place,** a peaceful spot to take a break. Keep heading south on 22nd Street, N.W., and turn right on R Street to the **Embassy of Mali** (*No. 2130, maliembassy.us*), where Franklin Delano Roosevelt once lived. One block away, turn right on 21st Street to end your tour at the **Phillips Collection ❼** (see pp. 166–169), one of Washington's most cherished museums.

ADAMS MORGAN

A culturally diverse enclave, Adams Morgan became in the 1980s and '90s the top apartment-and-nightlife nexus for artists and hip young professionals alike. With its international restaurants, funky shops, and rocking nightclubs, the neighborhood sprang to life with a personality all its own, a bastion of bohemian flair in the center of staid Washington. Never mind that this popularity meant there was no longer any place to park—especially on weekend evenings.

The name itself alludes to the neighborhood's melting pot mix: By combining the names of two schools—the mostly white Adams School and the predominantly black Morgan School—local citizens coined the term Adams Morgan in the 1950s for an area that had been part of four neighborhoods. In that same decade, the Spanish-speaking population swelled as an influx of students from Latin America and Mexican professionals added to the existing community of embassy workers.

The early 1960s saw an increase in Cuban immigration, followed by large numbers from South and Central America through the next few decades. The ethnic influence here still tends toward Latin—Spanish is heard on the streets as often as English—but in the smorgasbord of restaurants and shops, you'll find many other cultures, including Ethiopian, Chinese, Thai, Indian, and Vietnamese.

The heart of Adams Morgan is the intersection of **Columbia Road** and **18th Street.** On the northeast corner a kiosk provides lists of upcoming cultural events. At the intersection's southwest corner is a plaza where vendors set up shop on weekends and sell fresh produce and breads. Most of

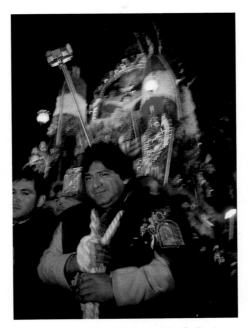

■ **Local Peruvians celebrate Our Lord of Miracles Day in Adams Morgan, a traditionally Hispanic neighborhood.**

the area's action—eating, drinking, and dancing—takes place south of the intersection on 18th Street between Columbia Road and Florida Avenue, and along a little branch west on Columbia Road to Belmont Road. That's pretty much it. Part of the neighborhood's appeal is its small size. Although the few attractions here are worth seeing, they do not draw crowds.

Adams Morgan

🗺 Map p. 165

✉ Within
Connecticut Ave.,
N.W., Calvert
St., Columbia
Rd., 16th St., &
Florida Ave., N.W.

🚇 Metro: Dupont
Circle (1.5 miles/
2.4 km S) or
Woodley Park–
Zoo/Adams
Morgan (0.75
mile/1.2 km NW);
Bus: 42, 90–92,
96, L2, Circulator

Visiting

The three-story, brightly painted
brick buildings lining the blocks of
18th Street south of the Columbia
Road–18th Street intersection hold
most of the ethnic restaurants,
bohemian bars, and boutiques. On
sultry summer evenings, the sidewalks buzz with people strolling,
walking dogs, or sipping and nosh-
ing at sidewalk cafés and bars.

Ethnic eateries abound, with
exotic cuisine just about routine
hereabouts. For some down-home

open afternoons, closed Mon.–Tues.),
features the work of emerging
artists and holds live performances
at night.

Columbia Road on both sides
of 18th also has several good restaurants—including **Perry's** *(1811
Columbia Rd., N.W., tel 202-234-
6218, perrysam.com),* the place to
be and be seen; its rooftop dining
(great sushi) is one of the city's
most pleasant experiences. Along
Columbia Road you'll also find
Latino grocery stores, outdoor

Gardens and houses in Adams Morgan

fare, including burgers, grilled
cheese, and pulled pork served
up with live music seven nights
a week, head over to **Madam's
Organ** *(2461 18th St., N.W., tel
202-667-5370, madamsorgan.com).*
The **District of Columbia
Arts Center** *(2438 18th St., N.W.,
tel 202-462-7833, dcartscenter.org*

jewelry stands, and vintage clothing and sundries shops.

Daytime Adams Morgan offers
different sights to see. For grand
interiors, walk down **16th Street.**
Just below Columbia Road, the
Mexican Cultural Institute
*(2829 16th St., N.W., tel 202-728-
1628, instituteofmexicodc.org, closed*

EXPERIENCE: Sample International Cuisines

Do you prefer Indian or Ethiopian? Thai or Caribbean? Take your pick in the eclectic neighborhood of Adams Morgan, with globe-spanning restaurants.

Washington has one of the largest concentrations of Ethiopian restaurants outside Addis Ababa, and **Zenebech** *(2420 18th St., N.W., tel 202-667-4700, zenebechdc.com)* provides a good introduction. The food is served on a communal platter; you pinch off pieces of *injera*—large, floppy pancake-like bread—and scoop up the spicy stews of vegetables and meat. One block away, you can try Nepalese food at **Himalayan Heritage** *(2305 18th St., N.W., tel 202-483-9300,* himalayanheritagedc.com). Momo (dumplings) is a popular choice.

Many locals think **Lauriol Plaza** *(1835 18th St., N.W., tel 202-387-0035, lauriolplaza.com)* has the city's best Mexican/Latin cuisine. Try the Cuban-style morsels of pork in hot *criollo* sauce and bitter oranges. **Mezè** *(2437 18th St., N.W., tel 202-797-0017, mezedc.com)* serves freshly made Turkish small plates such as *dolma* (stuffed grape leaves) and *köfte* (lamb meatballs). Caffeine aficionados will like **Tryst** *(2459 18th St., N.W., tel 202-232-5500, trystdc.com)* and its selection of coffees and teas from around the globe.

Sat.–Sun.), in a 1911 Italianate house, holds a huge tile-covered solarium, a lively stairwell mural, and ornately furnished salons; exhibitions, live music, and events are presented on two floors.

A few blocks farther, **Meridian International Center** *(1624 & 1630 Crescent Pl., N.W., tel 202-667-6800, meridian.org, closed Mon.–Tues.)* promotes international understanding through cultural exchanges. The adjoining houses, with free art exhibits, were designed by John Russell Pope in 1911 and 1921; the 1630 address has antique French furnishings and a courtyard with 40 linden trees.

Pope also designed the glorious 1911 **Scottish Rite of Freemasonery Headquarters** *(1733 16th St., N.W., tel 202-232-3579, scottish rite.org, free tours, closed Fri.–Sun.),* just beyond Adams Morgan at S Street; he modeled the building after the Mausoleum at Halicarnassus in Turkey.

INSIDER TIP:

Grab a window seat at one of the communal tables at Tryst *[2459 18th St., N.W.]* and linger over a latte as you observe the Adams Morgan scene.

—LUBA VANGELOVA
*National Geographic Traveler
magazine writer*

The northwest portion of Adams Morgan, up 18th and onto Adams Mill Road and Calvert Street, is more residential, with closely packed houses. Just off Adams Mill is one of the area's many colorful wall murals, this one dating from the 1970s and depicting life in Washington's barrio. If you follow Calvert, you'll come to the **Duke Ellington Memorial Bridge** over Rock Creek *(toward Woodley Park–Zoo/Adams Morgan Metro station).* ∎

U STREET CORRIDOR

Known as Washington's "Black Broadway" in the early 20th century, U Street was legendary for several decades as the heartbeat of urban African-American life. Intellectuals and professionals shared the streets with families of all economic levels, while the musical genius of Duke Ellington and others fueled a world-famous club scene. Today the area has undergone a renewal that's once again made it a vibrant community with a lively street life and rich cultural vibe.

■ American cuisine at its best: Ben's Chili Bowl on U Street

During the Civil War, two military camps and a hospital occupied the area. The surrounding Shaw neighborhood got its name from Robert Gould Shaw, the white colonel of the war's first black regiment (from Massachusetts).

With the rise of nearby Howard University (see sidebar p. 178) in the late 1860s, local residents developed a respect for academic achievement that inspired generations of black leaders. Elegant late Victorian row houses, many still surviving, marked the neighborhood's prosperity. By the 1920s, more than 300 businesses made the U Street area a bustling district of commerce and entertainment. Evenings and weekends, parades of people in their finest attire flocked to movie theaters, nightclubs, and ballrooms. On Sundays they

gathered at the churches, some dating from the Civil War, when the city had a large free-black population.

In the 1930s and '40s, clubs featured such luminaries as Cab Calloway, Pearl Bailey, Sarah Vaughan, and native son Duke Ellington, honored with a 20-foot-tall (6.2 m) statue adjacent to the historic Howard Theater at **Ellington Plaza** (Florida Ave. & T St., NW.), erected in 2012. So great was the area's reputation as a musical mecca that patrons included many white people, in a rare exception to Washington's rigid lines of racial segregation. Ironically, desegregation in the 1950s sparked a decline as residents moved to the suburbs. The 1968 riots further devastated the neighborhood, and by the 1970s blight and safety fears kept people away.

Since the 1990s a steady influx of businesses has created a mix of cafés, restaurants, boutiques, and nightclubs, plus new condo-loft complexes, that draw a diverse crowd and have infused new energy into the neighborhood. **Busboys & Poets** (2021 14th St., N.W., busboysandpoets.com) is a popular bookstore cum café. For years the **9:30 Club** (815 V St., N.W., 930.com) has been one of the city's hottest concert venues, with top acts. ■

EXPERIENCE: Relive Black History—on Foot

The history of African Americans in Washington, from Civil War days until the present, is a richly faceted one that prompts a wide spectrum of emotions. The city is rich in landmarks that help locals and visitors see and understand how African Americans have shaped history.

A group called Cultural Tourism DC (*culturaltourismdc.org*) offers a self-guided Heritage Trail walk in the U Street (see p. 176) area, free to download. Here are some neighborhood highlights.

If you exit the Metro at the the U Street/African-American Civil War Memorial/ Cardozo station, on Vermont Avenue, you'll see the **African-American Civil War Memorial** (*1925 Vermont Ave., N.W.*). A small nearby museum (at the Thurgood Marshall Center) chronicles the role of the 200,000 "colored troops" who fought alongside Union soldiers.

At 11th and U Streets you'll pass the former **Bohemian Caverns**, site of performances by jazz greats such as John Coltrane and Miles Davis. The legendary club closed in 2019.

A block away, the lavishly Italianate 1903 **True Reformer Building** (*12th & U Sts., N.W.*) was built by African-American architect John

INSIDER TIP:

Cap off your walk with a scoop or two of creative flavors at Ice Cream Jubilee [*1407 T St., N.W.*], voted best ice cream in D.C.

—CHRISTOPHER P. BAKER
National Geographic author & photographer

Lankford. Down the street, the **Thurgood Marshall Center** (*1816 12th St., N.W., tmcsh.org*) opened in 1853 as the country's first YMCA for blacks. Its patrons over the years included poet Langston Hughes and boxer Joe Louis.

Nearby are two **Duke Ellington houses** (*1805 & 1816 13th St., N.W.*), where he lived from ages 11 to 18, absorbing the influences of church choirs, traveling pianists, and local music teachers. The **former Whitelaw Hotel**

(*1839 13th St., N.W.*) opened in 1919 to offer African-American travelers first-class accommodations in segregated Washington. Its restaurant and ballroom were a favored location for elite parties. Big bands also performed in the Colonnade room of the **Lincoln Theatre** (*1215 U St., N.W.*), which opened in 1922. After renovation, it now offers a range of entertainment. To its east is **Ben's Chili Bowl** (see sidebar) and **Ben Ali Way,** an alley painted with murals of Duke Ellington, Barack and Michelle Obama, political activist Harriet Tubman, and other icons of black culture. The baroque 1910 **Howard Theatre** (*620 T St., N.W., thehowardtheatre.com*) was the country's first legitimate theater built for blacks.

Meridian Hill Park (*16th & Euclid Sts., N.W. nps.gov/ places/meridian-hill-park.htm*), inspired by 18th-century European gardens, completed in 1936, and also known as Malcolm X Park, is a lively anchor for the area's multicultural community.

Ben's Chili Bowl

When this tiny diner opened in 1958 at its present location (*1213 U St., N.W., tel 202-667-0909, benschilibowl.com*), Eisenhower was president and jazz artists often hung out at Ben's after playing local gigs. More recently, Barack Obama stopped by for a half-smoke with chili sauce a few days before his Inauguration. The founder of

Ben's, who died in 2009, turned the place into a multimillion-dollar business—and a Washington institution. His obituary revealed that while Mahaboob Ben Ali had created a small empire, he'd never actually tasted one of the dogs he made so famous: He was Muslim and didn't eat pork.

More Places to Visit in Dupont Circle & Beyond

Anderson House–Society of the Cincinnati

This spectacular 1905 mansion serves as the headquarters and museum of the **Society of the Cincinnati,** a patriotic organization whose first president general was George Washington. The house was once the winter residence of diplomat Larz Anderson III, whose wife, Isabel Weld Perkins, inherited $17,000,000 from her grandfather's shipping fortune. After Anderson died in 1937, his widow gave the mansion to the society, of which Anderson had been a member. The 3,800 members descend from officers in the Continental Army or Navy. Its name comes from the Roman senator Cincinnatus.

Among the treasures are walnut choir stalls from 16th-century Italy and a ballroom with Verona marble columns. The Billiard Room holds two temporary exhibits each year, primarily on the history of the Revolutionary War and the society's founding. A 45,000-title research library (closed Sat.–Sun.) focuses on the era of the American Revolution. Guided tours offered. societyofthecincinnati.org 🅼 Map p. 165 ✉ 2118 Massachusetts Ave., N.W. ☎ 202-785-2040 🕐 Closed Mon. & a.m. 🚇 Metro: Dupont Circle

Heurich House Museum

Built in 1894 for brewer Christian Heurich, this Romanesque dark stone castle is now a landmark building on the National Register of Historic Places. Heurich, a German immigrant, came to the United States in 1866. He purchased this property just off Dupont Circle in the late 1870s. He lived here and ran a brewery on what is now the site of the Kennedy Center. In 1956 his third wife, Amelia, deeded the house to the organization that became the Historical Society of Washington (since relocated). A guided tour takes you through 11 rooms on three levels. Sumptuous elements include a marble mosaic floor in the main hall and beautifully carved furniture in the dining room. heurichhouse.org 🅼 Map p. 165 ✉ 1307 New Hampshire Ave., N.W. ☎ 202-429-1894 🕐 Tours offered; garden open Tue.–Thurs. 🆂 $ 🚇 Metro: Dupont Circle

Howard University

General Oliver Otis Howard (1830–1909) came to Washington after the Civil War and took charge of the new Bureau of Refugees, Freedmen, and Abandoned Lands (better known as the Freedmen's Bureau). Under Howard's leadership, the bureau bought the Barry Farm near what would become the Anacostia neighborhood, in Southeast Washington, and sold off parcels to black families. The Freedmen's Bureau also helped fund and establish educational programs for freed people. In 1867, Howard University (6th & Bryant Sts., N.W.) was founded (and named for the general against his wishes) on land purchased by the bureau. It is now the country's leading black university, with an enrollment of more than 10,000 students.

Mary Church Terrell House

The LeDroit Park neighborhood (S of Howard University) has been the home of many prominent African Americans since the 1890s. Civic leader Mary Church Terrell, wife of the city's first black municipal judge, lived a long, active life. In 1950, at age 86, she headed a campaign to reinstate antidiscrimination laws that had been written in the 1870s. She lived in a three-story brick house (326 T St., N.W., private). Other blacks who lived in this area include poet Paul Laurence Dunbar and Walter Washington, the city's first elected mayor. 🅼 Map p. 195

From the bucolic (Rock Creek Park) to the divine (Washington National Cathedral)—respite from standard sightseeing

CLEVELAND PARK & BEYOND

■ Arches soar inside the vast Washington National Cathedral.

CLEVELAND PARK & BEYOND

Just north of Dupont Circle, the leafy neighborhood of Cleveland Park offers a pleasant afternoon of relaxed sightseeing or lounging in a loved-by-locals café. Higher elevations and the nearness of Rock Creek Park provide relief from the downtown heat.

■ **Washington National Cathedral is the fourth-largest building in Washington D.C.**

The tony neighborhood of Cleveland Park is named for President Grover Cleveland, who spent the summers of his second administration (1893–1897) at Woodley *(3000 Cathedral Ave., N.W.),* a Georgian mansion built about 1800.

Visitors who venture this far from the Mall usually come for the zoo. It's a fine reason to head this way, made easy by the Metro's Red Line to Cleveland Park or Woodley Park–Zoo/Adams Morgan stations. And maybe a nearby site could land on your list of D.C. favorites.

When the city's trolley tracks were extended across Rock Creek Valley at Calvert Street in the 1890s and then up Connecticut Avenue, the area took on a fashionable cachet. Today Connecticut Avenue is still lined with big apartment buildings (the more ornate ones from the 1920s and '30s) and fine old houses with wide front porches. Indeed, the luxury apartment building called the Wardman Tower *(Woodley Rd. & Connecticut Ave.),* built in 1928, was until recently the city's largest hotel. The tower's residents have included Herbert Hoover, Earl Warren, and Clare Booth Luce. Across Calvert Street, the 1930 Omni Shoreham has hosted Inaugural Balls since Franklin Delano Roosevelt took office in 1933. Farther up Connecticut Avenue is the almost pastoral 163-acre (66 ha) Smithsonian's National Zoo. It abuts Rock Creek Park, a delightful preserve of trees, meadows, and cycling paths.

A mile (1.6 km) west of the zoo, Washington National Cathedral towers gloriously on its high hill. Scores of stonemasons labored 83 years to complete this architectural masterpiece. The Hillwood Estate to the north is a jewel box of Russian and French antiques. Afterward, settle in with a cappuccino or a meal at one of the many eateries clustered near the Metro stops along Connecticut Avenue. Shoppers should keep heading northwest to Friendship Heights for the upscale Mazza Gallerie and neighboring high-end retailers. ■

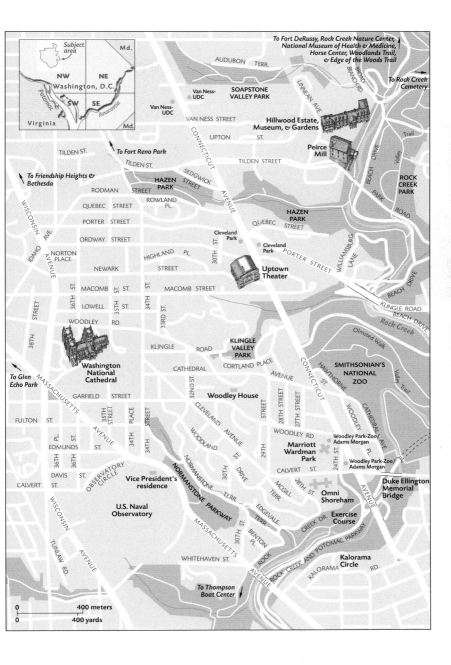

SMITHSONIAN'S NATIONAL ZOO

The National Zoo was conceived as "a home and a city of refuge for the vanishing races of the continent." In 1887, Smithsonian taxidermist William T. Hornaday corralled some of North America's vanishing bison and a few other animals in a small zoo on the Mall. Two years later, Congress set aside acreage along a bend in Rock Creek to create the National Zoo "for the advancement of science and the instruction and recreation of the people."

Prowling among native vegetation, this Sumatran tiger lives in the zoo's Great Cats exhibit.

National Zoo

Map p. 181

3001 Connecticut Ave., N.W.

202-633-4888

Parking: $$$$ per day

Metro: Cleveland Park, Woodley Park–Zoo / Adams Morgan; Bus: 96, L1–L2, Circulator

nationalzoo.si.edu

Part of the Smithsonian Institution, the 163-acre (66 ha) biological park opened in 1891 and is home to more than 2,500 animals representing almost 400 species. Nearly a third of the species—including Asian elephants, cheetahs, Sumatran tigers, giant pandas, western lowland gorillas, and Komodo dragons—are endangered.

The animal enclosures at the National Zoo were designed to re-create natural habitats. Meanwhile, at the zoo's 3,000-acre (1,214 ha) Smithsonian Conservation Biology Institute in Front Royal, Virginia, zookeepers have bred golden lion tamarins, red wolves, and black-footed ferrets for reintroduction to the wild.

Visiting

Given the zoo's 5 miles (8 km) of hilly paths, it's hard to avoid

INSIDER TIP:

On the National Zoo's Asia Trail, kids gravitate to the red pandas—they look like little raccoons, eat bamboo, and are on the threatened-species list.

—DANIEL R. WESTERGREN
National Geographic Traveler magazine director of photography

at least some uphill walking. To plan your route pick up a map at one of the information stations at either end of the zoo's main east-west thoroughfare, the Olmsted Walk (Frederick Law Olmsted designed the zoo's original layout).

With more than 30 animal exhibit areas to choose from, you may want to hit a few of the highlights and save the rest for another day. Fall and winter are the least crowded seasons at the zoo, but the buildings close early November through March.

If you begin at the visitor center inside the Connecticut Avenue entrance, the **Olmsted Walk** will lead you past the cheetahs, zebras, and other mammals to the **Giant Panda Exhibit.** This indoor-outdoor area features Tian Tian and Mei Xiang, a pair of pandas on long-term loan from China, and their cub Xiao Qi Ji (see sidebar right). Within days of arriving in December 2000, the pandas had adapted so well that they were devouring the decorative plantings of ornamental bamboo.

The exhibit outlines efforts to save the panda, whose numbers have seriously dwindled.

Continue downhill and east past the Elephant House to reach the **Small Mammal House,** where the challenge is to spot the golden lion tamarins, pygmy marmosets, two-toed sloths, and three-banded armadillos that occupy the glassed-in jungle.

The **Great Ape House,** next door to the little mammals, is home to gorillas and orangutans. The latter can climb over an aerial pathway called the O Line to **Think Tank,** where animal thinking, tool use, and problem-solving are studied.

A popular stop nearby, the **Reptile Discovery Center** features Komodo dragons, huge Aldabra tortoises, and spiky mata-mata turtles among the 70 or so

Panda Report

Two giant pandas that have thrilled zoo-goers for the past two decades—Mei Xiang and Tian Tian—arrived here in December 2000 from a research center in Sichuan, China, to become part of the Asia Trail exhibit. The male and female pair are on long-term loan from China as part of a research, conservation, and breeding program. Immediately, they charmed visitors and became one of the zoo's biggest draws.

Mei Xiang and Tian Tian have sired seven cubs, three of which have survived, including Xiao Gi Ji, born in August 2020. Huge crowds line up daily hoping for a glimpse of the young male cub.

Today, fewer than 1,900 giant pandas are left in the wild; another 600 live in zoos and breeding centers around the world, such as the National Zoo in Washington.

species of reptiles and amphibians represented here. Also on hand are multimedia exhibits.

Beyond the center you'll find the **Great Cats,** where Sumatran tigers and African lions roam their terraced exhibits. Their offspring are typically sent to other zoos to live with other young felines. **Lemur Island** is home to ring-tailed and red-fronted lemurs (red-ruffed lemurs can be found in the Small Mammal House).

At the south end of the zoo, near Parking Lot D, is a 2-acre (0.8 ha) **Kids' Farm** that is designed to introduce young children to farm animals and the basics of animal care. Kids can interact with alpacas, dwarf goats, and a miniature donkey.

Next, head to the warm, humid **Amazonia** exhibit, the zoo's largest and most complex, which simulates a journey through a rain forest; here parrots and other tropical birds flit through kapok and mahogany trees beneath a domed 50-foot-high (15 m) ceiling. After Amazonia, the American Trail features North American species such as beavers, bald eagles, gray wolves, seals, and sea lions. ∎

■ The endangered golden lion tamarin, a small monkey, is native to coastal Brazil, where its habitat is dwindling. At the zoo they eat fruit, crickets, mealworms, and the occasional stray roach or mouse.

ROCK CREEK PARK

When you need to get away from urban living (or touring), a peaceful Washington park awaits. Rock Creek Park, administered by the National Park Service, runs in a long strand of hilly woods and meadows from the National Zoo to the Maryland border 4 miles (6.4 km) north; tendrils of green branch off into other parts of the city. At 1,739 acres (704 ha)—more than twice the size of New York's Central Park—Rock Creek is one of the nation's largest urban parks.

Bridges, trails, and seasonal glories are among the enticements of this sprawling urban sanctuary.

For some 5,000 years, Algonquin Indians camped in the woods around Rock Creek above its run-in with the Potomac. They gathered fruits and nuts; hunted deer, bear, and elk; and quarried the valley, extracting quartz for tools and soapstone for bowls and other implements. By the early 1700s, the Indians had been displaced by white settlers who'd cleared out more of the forest and built mills along Rock Creek. The only one of these that remains is the 19th-century **Peirce Mill** (Tilden St. & Beach Dr., N.W.), whose adjacent barn is open several hours on weekends.

During the Civil War, a ring of 68 forts went up to protect against Confederate attack. You can see some earthworks from **Fort DeRussy** half a mile (0.8 km) north of the nature center. Other fort sites, most long since reduced to picnic and ball-playing areas, include **Fort Bayard Park** (River Rd. & Western Ave., N.W.); **Fort Reno Park** (Chesapeake St. & Belt Rd., N.W.), occupying the highest point of land in Washington and partially reconstructed; and **Fort Stevens Park** (13th St., N.W., N of Military Rd.), the only Washington-area battlement that came under enemy fire.

Rock Creek Park

Map p. 181

202-895-6000 & 202-895-6070

nps.gov/rocr

**Rock Creek
Nature Center &
Planetarium**

🗺 Map p. 181

✉ 5200 Glover
Rd., N.W., S of
Military Rd.

☎ 202-895-6070

🕐 Closed Mon.–
Tues. & major
holidays

Set aside in 1890, Rock Creek Park is the city's playground. About 85 percent of the park is forested; the remainder is mainly meadows and fields. Over the years, Theodore Roosevelt, Ronald Reagan, and other presidents have availed themselves of the park's walking and bridle trails. Today, people come for the tennis courts, an 18-hole golf course, playing fields, nature center and planetarium, and more than 32 miles (51 km) of trails for jogging, hiking, biking, and horseback riding.

Visiting

Start your visit at the **Rock Creek Nature Center & Planetarium.** Here you can learn about the park's flora and fauna, scope out its cycling and running paths, and pick up a trail map. The center's excellent offerings include a bee colony and astronomy programs.

Two short nature loops—the **Woodland Trail** and the wheelchair-accessible **Edge of the Woods Trail**—have signs identifying trees and plants. Come spring, dogwoods, redbud, and azalea blooms emerge in a gaudy show.

From the nature center, you can also access the park's larger trail network. Some pathways are open to bikes and horses (see below). Hikers gravitate to the moderate, 5.6-mile (9 km) **Valley Trail,** which winds along the east side of Rock Creek from Boundary Bridge on the Maryland line down to Bluff Bridge at the park's southern end. Its analogue on the western edge is the strenuous, green-blazed, 4.6-mile (7.4 km) **Western Ridge Trail.**

Just south of the nature center, sign up for a trail ride or lesson at the **Rock Creek Horse Center** *(tel 202-362-0117, rockcreekhorse center.com).* Much farther south, where Rock Creek joins the Potomac River, **Thompson Boat Center** *(tel 202-333-9543, boat ingindc.com)* rents canoes, kayaks, and bicycles. ∎

EXPERIENCE: Hiking & Biking Rock Creek Trail

Running north–south, the scenic Rock Creek Trail extends a total of 25 miles (40 km), starting at the Lincoln Memorial in Washington, D.C., and going all the way to Lake Needwood Park in Montgomery County, Maryland. For biking, walking, jogging, or picnicking, the trail can be accessed from the **Rock Creek Park Nature Center & Planetarium.**

The northern trail—the portion that goes beyond D.C. and crosses 14 miles (22.5 km) into Maryland—is entirely on paved roadways. It connects with **Beach Drive,** usually a pulsing commuter artery but pleasant on weekends when sections of it are closed to motor vehicles, giving cyclists an unobstructed ride all the way from the Maryland border south to Broad Branch Road.

Rock Creek Trail's southern route runs alongside Rock Creek and the Potomac Parkway until it reaches Memorial Bridge. Although paved, the path is narrow, windy, and rough in patches. Be on the alert for children, pets, and others. About halfway along this stretch of trail, near Calvert Street and Connecticut Avenue, you'll find a 1.5-mile (2.4 km) exercise course with fitness apparatus.

HILLWOOD ESTATE, MUSEUM, & GARDENS

A hidden gem, Hillwood was the final home of heiress Marjorie Merriweather Post (1887–1973). With her fabulous collection of imperial Russian and 18th-century French decorative arts, she furnished the house with the idea that it would become a museum after her death. The site opened to the public in 1977, and Hillwood, with 13 acres (5.2 ha) of formal gardens, is now one of the top art collector's house museums in the country.

As the only child of cereal magnate C. W. Post, Marjorie inherited a fortune at age 27 when her father died (just two years after her mother). She and her husband bought a mansion on Fifth Avenue in New York and began furnishing it with the help of renowned art dealer Sir Joseph Duveen, who became Post's mentor. She also educated herself by taking classes on tapestries, porcelain, and furniture at the Metropolitan Museum of Art.

In the course of a long and extraordinary life, Post married and divorced four times and amassed a tremendous collection of European artwork. An astute businesswoman, she also donated millions of dollars to charities and other organizations, including $100,000 to help build the Kennedy Center (see pp. 126–127).

It was after her third divorce, in 1955, that Post purchased Hillwood—a 1926 Georgian house on the woodsy edge of Rock Creek Park. She spent two years renovating and enlarging the house, transforming it into a residence where she could entertain in legendary style. Hillwood parties routinely exceeded 200 guests, the politicians mixing with celebrities in the gardens. At formal dinners, guests ate off Post's antique porcelain; informal dinners sometimes wound

■ A painting by Karl Bryullov in the Hillwood Museum, ca 1832

down with square dancing in the pavilion.

In the interstices between soirées, Post expanded her art collection, eventually turning Hillwood into a stunning showcase of decorative and fine arts. Today the museum is best known for its collection of 18th- and 19th-century Russian imperial art—the most comprehensive outside Russia—and for its French decorative art.

Hillwood Estate, Museum, & Gardens

- Map p. 181
- 4155 Linnean Ave., N.W.
- 202-686-5807
- Closed Mon., & most of Jan.
- $$$$
- Metro: Van Ness–UDC; Bus: L1–L2

hillwoodmuseum.org

Visiting

Get oriented to the museum and gardens with a 15-minute film at the visitor center. You can take a one-hour **guided tour** of the house, usually offered several times a day, or a self-guided audio tour or mobile app tour (download it from the website), and then stroll the gardens. There's a café on-site that serves lunch and afternoon tea; call for reservations *(tel 202-686-5807)*.

The imposing exterior of the brick house and the inside customarily prompt a chorus of oohs and aahs. One highlight, the **Russian Porcelain Room,** contains Imperial Glassworks pieces from the 1730s.

More tsarist treasures are on display in the outstanding **Icon Room,** where you can feast your eyes on the diamond wedding crown worn in 1894 by Russia's last empress,

Alexandra Fedorovona; two Fabergé Easter eggs (one dates from 1914 and is studded with gold, diamonds, and pearls); and Russian Orthodox icons from the 16th century. Post discovered her love of Russian decorative and liturgical art while living

INSIDER TIP:

Marjorie Merriweather Post created a pet cemetery after her beloved dog died. Every October, dogs and their owners are invited to the Spooky Pooch Parade.

—SUSAN O'KEEFE
National Geographic Traveler magazine associate editor

in the Soviet Union from 1937 to 1938 with her third husband, U.S. Ambassador Joseph E. Davies.

The elegant **French Drawing Room** is furnished in the style of Louis XVI, with 18th-century tapestries designed by painter François Boucher and furniture by David Roentgen. Upstairs, Post's bedroom is likewise decorated in Louis XVI style; a display of her clothing and jewelry adds life and personality to the collection.

Equally impressive are the 12 acres (4.8 ha) of lawns and formal gardens and 13 acres (5.2 ha) of native woodlands. A French parterre with a fountain, a circular rose garden, a lunar lawn, a Japanese-style garden, a cutting garden, and an orchid-filled greenhouse round out the grounds. It all makes strolling through Hillwood a delight in any season. ■

■ **Post's treasures included ornate jewel-studded Russian imperial Easter eggs created by Fabergé.**

WASHINGTON NATIONAL CATHEDRAL

Dominating the cityscape, Washington National Cathedral is visible from points all over the district. Conversely, its lofty perch on Mount St. Alban gives cathedral visitors a commanding vista of the urban skyline. Officially known as the Cathedral Church of St. Peter and St. Paul, this towering Gothic church is one of Washington's most magnificent architectural achievements. The cathedral is undergoing lengthy restoration following the 2011 earthquake.

The idea of a national church featured in Pierre-Charles L'Enfant's Federal City plans. He envisioned a house of prayer for national services, open to all rather than reserved for a particular denomination. It took nearly a century for the idea to gain adequate support. In 1893 the Protestant Episcopal Cathedral Foundation obtained a charter allowing the church to be established.

After the 57-acre (23 ha) site atop Mount St. Alban was selected and public donations were obtained, President Theodore Roosevelt and a crowd of 10,000 were on hand in 1907 for the laying of the foundation stone. The Bethlehem Chapel, named for one of its stones that came from a field near Bethlehem, opened first, in 1912. Services have been held here ever since, even though construction of the building actually took 83 years. President George H. W. Bush dedicated the west towers in 1990.

For half a century, construction of the cathedral was guided by Philip Hubert Frohman, who had dreamed of becoming its architect; he got the job after the two initial designers died in 1917. Obsessed with detail, Frohman once ordered that all the molding on the central tower be shifted by one-eighth of an inch (0.3 cm). He died in 1972,

■ The imposing St. Peter and St. Paul towers on the west facade of Washington National Cathedral bask in the honey-gold sunshine of late afternoon.

Visiting

Half-hour docent-led tours are offered several times at midday *(donation),* beginning at the west end of the nave. For groups, reservations are required *(tel 202-537-6200).* You can also wander on your own with an audio tour *($$).* Tours may be unavailable, however, if the cathedral is being used for a special event; check the website, which also has the schedules of services and musical events.

Stroll outside to admire the flying buttresses, the arches, and some of the **112 gargoyles** whose expressions range from silly to fiendish. In addition to supposedly warding off evil, the gargoyles funnel rainwater away from the building during storms. The figures include a bear, an American rattlesnake, and even Darth Vader, plus several caricatures of people who were central to the construction of the cathedral. Binoculars are handy for inspecting the higher ones.

Outside is also the best place to absorb the immensity of the sixth largest cathedral in the world, and the second largest in the United States (only New York's St. John the Divine is bigger). The central Gloria in Excelsis Deo tower rises 300 feet (91 m), while the nave measures one-tenth of a mile (0.16 km).

The west entrance portal features Frederick Hart's tympanum sculpture, "Ex Nihilo," in which the Christian idea of creation is expressed through half-formed men and women.

Faithful to its Gothic style, the church was built in a cruciform shape. Stand at the crossing and look up; the massive piers rise

■ "History of the Baptism" illuminates the south transept.

Washington National Cathedral

🗺 Map p. 181

✉ Massachusetts & Wisconsin Aves., N.W.

☎ 202-537-6200

🚌 Bus: 31–32, 36–37, 96–97, N2–N4

cathedral.org

at the age of 85, after being struck by a car while walking to work from his home.

Others who dedicated their lives to the cathedral were the many masons, stone carvers, and stained-glass artisans who applied 14th-century skills to modern times. Their legacy includes more than 200 stained-glass windows, 3,000 stone sculptures, and many other artfully crafted works. Most of the building was constructed of grey Indiana limestone, selected for its endurance without the need for major restoration over time.

98 feet (30 m) to the vaulting overhead. The pulpit, from which Dr. Martin Luther King, Jr., gave his final sermon on March 31, 1968, was carved from stone donated by England's Canterbury Cathedral. The 10,500 pieces of glass in the spectacular **West Rose Window** cast late afternoon rainbows.

Running along the nave are memorial alcoves, or bays. The **Woodrow Wilson Bay** honors the life of the 28th president, the only U.S. president whose final resting place is Washington, D.C. The floor of the **Lincoln Bay** is inset with 33 Lincoln-head pennies—one for each state in the Union at the time of the Great Emancipator's assassination.

About halfway down on the right (south) side, the modernistic **Space Window** has a moon rock from the Apollo 11 lunar landing embedded in the center lancet.

Scattered throughout, nine chapels vary from the tiny **Good Shepherd Chapel** to the church-size **Bethlehem Chapel** on the crypt level. Especially appealing is

the intimate **Children's Chapel,** where every item has been scaled to a size befitting a six-year-old. Also, look for busts of such humanitarians and human rights activists as Dietrich Bonhoeffer, Martin Luther King, Jr., Helen Keller, Rosa Parks, Albert Schweitzer, and Mother Teresa.

For a closer look at the cathedral's towers and gargoyles (and a panoramic view of the city), take an elevator to the **Pilgrim Observation Gallery** on the seventh floor of the St. Peter and St. Paul towers. In nice weather, stroll in the beautifully landscaped **Bishop's Garden,** which was designed by Frederick Law Olmsted. ■

INSIDER TIP:

See the cathedral's gargoyles up close on a behind-the-scenes tour. For information, call 202-537-6200

—BARBARA NOE
*National Geographic Travel
Books senior editor*

Bell Appeal

National Cathedral's central tower holds ten peal bells and a 53-bell carillon. It is the only cathedral in North America blessed with both kinds of bells in a single tower.

Each peal bell is mounted on a wheel, from which a rope hangs down to the ringers' chamber. The pull must be smooth and even, so one ringer is assigned to each bell. Weighing 600 to nearly 3,600 pounds apiece (272 kg–1,632 kg), the bells cannot be rung fast

enough for a melody; instead, sequences of notes called "changes" are played. Change ringing is difficult and dangerous: Lose your concentration and you not only sabotage the change but risk injury when the bell's momentum jerks you high off the floor. Peals *(Sun. after a.m. service)* can last from several minutes to the rare "full peal," a three-hour extravaganza of 5,000 changes. The joyous noise can be heard at the White House, 3 miles (4.8 km) away.

More Places to Visit in Cleveland Park & Beyond

National Museum of Health & Medicine

Though it now stresses serious science over sensational spectacle, this museum is not for the squeamish: Exhibits range from preserved human fetuses and a stomach-shaped hair ball to a leg swollen by elephantiasis and a hands-on brain. Also on display: the bullet that killed President Lincoln and a tent hospital from Iraq. The collection was begun during the Civil War as a research tool for military medicine and surgery. Today the museum's vast collection of skeletal specimens, organs, and models is employed for research on human anatomy. *medicalmuseum. mil* 🗺 Map p. 181 ✉ 2500 Linden Lane, Silver Spring, MD ☎ 301-319-3300 🚇 Metro: Forest Glen

Rock Creek Cemetery

A mile and a half (2.4 km) east of Rock Creek Park in the Petworth neighborhood, this 86-acre (35 ha) site exudes the feel of an old country parish. Set amid this pastoral glebe, St. Paul's Episcopal (or "Rock Creek") Church is the city's sole surviving colonial church. It was founded in 1719, long before Washington was a city; although the current building dates from 1775, only the walls are original.

Some of the city's finest cemetery memorials reside here. They honor crusading novelist Upton Sinclair, Cabinet members, Supreme Court justices, and National Geographic Society founder Gilbert H. Grosvenor. The cemetery also houses one of the finest works by one of America's greatest sculptors: The Adams Memorial (1890) by Augustus Saint-Gaudens was commissioned by historian Henry Adams to honor his wife, Clover. It depicts a seated figure wearing a heavy cloak, the face obscured by shadows. Mark Twain remarked that the sculpture embodied all of human grief. *rockcreekcem etery.org* 🗺 Map p. 181 ✉ 201 Allison St., N.W. ☎ 202-726-2020

Uptown Theater

Opened in 1936, the art deco Uptown was Washington's premier movie palace, a blast from the past that underscored the erstwhile power of the big screen. Its original 1,500 seats, including a balcony, made it the city's largest cinema theater. A curved screen, 72 feet (23 m) long and 32 feet (9.7 m) high, wrapped viewers in movie magic, while a Dolby digital sound system kept the illusion up-to-date. It closed permanently in March 2020, but is protected as a historic building 🗺 Map p. 181 ✉ 3426 Connecticut Ave., N.W. 🚇 Metro: Cleveland Park

U.S. Naval Observatory

Established as a national observatory in 1842, this military scientific facility enclosed by Observatory Circle is tasked with establishing precise positioning, navigation, and timing for the U.S. Navy and Department of Defense. It maintains the atomic "master clock" used by the U.S. government for standard time to 1/10th of a nanosecond, as well as the world's largest library of astronomical and astrophysical books.

A manse built in 1883 *(Number One Observatory Circle)* was originally intended for the superintendent of the USNO, but the Chief of Naval Operations liked it so much he ousted the superintendent and moved in himself. It has traditionally served as the vice president's official residence since Walter Mondale's family occupied it in 1977–1981.

The USNO offers free guided tours on certain Monday nights (see website), including a chance to view the sky through a 26-inch (0.6 m) refractor telescope. Requests for tours must be made in advance. *usno.navy.mil/USNO* 🗺 Map p. 181 ✉ 3450 Massachusetts Ave., N.W ☎ 202-762-1401 🚇 Metro: Woodley Park–Zoo/ Adams Morgan; Bus: Circulator

Discoveries off the beaten path—a museum honoring African Americans, a dazzling basilica, gardens, and more gardens

EAST & NORTH OF THE CAPITOL

■ Asters flourish at the U.S. National Arboretum.

EAST & NORTH OF THE CAPITOL

It's an area rich in African-American and military history, as well as botanic treasures, marshes, and woods. Architecture lovers will find one of the city's most awe-inspiring buildings here, the nation's largest Catholic church.

■ Reverend Willie Wilson plays washboard at Union Temple Baptist Church in Anacostia.

The history of this part of the city is tied to its river, the Anacostia, first seen by a European, explorer John Smith, nearly 400 years ago. Back then the Nacotchtank Indians (whose

corrupted name, Anacostan, would be given to this East Branch of the Potomac) lived here. The arrival of white settlers meant the Indians' demise and the spread of tobacco plantations. In 1790 the lower Anacostia became part of the new capital. Soon developments arose on the northwest riverfront—the Washington Navy Yard (1799) and the U.S. Arsenal (1803).

Across the river from the Navy Yard, the city laid out its first whites-only suburb, Uniontown, in 1854. During the Civil War, the military erected several forts east of the river. After the war, the Freedman's Bureau bought nearby 375-acre (151 ha) Barry farm and sold lots to 500 black families. Still the community, renamed Anacostia in 1886, remained mostly white until the 1950s, when whites migrated to the suburbs. By 1970, Anacostia was 86 percent black. The District government and private corporations have been investing millions of dollars to develop the Anacostia waterfront, while

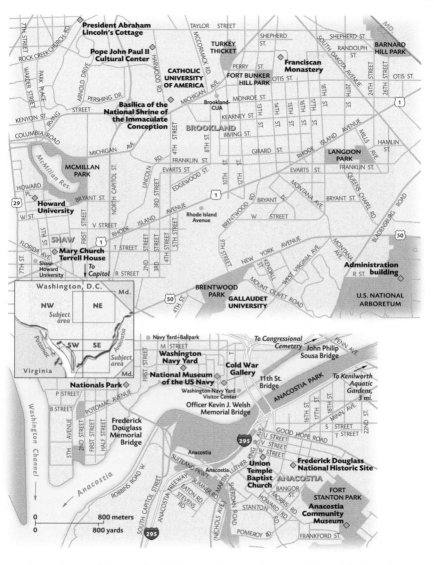

the superb National Museum of the U.S. Navy is being given a 21st-century remake.

On the other side of the river, the Northeast quadrant is anchored by the U.S. National Arboretum and the Catholic University of America. Also in this area is Gallaudet University, the premier U.S. school for the deaf.

Sports fans know the area as the site of Langston Golf Course, Nationals Park baseball stadium, and the defunct RFK Stadium, once home to the Washington Redskins football team. ■

U.S. NATIONAL ARBORETUM

A little off the beaten tourist path, this delightful oasis of fields, ponds, fountains, gardens, and flowering trees is just the tonic for those in need of some outdoor beauty. Established by an act of Congress in 1927, the National Arboretum is run by the Department of Agriculture as a living museum and a research and education facility. The arboretum's 446 acres (180 ha) include 9.5 miles (15 km) of gentle roadways that wind past a dozen garden areas.

Children create their own floral tableau beneath a flowering "Tonto" crape myrtle at the arboretum.

U.S. National Arboretum

Map p. 195

24th & R Sts., N.E., or 3501 New York Ave., N.E.

202-245-4523

Metro: Stadium–Armory (2 miles away); Bus: B2

usna.usda.gov

A pleasure any time, the arboretum is especially beautiful in spring, with 15,000 multicolored azaleas and blossoming dogwoods, cherries, and crab apples blushing on the hillsides. In summer, delicate flowers and high grasses stipple meadows, while daylilies and crape myrtles take to the heat with ease, and water lilies bloom in the koi pool near the administration building. Fall enriches the color palette with the vivid yellows of hickory and tulip poplar and the wine reds of sweet gum and dogwood. The late flowers of witch hazel and spider lilies fan the flames. In the cold quiet days of winter, the bright red berries of holly glisten like little beads, and dwarf conifers and other evergreens are sometimes rimed with ice. Ornamental grasses and dry leaves chatter in the breeze.

Visiting

On the way to the administration building from the New York Avenue entrance, you'll notice

The Story of the Anacostia River

Since the arrival of Europeans nearly 400 years ago, the Anacostia watershed has been used, overused, and abused. Runoffs from big farms in the 18th century silted the river, and urban growth has troubled the waters ever since. In the early 20th century, efforts to reshape the waterway and "reclaim" the adjoining swamps for development nearly killed the Anacostia.

Government agencies as well as several citizen groups, such as the Anacostia Watershed Society (anacostiaws.org), are working to protect this valuable ecosystem, a vital part of the country's largest estuary—the Chesapeake Bay.

In recent years, thousands of tons of debris have been cleaned up, thousands of trees have been planted, and in 2016 a tunnel was completed to carry street drainage and unfiltered sewage that once flowed into the river to a waste treatment plant. In 2021, river otters returned for the first time in decades. With an eye on the future, the Anacostia Watershed Society has enlisted thousands of city youths to help clean up the river.

beehive-shaped **brick kilns.** When the brickyard, dating from 1909, shut down in 1972, the acreage and buildings were sold to the arboretum. At the administration building, you'll find maps and a list of gardens in bloom.

Next to this building, the **National Bonsai & Penjing Museum** has an outstanding collection of miniature trees from Japan, China, and North America. Breezes lilt through feathery Japanese maples and paths meander among bonsai pavilions.

Across the drive, the 2.5-acre (1 ha) **National Herb Garden** features some 800 varieties of herbs. Standing like unexpected ruins in a nearby field are 22 sandstone Corinthian columns, removed from the Capitol's east central portico in 1958 when the Senate side of the building was enlarged. You can drive or bike to most gardens by looping the outer road, but check if the guided 35-minute open-air tram tour (weekends, seasonal, $) is running from the R Street entrance.

Heading southwest from the administration building, you come to the **National Boxwood Collection**—around 150 types on 5 acres (2 ha). Adjoining perennials include irises, peonies, and daylilies. Continue to the **Azalea Collections,** which peak in late April. To the east, on Crabtree Road, is **Fern Valley;** a half-mile (0.8 km) wooded path winds past wildflowers, a meadow, prairie, and a stream.

At the arboretum's far eastern end are the well-loved **Asian Collections,** with flora planted on a hillside so that from strategically placed benches you have glimpses of a pagoda and views down to the Anacostia River. To the north, the **Gotelli Collection** of dwarf and slow-growing conifers is considered among the world's best.

The setting of the **Dogwood Collections** nearby offers a fine view of the Anacostia River. South of the Asian collections, the glossy **hollies and magnolias** are striking in all seasons. ∎

BASILICA OF THE NATIONAL SHRINE OF THE IMMACULATE CONCEPTION

The blue dome and 329-foot-tall (100 m) campanile of the National Shrine preside over the skyline of Northeast Washington. Built along Byzantine and Romanesque lines, the National Shrine is the country's largest Roman Catholic church. One of the most impressive pieces of architecture in a city renowned for its monuments, it rivals the great sanctuaries of the world.

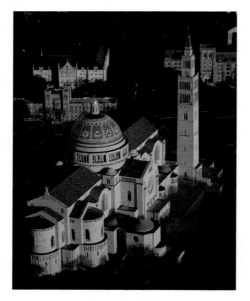

■ The National Shrine's dome and bell tower punctuate the skyline.

Basilica of the National Shrine of the Immaculate Conception

🗺 Map p. 195

✉ Michigan Ave. & 4th St., N.E.

☎ 202-526-8300

🚇 Metro: Brookland–CUA; Bus: 80, H1–H4

nationalshrine.com

The idea of giving Washington a magnificent Catholic church in the manner of Old World cathedrals was first proposed in 1846. In 1913, the rector of the Catholic University of America presented Pope Pius X with plans for building a shrine to the Blessed Virgin Mary on the campus. With the pope's support, work began in 1920; the building was dedicated in 1959. In 1990, John Paul II designated the shrine a basilica because of its significance as a national center of worship.

You can take a free group tour or pick up a floor plan near the entrance and wander on your own. More than 70 chapels and oratories circle the perimeter of the crypt level and upper church. Enter on the upstairs level, where the grandiose **Great Upper Church** soars to a height of 100 feet (30.5 m). Natural light floods the vast interior, stained glass casts rich color on walls and floors, and mosaics and candles sparkle in almost every niche and dome. Notice the swirling cosmos and the Creation depicted above the east transept and, in the west transept, the people rising toward a cloud-enthroned Jesus. The chancel dome holds a huge mosaic titled "Descent of the Holy Spirit." A soothing contrast is the trickling fountain of the **Mary Queen of All Hearts chapel.**

Stairs lead to the **crypt level,** where marble walls and pillars adorn **Memorial Hall,** honoring the shrine's donors. Also on this level, the **Crypt Church** was modeled on Roman catacombs. Between the hall and church is the Hall of American Saints. ■

PRESIDENT ABRAHAM LINCOLN'S COTTAGE

It was in a handsome "country cottage" on a hill, about 3 miles (5 km) from the center of the city, that President Abraham Lincoln and his family spent most of June–November in 1862, 1863, and 1864, in retreat from the heat. Most days, Lincoln would commute to his office via horse, passing temporary shelters housing former slaves who had escaped to freedom.

The 10,000-square-foot (930 sq m) home was built in 1842 as the summer house of George Washington Riggs, a prominent banker. In 1851, he sold the property to the government; later that year, Congress passed legislation that established the home as a place for retired or disabled soldiers.

After a $15 million renovation by the National Trust for Historic Preservation, the cottage, located on the Armed Forces Retirement Home campus in Northwest Washington, was opened to the public for the first time in 2008. Now you can walk the grounds where Lincoln pondered difficult decisions surrounding the Civil War.

Far from a log cabin, the 34-room house served as the setting for important meetings; it's also where Lincoln drafted the Emancipation Proclamation. Admission is by guided tour only, and tickets are required. ∎

President Abraham Lincoln's Cottage

- Map p. 195
- Rock Creek Church Rd. & Upshur St., N.W.
- 202-829-0436
- Guided tours hourly, 10 a.m.– 3 p.m.
- $$
- Metro: Georgia Ave.–Petworth (1 mile/1.6 km away); Bus: H8

lincolncottage.org

H Street Corridor

The H Street Northeast area, just beyond Union Station and the U.S. Capitol, got hit hard by the rioting that occurred after Rev. Martin Luther King, Jr., was assassinated in 1968. Recovery was slow in coming, but today the neighborhood offers one of the hippest club scenes in Washington D.C.

In 2003, the city adopted a plan to develop the H Street Corridor (hstreet.org) as an arts and entertainment zone to drive social and economic revitalization. Philanthropist Jane Lang spearheaded renovation of a 1930s art deco movie theater into the **Atlas Performing Arts Center** (1333 H St., N.E., atlasarts.org). It opened in 2006, providing 60,000 square feet (5,575 sq m) of space for theater, dance, choral, and orchestral groups. An influx of new businesses followed the installation of a streetcar line (dcstreetcar.com), which began service in 2016. Clubs and coffee shops have sprung up, many with unvarnished decor and eclectic themes, such as **Little Miss Whisky's** (1104 H St., N.W., littlemiss whiskeys.com) for karaoke and dance parties; **H Street Country Club** (1335 H St., N.E., thehstreetcountryclub.com) with Mexican food and indoor miniature golf; and **Sticky Rice** (1224 H St., N.W., sticky ricedc.com) for top 40s past and present. **Dr. Granville Moore's** (1238 H St., N.E., granvillemoores.com), a spot named for the physician whose name is still above the door, specializes in mussels and Belgian beer. If you want to try the dining scene, there's **Ethiopic** (401 H St., N.E., ethiopic restaurant.com) and **Pie Shop** (1339 H St., N.E., pieshopdc.com) for fresh pizzas, pies, and live music.

FREDERICK DOUGLASS NATIONAL HISTORIC SITE

Situated among the row houses of Anacostia, Cedar Hill—former home of abolitionist Frederick Douglass—was built in the 1850s atop a grassy knoll. The 21-room tan brick house offers a commanding view of Washington from its gracious front porch. A visit to this National Park Service site provides a fascinating glimpse into the life and work of the "sage of Anacostia," the most prominent African-American orator of the 19th century.

■ **The Douglass house contains many of the early civil rights leader's personal effects.**

Frederick Douglass National Historic Site

⛰ Map p. 195

✉ 1411 W St., S.E.

☎ 202-426-5961 or 877-444-6777 for tour reservations

$ $

🚇 Metro: Anacostia, then Bus B2

nps.gov/frdo

Frederick Douglass was born a slave in Maryland's Talbot County in 1818, son of a black mother and a white father, possibly his owner. Sent to Baltimore as a servant, he taught himself to read; at 20 he escaped to New York, then Massachusetts, where he lectured for the Massachusetts Anti-Slavery Society. To elude slave hunters after publishing his autobiography, in 1845, he fled to Europe. The purchase of his freedom by friends allowed him to return two years later. He began the *North Star* newspaper and kept working for the rights of blacks and women.

After the Civil War, he moved to Washington, D.C. Appointed U.S. marshal of the District in 1877, he bought 9-acre (3.6 ha) Cedar Hill. Cedar Hill was originally a farm estate with chicken coops, barn, and carriage house. He expanded it to 15 acres (6 ha) and enlarged the house by seven rooms. After his 1895 death, his widow, Helen, preserved Cedar Hill, which was later turned over to the National Park Service.

The guided 30-minute tour begins with a 17-minute film. Among items on display is a Lincoln cane given to Douglass by the president's widow. After the film, you climb the hill (via steep steps) to the **Victorian house.** Inside, the tastefully appointed parlors, library, and dining room look much as they did in Douglass's time—some 70 percent of the furnishings are original.

Upstairs, Douglass's bedroom is replete with a 19th-century bootjack and pair of shoes tucked by a chair. To see the different styles of his two wives, peek into their separate bedrooms.

Outside, you will find the **Growlery** (a reconstruction), the private study to which Douglass often retreated. ■

More Places to See East & North of the Capitol

Anacostia Community Museum

Located in Fort Stanton Park, site of a Civil War fortification, this Anacostia museum opened in 1967 as a neighborhood museum devoted to the interpretation of the African-American experience, particularly in Washington, D.C.

Now part of the Smithsonian Institution, the museum offers a changing program of exhibits, music, art, dance, storytelling, and poetry. One of the permanent exhibits, for example, focuses on black baseball teams in D.C., from Reconstruction to the second half of the 20th century.

Other exhibits have included retrospectives on black photographers, such as New Orleans's Jules Lion and inventors such as Benjamin Banneker, who helped plan the capital city. In addition, the museum has staged exhibits covering topics as diverse as African-American quilts, black churches, the antebellum South, the civil rights movement, Malcolm X, the 1920s renaissance, and the meaning and celebration of the Kwanzaa and Juneteenth holidays. *anacostia.si.edu* Map p. 195 1901 Fort Pl., S.E. 202-633-4820 Metro: Anacostia, then Bus W2–W3

Congressional Cemetery

Founded by residents of Capitol Hill in 1807, this cemetery came to be reserved for members of Congress who died in office. Beginning in 1839, sandstone monuments were created for every member of Congress. (Fewer than 90 of the monuments have bodies buried beneath them; the rest honor people who are buried elsewhere.) Congress stopped the practice in 1877 after a furious debate, in which Senator George Hoar of Massachusetts argued that being buried under one of the massive monuments added "a new terror to death." Among the cemetery's famous residents are Capitol architect William Thornton (1828), Civil War photographer Mathew Brady (1916), Marine Corps bandmaster John Philip Sousa (1932), and J. Edgar Hoover (1972), director of the FBI. Visitors can stroll the hilly grounds; a map is available at the entrance. Guided tours are offered Sunday at 1 p.m. by reservation. *congressionalcemetery.org* Map p. 195 1801 E St., S.E. 202-543-0539 Metro: Potomac Avenue

Franciscan Monastery

If a trip to the Holy Land is on your must-do list, this working monastery near the National Shrine of the Immaculate Conception offers a more accessible alternative. Tours are offered hourly, and you can wander the gardens freely. Built in 1899 to educate missionaries, the monastery contains full-scale reproductions of such sacred places as the Grotto of Lourdes, the Grotto of Gethsemane, the Tomb of the Virgin

■ **A monk leads a tour down into the catacombs of the Franciscan Monastery.**

Mary, and the Holy Sepulchre of Christ. The Byzantine-style church is laid out in the shape of a Crusader's cross, with chapels in the four corners. Especially memorable are the Roman-style catacombs down below. In spring the gardens grace the monastery with flowering rose bushes, dogwoods, and cherry trees. Themed 45-minute guided tours are offered. *myfranciscan.org* 🅰 Map p. 195 ✉ 1400 Quincy St., N.E. ☎ 202-526-6800 🚇 Metro: Brookland–CUA

Kenilworth Park & Aquatic Gardens

A cool feast of water lilies and lotuses floats on the waters of the Kenilworth Aquatic Gardens, on the east bank of the Anacostia River. Started in 1880 by Civil War veteran Walter B. Shaw, this lovely 14-acre (5.6 ha) sanctuary—now managed by the National Park Service—is in full bloom in the middle of the summer. Garden tours are offered mornings on weekends during summer months.

A **visitor center** near the gardens' parking lot has exhibits on the area. With 40 ponds and a 335-yard (306 m) boardwalk extending into marshes, the gardens offer

fine opportunities for viewing birds and other wildlife, such as osprey, snapping turtles, and muskrats.

The 0.7-mile (1.1 km; one way) **River Trail** offers a closer look at 77-acre (31 ha) Kenilworth Marsh, which borders the gardens and is rich in bird and plant life. Here American bittern, long-billed marsh wrens, and spotted salamanders live in a cattail-fringed wetland.

The best time for seeing wildlife and catching night-blooming lilies is in the early morning. The gardens are open 7 a.m.–5 p.m. *nps.gov/keaq* 🅰 Map p. 195 ✉ 1550 Anacostia Ave., N.E. ☎ 202-692-6080 🚇 Metro: Deanwood, then walk across Kenilworth overpass to Douglas St. & Anacostia Ave.; Bus: V7

National Museum of the U.S. Navy

The museum occupies the sprawling Washington Navy Yard, which was a major shipbuilding facility between 1799 and 1886, and thereafter served until 1961 as the Navy's main ordnance plant. Ever since it has served as home to the Chief of Naval Operations—the administrative center for the U.S. Navy. The National Museum of the U.S. Navy *(Bldg. 76)*, in the yard's southeast corner, displays an impressive array of artifacts that span conflicts from the Revolutionary War to World War II, including almost 100 scale models, from the U.S.S. *Maine* to the German battleship *Scharnhorst*. Experience submarine warfare first-hand with the **"Dive! Dive! Dive!"** simulated submarine combat center. The museum's **Cold War Gallery** (see sidebar left) covers the Navy's history from the Korean War to today. In October 2020, plans were announced to build an entirely new, state-of-the-art museum. *history.navy.mil* 🅰 Map p. 195 ✉ 11th & O Sts., S.E. (weekdays); 6th & M Sts., S.E. (weekends) ☎ 202-685-0589 (Navy Museum), 202-433-3738 (access) 🕐 Closed Sun. 🚇 Metro: Eastern Market, Navy Yard–Ballpark

Relive the Cold War

The Cold War Gallery, in Building 70 at the National Museum of the U.S. Navy *(see opposite)*, offers a chance to relive the chilling "Cold War" with the Soviet Union following World War II, including the Korean and Vietnam wars, and the Navy's role in deterring a nuclear attack on the United States. A Vietnam-era Swift Boat sits outside, while a Trident I missile dominates the entrance. The "Covert Submarine Operations" exhibit includes scale models of U.S. and Soviet submarines; a Control Room from U.S.S. *Trepang* (SSN-674); and reconstructions of a mess and bunk area in "Life Aboard a Submarine."

On the Virginia side of the Potomac, from Alexandria to Arlington, you can visit lots more of the country's past

ACROSS THE POTOMAC

■ Welcome to Alexandria: A pineapple door knocker symbolizes hospitality.

ACROSS THE POTOMAC

The Northern Virginia region just beyond Washington proper is an exciting, densely populated mix of historic sites, residential neighborhoods, restaurants, and shops. Arlington and Alexandria especially have much to offer residents and visitors alike. Both bustling communities originally belonged to the District of Columbia, which once straddled both sides of the Potomac River.

■ Theodore Roosevelt Memorial Bridge connects Washington with the Virginia burbs.

Though Virginia took back roughly a third of the city in 1846, the fortunes of the reclaimed areas remain tied to Washington. Separated by the Crystal City high-rises around Ronald Reagan Washington National Airport, the communities of Arlington and Alexandria are connected by the Metro system and highly scenic George Washington Memorial Parkway.

Already a tobacco port, Alexandria got its official start in 1749 as a 60-acre (24 ha) town site. Both George Washington, who lived 9 miles (14.5 km) south at Mount Vernon, and Robert E. Lee considered it their hometown. Alexandria has prospered of late with the sprucing up of its waterfront and the restoration of 18th-century town houses. Now a tony residential area, the town draws a steady stream of visitors to its bars, restaurants, and shops. Historical sites give insight into the lives of Washington, Lee, and other prominent locals.

One of the nation's smallest counties, with no incorporated cities or towns, Arlington did not exist as a separate entity until after 1846, when the land was returned from Washington to Virginia. Today it is home to Arlington National Cemetery and the Pentagon. The moving Marine Corps War Memorial, Theodore Roosevelt Island, the string of Potomac River parks along the parkway, and the restaurants along the Ballston/Clarendon corridor are other good reasons for venturing to the Virginia side of the river. ■

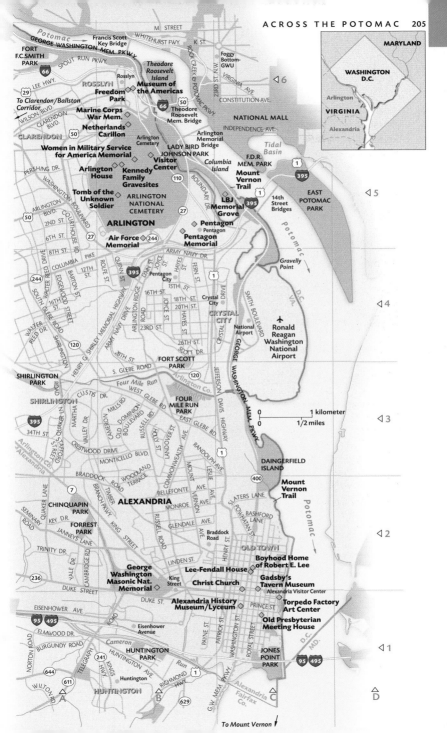

ARLINGTON

Originally part of the area surveyed for the nation's capital, the land on the west bank of the Potomac River was returned to the Commonwealth of Virginia by the U.S. Congress in 1846. Sites with historic resonance abound, along with 86 miles (138 km) of hiking and biking trails.

■ Hundreds of thousands of servicemen and women lie buried beneath Arlington's green expanses.

Arlington National Cemetery

🗺 Map p. 205 B5

✉ 1 Memorial Ave., off Va. 110

☎ 703-607-8000 or 877-907-8585

🕐 Changing of the Guard, every hour Oct.–March, every half hour April–Sept.

💲 $ (parking fee), $$ (tourmobile)

🚇 Metro: Arlington Cemetery

arlingtoncemetery .mil

Arlington National Cemetery

Rows of white headstones on rolling hills, the Changing of the Guard at the Tomb of the Unknowns, the eternal flame at John F. Kennedy's grave: These enduring images immediately bring to mind the nation's most famous national cemetery.

The nearby mansion atop the hill is Arlington House, once the home of Robert E. Lee and his wife, Mary. Lee's father-in-law—George Washington Parke Custis, the first president's adopted grandson—built the Greek Revival mansion in 1802–1817; it anchored a 1,100-acre (445 ha) plantation worked by slaves. Lee

and his wife lived here on and off for 30 years.

Soon after Lee left to fight for the Confederacy in 1861, the federal government confiscated the estate. In 1864, the mansion and 200 acres (91 ha) were set aside for a national cemetery at the urging of Union Quartermaster Gen. Montgomery Meigs. Later that year, his son was killed in the war; a high-relief tomb effigy of him lying slain by the side of the road is one of the cemetery's most distinctive memorials.

Despite the objections of Meigs, Confederate soldiers were allowed burial in the Arlington cemetery, but without any official observances. In 1900

Congress finally designated a Confederate section of the cemetery, and in 1914 the **Confederate Memorial** was dedicated by President Woodrow Wilson.

As for the Lee family's fate, Lee's son, G. W. C. Lee, sued the government after the Civil War for confiscating the land. The Supreme Court ruled that he should be paid the market value, $150,000.

The 639-acre (259 ha) cemetery is now the final resting place for more than 400,000 service people. With 135–150 funerals conducted every week, the cemetery is expected to be filled by 2060, at which time it may expand onto other government-owned land. For burial here, a service person must have died on active duty, retired from active duty service, or been awarded a high military decoration; the cremated remains of any veteran with an honorable discharge can be placed in the Columbarium. For a funeral with full military honors, a flag-draped casket is accompanied by an honor guard. After three rifle volleys, "Taps" is played. The honor guard then presents the folded flag to the next of kin.

Visiting: Entering the cemetery via Memorial Avenue, you'll see the semicircular building of the **Women in Military Service for America Memorial.** Dedicated in 1997, it honors the nearly two million women who have served since 1776. Begin your tour in the **visitor center,** which has exhibits, a 12-minute film, and a map of the cemetery. You can stroll on your own among the quiet, tree-shaded pathways or board a tourmobile, which stops at major points of interest.

From behind the visitor center, head up the pathway to find the **gravesite of President John F. Kennedy.** At his funeral in 1963, his widow, Jacqueline, lit an eternal flame that continues to flicker even in the rain. She and their two infant children also are interred here. The site offers a grand view of familiar monuments across the river in Washington. Nearby, white wooden crosses mark the **graves of Senators Robert F. Kennedy and Edward M. Kennedy.**

INSIDER TIP:

Two presidents are buried at Arlington National Cemetery: William Howard Taft (1930) and John F. Kennedy (1963).

—LARRY PORGES
National Geographic Travel Books editor

The best view of Washington, however, is farther up the hill at **Arlington House.** The Union Army used the house as a defense post headquarters. After the war, the cemetery superintendent lived and worked here for many years. In 1955 it was officially designated the Robert E. Lee Memorial.

Restored to its antebellum appearance, the house looks much as it did during the Lee years. Though many heirlooms in the 15 rooms were looted, about

Arlington House

🏛 Map p. 205 B5
✉ Arlington National Cemetery
☎ 703-235-1530

nps.gov/arho

Arlington Visitor Information

🏛 Map p. 205
✉ Arlington Convention & Visitor Center, 100 N. Glebe Rd., Ste. 1500
☎ 800-677-6267

stayarlington.com

Marine Corps War Memorial

- Map p. 205 B6
- N. Marshall Dr., just N of Arlington Cemetery
- 703-289-2500
- Metro: Arlington Cemetery or Rosslyn

nps.gov/gwmp

a third of the furnishings are original. In the slave quarters and museum out back are exhibits on the Lee and Custis families.

About a half-mile (0.8 km) walk south of the house, adjacent to the amphitheater, the **Tomb of the Unknowns** holds the remains of unidentified servicemen, one each from the two World Wars and Korea (the Vietnam veteran's remains were removed in 1998 when they were identified).

Restaurants & Shops Along Arlington Corridor

This busy commercial and residential area, served by several stops along Metro's Orange Line, has become a popular destination for dining and shopping. **The Clarendon** (2800 Clarendon Blvd., marketcommonclarendon.com) has a walkway that will deliver you to chain stores as well as small shops and coffee hangouts. Close-by restaurants include **Cava Mezze** (2940 Clarendon Blvd., tel 703-276-9090, cavamezze. com), which specializes in Greek small plates, and **Le Pain Quotidien** (2900 N. Clarendon Blvd., tel 703-465-0970, lepainquo tidien.com) for casual munching on quiche and pastry. Another good choice is **Mussel Bar & Grille** (800 N. Glebe Rd., 703-841-2337, musselbar.com) for its plump mussels in creamy sauces from classic white-wine broth to Thai curry.

A 24-hour guard patrols this symbolic site, carrying an M-14 rifle with a ceremonial bayonet. The sentinel takes 21 steps on the plaza (symbolic of a 21-gun salute), then turns to face the tomb for 21 seconds. Among those buried at Arlington are polar explorer Robert Peary, boxer Joe

Louis, 229 sailors from the U.S.S. *Maine* (sunk in Havana harbor in 1898), and the city designer of Washington, Pierre-Charles L'Enfant, whose grave lies in front of the mansion. Another is Gen. John J. Pershing, commander of the American Expeditionary Forces in World War I, who lies buried among those with whom he served. Section 60, one of the cemetery's active burial sections, is the final resting place for almost 7,000 service members killed in Iraq and Afghanistan.

Marine Corps War Memorial

Located a short distance from Arlington National Cemetery, the Marine Corps War Memorial (or Iwo Jima Memorial) depicts an actual event. On February 23, 1945, four days into a vicious struggle for control of Iwo Jima, a detachment of U.S. Marines made it to the top of Mount Suribachi and raised a small American flag. Later that day, after the slopes had been cleared of enemy resistance, five Marines and a Navy hospital corpsmen raised a larger flag—inspiring the iconic image that won news photographer Joseph Rosenthal a Pulitzer Prize. The Marines' capture of the island three weeks later was a key victory in the Pacific campaign. President Eisenhower dedicated the memorial, cast in bronze by sculptor Felix de Weldon, in 1954. On Tuesday evenings in summer, the U.S. Marine Drum and Bugle Corps holds Sunset Parades.

Air Force Memorial

The sleek stainless-steel spires of the Air Force Memorial, completed in 2006, soar skyward from a promontory near the Pentagon. The novel design is by architect James Ingo Freed, who drew his inspiration from the "bomb burst" formation of Air Force jet maneuvers. Three spires—the tallest reaches 270 feet (82 m)—represent the three core values of the Air Force (integrity, service before self, and excellence) and its three divisions (active, guard, and reserve). In granite beneath each spire is the Air Force star.

Pentagon & National 9/11 Pentagon Memorial

No one today can look at this massive headquarters without recalling the tragedy of September 11, 2001, when a hijacked jetliner crashed into the building's south side, now rebuilt. Millions of dollars in donations were collected to construct a memorial park to honor the 184 civilian and military victims of that incident.

The world's largest office building, the 6.5-million-square-foot (603,870 sq m) **Pentagon** was built in just 16 months during World War II to combine the offices of the War Department under one roof. The number five has no particular significance; the building originally conformed to a five-sided site, and since President Roosevelt liked the unique shape, it was kept.

Today the Pentagon is a city unto itself, housing 23,000 military, civilian, and support

■ The Air Force Memorial's three steel spires stretch to the sky.

personnel working to protect national interests. On weekdays, enlisted members from the military services conduct 60-minute tours along more than a mile (1.6 km) of corridors, where military art, model planes, and portraits of military leaders are on display. Out of sight are the top-secret War Room and other situation rooms. Reservations are mandatory for Pentagon tours and should be made online at least two weeks in advance.

The adjacent 2-acre (0.8 ha) **Pentagon Memorial** occupies a site near where American Airlines Flight 77 hit the Pentagon. In an open competition, the winning design for the memorial was submitted by a pair of young architects, Julie Beckman and Keith Kaseman. It features lighted reflecting pools, maple trees, and rows of steel benches—one bench for each of the victims.

Air Force Memorial

⬥ Map p. 205 B5

✉ 1 Air Force Memorial Dr., off the 1400 block of Columbia Pike

☎ 240-612-6464

🚇 Metro: Pentagon or Pentagon City, then a mile (0.6 km) walk

airforcememorial.org

Pentagon & Pentagon Memorial

⬥ Map p. 205 B5

✉ I-395 & Jefferson Davis Hwy. (Va. 110)

☎ 703-697-1776

🕐 Closed Sat.–Sun. & federal holidays

💲 $ (parking fee Pentagon City)

🚇 Metro: Pentagon

pentagontours.osd.mil
pentagonmemorial.org

Theodore Roosevelt Island

- Map p. 205 B6
- Potomac River, 0.25 mile/0.4 km N of Theodore Roosevelt Bridge via George Washington Memorial Pkwy. N (no vehicle access southbound)
- 703-289-2500
- Metro: Rosslyn

nps.gov/this

The 125 benches are arranged so that visitors will see the names of the victims and the Pentagon at the same time; the benches dedicated to the 59 airline passengers are oriented toward the flight path. Each bench bears the name of one victim, organized on an age line (ranging from 3 to 71). A Visitor Education Center and shuttle tour are planned.

The site can be approached from the Pentagon's south parking lot and nearby Metro station or from public parking lots at Pentagon City.

Theodore Roosevelt Island

An arcadia of wooded paths and bird-filled marshes, this 91-acre (37 ha) island opposite the Kennedy Center is a favorite lunchtime retreat for office workers. Some 2.5 miles (4 km) of trails are just right for walking, running, bird-watching, and general relaxing from city stresses.

In 1967, the island was turned into a memorial to the charismatic, conservation-minded U.S. president. Many people heading over the footbridge for a walk

---

INSIDER TIP:

Leave your wheels behind. Neither cars nor bicycles are allowed on Theodore Roosevelt Island, a place of green in the Potomac River.

—JONATHAN TOURTELLOT
National Geographic fellow

---

are surprised to find, tucked in the middle of the woods, a rather grandiose **memorial** featuring a 17-foot-high (5 m) bronze of Roosevelt, fountains, and several enormous granite tablets inscribed with his words.

After a look at the memorial, you can choose between wooded or river-edged paths. One of the most delightful areas is the **boardwalk** through the swamp and marsh on the island's east side. Along here, herons stalk prey among cattails and pickerelweed, while bald cypresses and gnarled oaks suggest a pre-Washington landscape. ∎

An island and statue honor President Theodore Roosevelt.

CRUISING THE GEORGE WASHINGTON MEMORIAL PARKWAY

Offering peerless views of the capital city, this stunning roadway lends the perfect excuse for a leisurely drive. Ambling along the Potomac River between Mount Vernon and the American Legion Bridge, it links historic sites, riverside parks, and overlooks.

Beginning south of Alexandria at **Mount Vernon** (see pp. 224–226), the parkway *(nps .gov/gwmp)* winds north through maples, oaks, beeches, and tulip poplars, chosen when the parkway was designed in the 1930s to give it the look of the Virginia countryside. Two miles (3.2 km) on sprawls **Fort Hunt Park,** preserving batteries that guarded the river approach to the city, 1898–1918. Look across the river to see its mate, **Fort Washington** (1824). Ahead, a right turnoff leads to **River Farm** *(tel 703-768-5700, ahsgardening.org, closed Sun.)*, once part of George Washington's estate. Beyond **Belle Haven Marina** spreads a wide upriver view—birders congregate here. For a closer look, stroll **Dyke Marsh** *(Belle Haven Marina)*, a 240-acre (97 ha) bird haven.

Within **Old Town, Alexandria** (see pp. 214–216), the parkway becomes Washington Street. Two blocks beyond King Street rises **Christ Church** (see pp. 212–213), on the left. Beyond town you'll spot **Daingerfield Island,** site of a small marina and restaurant with a view.

Just north of Ronald Reagan Washington National Airport you'll see the **Washington skyline** and its parade of monuments: the Capitol, Jefferson Memorial, Washington Monument, and Lincoln Memorial. Beyond the 14th Street Bridge rises the **Navy and Marine Memorial.** Farther, you'll pass through the **LBJ Memorial Grove** and **Lady Bird Johnson Park** (see sidebar below). About a quarter mile (0.4 km) beyond Roosevelt Bridge is the turnout for **Theodore Roosevelt Island** (see p. 210). The road passes beneath Key Bridge, with **Georgetown University's** spire looming across the river. The road then climbs above the Potomac. About 1.5 miles (2.4 km) beyond **Turkey Run Park,** the parkway ends at I-495 and the **American Legion Bridge.**

> **INSIDER TIP:**
> Pull off at Gravelly Point in Arlington and watch jetliners take off and land—seemingly just above your head. Ronald Reagan Washington National Airport is that close.
>
> —BARBARA NOE
> *National Geographic Travel Books*
> *senior editor*

Lady Bird's Legacy

Thousands of daffodils, hundreds of red tulips, and groups of golden willows and dogwood trees—that's just part of the plantings at **Lady Bird Johnson Park** *(tel 202-235-1530)*, a 17-acre (7 ha) site on Columbia Island, across the Potomac River from Washington. During her 1960s White House years, the first lady took up the task of beautifying the landscapes of both the nation and its capital (among those efforts was the planting of wildflowers along blighted patches of highway). The nearby memorial to her husband, Lyndon Baines Johnson, is a granite sculpture set in a grove of trees. Access to both parks off the George Washington Parkway is from the southbound lanes only, south of the Arlington Memorial Bridge.

ALEXANDRIA

With its brick sidewalks, federal town houses, and quaint shops and restaurants, Alexandria's Old Town reminds many people of Georgetown. No coincidence here, since both arose as tobacco ports in the mid-1700s, a mere eight river miles (13 km) from one another.

■ Local color: King Street's panoply of shops and restaurants fills centuries-old row houses.

Alexandria

Visitor Information

🗺 Map p. 205 C1

✉ 118 Alexandria Visitor Center 221 King St.

☎ 703-838-5005 or 800-388-9119

visitalexandriava. com

Christ Church

🗺 Map p. 205 C2

✉ 118 N. Washington St.

☎ 703-549-1450

🚇 Metro: King St.– Old Town; Bus: 10A

historicchrist church.org

Scotsman John Alexander, for whom Alexandria is named, purchased much of present-day Alexandria in 1669 from an English ship captain for 6,000 pounds (2,720 kg) of tobacco. Incorporated in 1749, the town thrived as a foreign port of entry. Strolling along Old Town's beautifully preserved wharf today, it's easy to visualize how Alexandria must have looked when tall-masted brigs and schooners docked at the piers, mariners caroused and captains strutted cobbled lanes. Slaves and grain as well as tobacco added to the early prosperity of this genteel Southern town.

The Civil War, however, changed all that. As a buffer for Washington, only 100 miles (160 km) north of

the Confederate capital of Richmond, Alexandria was occupied and soon overrun with Union forces. The fortified town became a crossroads for men and supplies—hundreds of thousands of soldiers tramped through on their way to postings and battles, and train after train rolled in with the wounded. Warehouses, churches, hotels, even large houses were requisitioned for use as military stations and hospitals. After the war, the small-town atmosphere was all but gone. As Washington grew, Alexandria deteriorated. In 1946 the City Council moved to protect the 18th- and 19th-century row houses, making Old Town the nation's third officially designated historic district.

Today, Old Town is a delightful place to stroll (see pp. 214–216). Especially on weekend evenings, crowds pack the restaurants and pubs, enjoying the vibrant nightlife against its historical backdrop.

Christ Church

This historic church has sat behind its iron-gated fence on Washington Street since before Alexandria was established. Completed in 1773 in Georgian country style, it has a brick exterior and whitewashed interior. The Palladian chancel window is unusual for its time.

George Washington was one of the first to buy a pew here, now marked by a silver plaque (No. 60). Tradition says that on the lawn he first declared to friends his intent to fight the war of American independence. Robert E. Lee was confirmed here on July 17, 1853 (marked by another silver plaque, on the chancel), and he worshiped here with his family.

The tree-shaded **burying ground** was used for Alexandrians until 1808; the earliest tombstone is dated March 20, 1791. Look for one of the latest tombstones, for actress Anne Warren. Her 1808 epitaph reads in part: "The unrivaled excellence of theatrical talents was surpassed by the mighty virtues ... which adorned her private life." Docents lead **tours** daily; meet at the church's front door.

Gadsby's Tavern Museum

Consisting of a 1785 tavern and a 1792 hotel, Gadsby's Tavern was colonial Alexandria's center of social, political, and business life. Balls, meetings, performances, and receptions once enlivened its rooms, earning it praise as the finest public house in America. Restored as a museum and restaurant, the tavern appears just as frequent visitor George Washington might have seen it. A 30-minute **guided tour** shows the taproom where patrons dined on whatever fare happened to be served that night—perhaps ham and cheese "pye" or cream of County Surrey peanut soup. You learn that the drink of choice was rum, sometimes mixed with fruit juice and imported sugar. You also see the dining room, ballroom, and assembly room, where local groups met. In the third-floor communal bedchambers, the beds and floors were shared by as many travelers as could fit the space. ■

Gadsby's Tavern Museum

- Map p. 205 C1
- 134 N. Royal St.
- 703-746-4242
- $
- Closed Mon.– Tues. Nov.– March
- Metro: King St.– Old Town; Bus: AT2–AT5

gadsbystavern.org

EXPERIENCE: Follow the Trail to Mount Vernon

Running along the Virginia side of the Potomac River, the **Mount Vernon Trail** (nps.gov/gwmp) extends nearly 18 miles (29 km) from Theodore Roosevelt Island to George Washington's estate. Walkers, joggers, and rollerbladers are a common sight, but there are other activities you can enjoy. Note that electric bikes are not allowed on the trail.

The best plan for biking to Mount Vernon is to start from Old Town Alexandria. Rent a hybrid or mountain bike from **Big Wheel Bikes** (2 Prince St., tel 703-739-2300, bigwheelbikes.com), then head south on the Mount Vernon Trail for 10 miles (16 km; note: It's somewhat hilly, especially as you approach the tail end). When you reach Mount Vernon, you can park your

bike and tour the estate and gardens (see pp. 224–226).

For a vigorous walk and great views of the monuments, start at **Theodore Roosevelt Island** (see p. 210). Travel south along the path to **Gravelly Point;** round-trip, you'll cover about 4 miles (6.4 km).

Gravelly Point Park attracts people straining to film the drama of giant planes landing and taking off at National Airport.

The **Washington Sailing Marina** (tel 703-548-9027, washingtonsailingmarina .com), 1.5 miles (2.4 km) south of the airport, is a favored spot for small sailboat racing. The marina offers weekend sailing lessons, and its waterfront **Triple Craft** restaurant serves up beer, burgers, and shakes.

OLD TOWN BY FOOT

Strolling is the best way to enjoy Old Town's colonial ambience, allowing you plenty of time to study the architectural details of historic row houses, admire postage-stamp gardens, visit historic buildings once frequented by Thomas Jefferson, George Washington, and Robert E. Lee, poke into specialty shops, and simply see what there is to see. The walk outlined here can be done in a couple of hours—more if you linger.

Along the Potomac River: The wharf offers pleasant waterfront views and breezes.

Begin in the heart of the historic core at the two-story, yellow-frame **Ramsay House Visitor Center** ❶ (221 King St., tel 703-838-5005), a reconstruction of the 1724 home of town founder William Ramsay. Across Fairfax Street, **Market Square** holds a Saturday morning market that dates from 1753, making it one of the country's oldest.

From the visitor center, walk south on Fairfax Street. About half a block down on the right, the **Stabler-Leadbeater Apothecary Museum** ❷ (105–107 S. Fairfax St., tel 703-746-3852, closed Mon.–Tues. Nov.–March, $) operated from 1792 to 1933. George Washington, James Monroe, and Robert E. Lee all knew these walls, stocked with all kinds of goods, including medical supplies. Preserved intact, the shop contains original potions, herbs, mortars, and journals.

NOT TO BE MISSED:

Torpedo Factory Art Center • Christ Church • Gadsby's Tavern Museum

Go back to King Street and turn right. On the river, the **Torpedo Factory Art Center** ❸ (105 N. Union St., tel 703-746-4570, torpedofactory.org) holds 80-odd studios where you can watch artisans sculpt, paint, weave, and more. A museum of local archaeological artifacts is on the third floor. Built in 1918, the factory turned out torpedo shell casings and other weaponry for both World Wars (look for the torpedo on the ground floor); the federal government used the building for storage until the city of

Alexandria bought it in 1969. The art center, opened in 1974, was incorporated into a major waterfront development a decade later. Out back, you can stroll along the docks or relax on a bench and enjoy the fresh air.

Walk south on Union and make a right on Prince Street. Known as **Captain's Row,** this cobblestoned block is lined with sturdy federal town houses, many of which were owned by ship captains in the 18th century. Cross Lee Street, and on the right stands the 1851 pink stucco Greek Revival **Athenaeum** (201 Prince St., tel 703-548-0035, nvfaa.org), which once functioned as a bank; with the onset of the Civil War, the bank closed and documents were hidden until after the war, when customers were reimbursed. Now owned by the Northern Virginia Fine Arts Association, the Athenaeum features a contemporary art gallery. A little farther up the block, William Fairfax,

an original trustee of Alexandria, lived at **207 Prince Street,** and next door at **209 Prince** lived Dr. James Craik, the surgeon-general who was with George Washington throughout the Revolutionary War, and who attended him at his death in nearby Mount Vernon.

At Fairfax Street, turn left and head south across Duke Street to the **Old Presbyterian Meeting House** (321 S. Fairfax St., tel 703-549-6670, opmh.org). Built in 1774, the church has an unadorned interior; in the churchyard lies the Tomb of the Unknown Soldier of the American Revolution.

△ See also area map p. 205
🅿 Ramsay House Visitor Center
🕒 3 hours, without stops
⟷ 2 miles (3.2 km)
🅿 Carlyle House

■ **An old church in Alexandria**

Proceed back up Duke Street to Washington Street, the main north-south thoroughfare, and head north. On the street's west side, the Greek Revival–style **Lyceum** *(201 S. Washington St., tel 703-838-4994, alexandriava.gov/Lyceum)*, built in 1839 as a cultural center and library, now houses the **Alexandria History Museum.** Outside, at the intersection of Washington and Prince, stood a bronze statue of a Confederate soldier, "Appotomax," facing south. Considered an insensitive segregation-era relic, it was removed in June 2020. A block north you're back at **King Street,** Old Town's main commercial avenue with a busy assortment of restaurants, bars, and boutiques. Antique shops pack the stretch to the west.

The monument rising on the hill a mile (1.6 km) or so west is the grandiose **George Washington Masonic National Memorial** *(King St. & Callahan Dr., tel 703-683-2007, gwmemorial.org)*, with views of Alexandria and Washington from the ninth-floor observation deck. The guided one-hour tour *($$)* lingers a bit much on Masonic history, but is worthwhile for the collection of Washington memorabilia, including his family Bible and leather field trunk.

Back at Washington and King Streets, the next block north holds historic **Christ Church** ❹ (see pp. 212–213). Three blocks farther north on Washington, the **Lee-Fendall House** ❺ *(614 Oronoco St., tel 703-548-1789, leefendallhouse.org,*

closed Mon.–Tues., $) was built in 1785 by lawyer Philip Fendall, who married an aunt of Robert E. Lee. Family heirlooms on display include portraits, letters, and books.

Across Oronoco Street is the **Boyhood Home of Robert E. Lee** (No. 607), where George Washington once dined and which the Marquis de Lafayette visited. The house is occupied by private owners and is not open to the public.

Head back down Washington and make a left on Cameron. To get a feel for how early Alexandrians dined, stop by the **Gadsby's Tavern Museum** ❻ (see p. 213). Then walk east to Cameron and Fairfax Streets and end your stroll at the Georgian Palladian-style **Carlyle House** *(121 N. Fairfax St., tel 703-549-2997, novaparks.com, closed Mon., $$),* built in 1753 by Scottish merchant John Carlyle. British Gen. Edward Braddock convened a meeting here in 1755 with five colonial governors to discuss the financing of the French and Indian War. Interesting tours showcase the lifestyles of an 18th-century Virginia family and their servants and slaves.

Alexandria—National Harbor by Water Taxi

Go by water from the Old Town, Alexandria, historic waterfront downriver to National Harbor—and vice versa. Water taxis *(potomacriverboatco .com, $$)* make the 20-minute trip (one way) several times a day year-round. Along the Maryland banks of the Potomac, National Harbor *(national harbor.com)* is a mix of hotels, restaurants, and shops, including the Gaylord National Resort and Convention Center. Among the special events along the National Harbor are a summer clambake and Oktoberfest, plus free movies alfresco and live performances by military bands on Saturday and Wednesday evenings.

A wealth of historic sites worth a peek even without the capital city nearby, plus a surprising on-the-water metropolis

EXCURSIONS

Even the grass seems to stand tall at the U.S. Naval Academy in Annapolis.

EXCURSIONS

With riverside parklands and cobble-laned villages, colonial plantations and busy harborfronts nearby, Washington is blessed with an abundance of easy escapes within an hour's drive away.

■ **Kids learn to curtsy at Gunston Hall in Virginia.**

Among the most accessible destinations is the Chesapeake & Ohio National Historical Park, which preserves the ruins of a 19th-century canal and its towpath. Beginning in Georgetown and paralleling the Potomac River for more than 180 miles (290 km) north,

it's especially popular with walkers, bikers, and campers. Great Falls—its most distinctive feature and probably the most spectacular natural attraction between the Blue Ridge and the Chesapeake Bay—is only 5 miles (8 km) beyond the Beltway (I-495). Great Falls Park on the Virginia side of the river is also a popular place to view the falls.

One of the most enriching attractions is the Udvar-Hazy Center, the National Air and Space Museum annex near Washington Dulles International Airport in Northern Virginia. The hangarlike facility houses notable aircraft too large to fit in the downtown museum, including the *Enola Gay* and a supersonic Concord.

You'll find history that goes even further back on the Potomac River south of Washington. More than 250 years ago, Virginia colonists established vast plantations and manor houses, such as Mount Vernon, the home of George Washington, and Gunston Hall. Built by the slaves of early citizens, these historic houses, and the younger Woodlawn, stand today as tributes to the quality workmanship and to the tireless efforts of preservationists.

Annapolis, some 30 miles (48 km) east of D.C. at the point where the Severn River spills into the Chesapeake Bay, is equally well pre-served. The Maryland state capital is a charming, history-steeped, seafood-proud water town. It's easy to fill a day exploring the town's colonial center and admiring the sailboats.

To the north, Baltimore, with its vibrant Inner Harbor, sits on the Patapsco River off the Chesapeake Bay. Boasting a world-class aquarium, stellar museums, and the only Civil War–era vessel still afloat today, this popular, newly revitalized city makes for another good waterside excursion. ■

NOT TO BE MISSED:

Views of the Potomac River from Great Falls Park   221

Jumbo historic aircraft at the National Air & Space Museum's Udvar-Hazy Center   222–223

Touring George Washington's home at Mount Vernon   224–226

Strolling historic Annapolis and eating seafood dockside   230–232

The Walters Art Museum and eerie manta rays at the National Aquarium in Baltimore   233–234

CHESAPEAKE & OHIO CANAL AND GREAT FALLS

Snaking 184.5 miles (297 km) northwest from Georgetown to Cumberland, Maryland, the Chesapeake & Ohio Canal National Historical Park is one of the longest, skinniest parks in the National Park system. The most dramatic section is certainly the Great Falls area, just north of Washington, where the Potomac River hurls over steep, ragged rocks in a spectacular series of thundering falls before flowing through narrow Mather Gorge.

A kayaker hones his technique in the holes and waves below Great Falls.

C & O Canal National Historical Park

🏔 Map p. 219 A5

✉ Georgetown Visitor Center, 1057 Thomas Jefferson St., N.W.

☎ 202-653-5190

✉ Great Falls Tavern Visitor Center, 11710 MacArthur Blvd., Potomac, MD

☎ 301-767-3714

💲 $

nps.gov/choh

President John Quincy Adams broke ground for the C & O Canal on July 4, 1828. It was considered a Great National Project that would link Georgetown in Washington with Pittsburgh on the Ohio River. Plagued with problems from the start, however, including stiff competition by the new Baltimore & Ohio Railroad, the canal only made it as far as Cumberland, Maryland.

Thousands of laborers toiled for 22 years to carve the trench, sometimes out of pure rock. A feat of engineering, its 74 lift locks raise it 605 feet (184 m) in elevation from beginning to end.

Mule-drawn barges hauled coal, hay, fertilizer, and cement from the Appalachian Mountains into Washington until 1924. Today, you can board a mule-powered canal boat in Georgetown and ride through a working lock (April–Oct., $$).

In the early 1950s, Supreme Court Justice William O. Douglas led a movement to preserve the abandoned canal. The C & O was designated a national historical park in 1971.

You can bike or hike the 14-mile (22.5) towpath stretch from Georgetown to Great Falls, a lovely stretch offering pretty river views; or you can drive, via MacArthur Boulevard, to the Great Falls Tavern section of the national historical park. The white stucco building overlooking the canal houses the **visitor center.** Built in 1831, the structure served as a lodge for travelers and boatmen for nearly a century. Exhibits tell about the canal's history.

To see the falls—and perhaps bald eagles—head a short way downstream on the towpath to the trail leading to **Great Falls Overlook.** A combination of boardwalk and bridges, the trail links the two sections of Olmsted Island, ending at roaring Great Falls as it narrows and tumbles 76 feet (23 m) over craggy boulders. Back on the towpath, continue downstream. Before the stop-lock bridge, pick up the **Billy Goat Trail,** a wild, 2-mile (3.2 km) romp over jagged rocks high on the river's edge, along Mather Gorge. In spring, trout lilies, jack-in-the-pulpits, and bluebells sprinkle the forest floor, and goose honks and songbird trills fill the air. Often kayakers play in the rapids below and rock climbers scale the gorge wall. The trail ends farther down the towpath, allowing an easy 1.25-mile (2 km) walk back to the visitor center.

The 4.2-mile (6.7 km) **Gold Mine Loop** behind the visitor center winds through post oaks and river birches to the Maryland Mine. Now in ruins, it operated from 1867 to 1939.

Great Falls Park

On the Virginia side of the falls, a short distance as the crow flies but some 12 miles (19 km) by car, is 800-acre (323 ha) Great Falls Park. Learn about local flora and fauna, kayaking, and rock climbing at the **visitor center.** Nearby overlooks provide fine views of the wide river. The blue-blazed **River Trail** heads downstream for about a mile and a half (2.4 km), edging the bluff above Mather Gorge. Here you'll find the ruins of the **Patowmack Canal,** started by George Washington in 1786 and closed in 1830 after work on the C & O had begun; five locks raised or lowered boats the height of the falls. A 2.2-mile (3.5 km) trail takes you past the ruins of **Matildaville,** a town that served the needs of the canal industry. ■

Great Falls Park

- Map p. 219 A5
- Intersection of Georgetown Pike (Rte. 193) & Old Dominion Dr., Mclean, VA
- 703-757-3101
- $

nps.gov/grfa

EXPERIENCE:
Trekking the C & O Canal Towpath

The C & O Canal towpath, part of the 830-mile-long (1,335 m) Potomac Heritage National Scenic Trail, begins in southern Maryland at the confluence of the Potomac River and Chesapeake Bay, passes though Washington, then extends northwest to Cumberland, Maryland, and on to Pittsburgh, Pennsylvania. Local groups manage sections of the trail. The **Allegheny Trail Alliance** (atatrail.org) has info on hiking and biking. You can plan side trips to attractions such as **Fallingwater** (falling water.org), Frank Lloyd Wright's landmark in southwest Pennsylvania, and **Fort Stevens** (nps.gov/places/fort-stevens.htm), site of the only Civil War battle fought within Washington, D.C.

STEVEN F. UDVAR-HAZY CENTER

This annex of the National Air and Space Museum (see pp. 77–83), located near Washington Dulles International Airport in Northern Virginia, was built to house additional aircraft and space artifacts too large and numerous to fit into the downtown building. But the splendid hangarlike facility, named the **Steven F. Udvar-Hazy Center** for its major donor, hardly plays second string to the more established museum when it comes to attractions.

The Boeing B-29 Superfortress *Enola Gay* targeted the atomic bomb on Hiroshima.

Steven F. Udvar-Hazy Center

✉ 14390 Air & Space Museum Pkwy., Chantilly, VA (S of Dulles Airport's main terminal, near Rtes. 28 & 50)

☎ 703-572-4118

🕐 Closed Christmas Day

💲 Entrance free, parking $$$

airandspace.si.edu/visit/udvar-hazy-center

In 1998, the Smithsonian and the Metropolitan Washington Airports Authority signed a long-term lease for the center's 17-acre (7.1 ha) site, which lies south of Dulles Airport's main terminal, in Chantilly, Virginia. The Steven F. Udvar-Hazy Center opened in December 2003—timed to coincide with the 100th anniversary of the Wright brothers' first powered flight.

The center continues adding to the items on display, which have grown to more than 300 aircraft and large space objects and more than 2,000 smaller artifacts. In

2011, the center opened the huge **Mary Baker Engen Restoration Hangar,** where visitors can witness specialists at work on the restoration and preservation of planes and other flight-related artifacts. Most exciting is the ongoing restoration of a Horten Ho 229 V3, the only extant example of the world's first all-wing jet aircraft, captured in Germany in April 1945.

Visiting: You enter the facility on the second level of the museum. Pick up a map inside the entrance to see the layout of the building, which is arranged according to different types, eras, and uses of flight, such as military, sport, general, and commercial. Begin your tour in the far southwestern corner of the building, with a display on helicopters and vertical flight.

The cavernous **Boeing Aviation Hangar** that makes up the core of the Udvar-Hazy Center rises ten stories high and extends as long as three football fields. The objects are displayed on three levels, with elevated walkways allowing a closer look at suspended aircraft.

Among the featured aircraft are the Boeing B-29 Superfortress *Enola Gay*, which dropped the first atomic bomb; an Air France Concorde, the first supersonic airliner; a sleek, black Lockheed SR-71A Blackbird, the fastest airplane in the world; the Boeing "Dash 80" prototype of the 707, America's first commercial jet airliner; and overhead such warbirds as a Curtiss Warhawk and a Vought F4U Corsair. The World War II German Aircraft gallery is particularly fascinating, with such rarities as a Dornier 335A and a Messerschmitt ME-163 B-1a Komet.

Other interesting objects in this hangar include engines, hang gliders and ultralights, and experimental flying machines. The exhibit on sport aviation, for example, explains how designers of home-built aircraft often used the most advanced ideas in aerodynamics, propulsion, and structures. Displays of aircraft models, aerial cameras, and "balloonamania"—popular culture items from the 18th

century—add further interest.

After you've covered the immense aviation hangar, head to the adjoining building, which houses the **James S. McDonnell Space Hangar.** The centerpiece here is the restored space shuttle *Discovery*. You can also view displays on satellites, missiles, rockets, Mars probe equipment, space capsules, and other equipment used in human space flight, such as the mobile quarantine unit used by the returning crew of the Apollo 11.

Circling back to the entrance area, visit the nearby **observation tower** to watch overhead traffic at Dulles Airport. Also in this area is an **IMAX theater** *(fee)*. Near the main stairs in the aviation hangar, you can climb inside a **simulator** to ride on a variety of history's greatest flying machines—from the Sopwith Camel to the F-5 Tiger—or take a 3-D journey around the International Space Station *(fee)*.

On your way out, take a closer look at the **Wall of Honor,** running along the entryway. The memorial bears the names of hundreds of people who have contributed to aviation and space exploration. ■

POTOMAC RIVER PLANTATIONS

In the 18th and early 19th centuries, landowners built magnificent plantation houses along the Potomac south of present-day Washington, D.C. Three—Mount Vernon, Woodlawn, and Gunston Hall—lie within easy reach of the city. A visit to any one of these mansions, each carefully preserved in period detail, immerses you in the early slave-holding aristocratic life.

■ Washington enlarged Mount Vernon—once a modest 1.5-story farmhouse—to its present size.

Mount Vernon

🅜 Map p. 219 B2

✉ 3200 Mt. Vernon Memorial Highway., Mt. Vernon, VA

☎ 703-780-2000

🚇 Metro: Huntington, then bus

💲 $$$$$

mountvernon.org

Mount Vernon

The stately Georgian-style home of George Washington sits on 500 acres (202 ha) of smartly kept grounds overlooking the Potomac. George Washington moved to Mount Vernon, home of his elder half brother Lawrence, when he was in his teens; he acquired the estate from Lawrence's widow in 1754 at the age of 22. As commander in chief of the Continental forces, Washington rarely saw his home between 1775 and 1783. He then spent the next six years farming, expanding the plantation to nearly 8,000 acres (3,237 ha) and the home to 21 rooms, run by a staff of 10

enslaved butlers, housemaids, waiters, and cooks. After serving as the country's first president (1789–1797), he had only a couple of years left to enjoy his beloved home before his death.

The Mount Vernon Ladies' Association purchased the estate from a Washington relative in 1858 and continues to own and operate it. Both the Confederate and Union Armies considered the estate neutral ground during the Civil War.

Visiting: Today, you could easily spend an entire day here learning about Washington during every stage of his life, through a dizzying array of films, museum displays, tours (including a visit to his nearby distillery; see sidebar p. 227), and interactive programs.

Visitors enter the estate through an **Orientation Center.** Audio-tour equipment is available if you want to get more information while wandering the 45-acre (18 ha) grounds on your own. A 20-minute film depicts pivotal moments in Washington's life as a citizen, soldier, and statesman.

The biggest attraction remains the famous red-roofed mansion and its gardens, pasture, and woodlands. The wood exterior of the mansion looks like stone; sand thrown onto wet paint created this impression. All details of the house's appearance, down to the exact color of the interior, are authentic to the period, and were most recently restored in 2021.

Inside, many of the furnishings are original to the house; others, 18th-century duplicates. Docents are on hand to provide information about each of the rooms. The large two-story green dining room, painstakingly reinterpreted to appear as it did in the Washingtons' lifetime, was used for many different functions; it held chairs and sideboards, but formal tables were installed only when the family entertained. Washington's study sits at the other end of the house. Various personal artifacts displayed here, including a telescope and an 884-volume library, reflect his varied interests.

A small staircase connects the study to the master bedroom on the second floor. This simply decorated bedroom contains the four-poster bed in which Washington died in 1799. After his death, his wife, Martha, could not bear to stay in the room; she moved to another room, on the third floor.

Back on the first floor, before you step onto the piazza, note the framed key hanging on a wall in the passageway. It's the key to the Bastille's west portal, which the Marquis de Lafayette sent to Washington as a gift in 1790. The piazza, looking east over a lawn that dips toward a deer park, offers a grand view of the Potomac River.

On the house's west side,

INSIDER TIP:

At Mount Vernon's reconstructed Blacksmith Shop, you can watch and listen as period-style tools and hardware are handcrafted.

—DIANA PARSELL
National Geographic writer

---

explore the **formal grounds** and **outbuildings.** The smokehouse, kitchen, washhouse, servant's hall, and other buildings suggest how much work it took to run a large, profitable 18th-century estate. Walled upper and lower gardens flank the bowling green.

Circle around the fruit garden and nursery to the iron-gated brick **tomb** that holds the remains of George, Martha, and other members of the family. A nearby

Slave Quarters

Blacksmith Shop

Entrance

Upper Garden

Woodlawn

Map p. 219 B2

9000 Richmond Hwy. (U.S. 1), 3 miles W of Mount Vernon

703-780-4000

Closed Tues.– Thurs. & Dec.– Feb.

$$

woodlawnpope leighey.org

memorial marks the estate's slave burial ground. Downhill is the site of a wharf where George Washington staged the transport of his goods to Alexandria.

Most of Mount Vernon's historic artifacts are now housed in the **Museum and Education Center,** tucked beneath a pasture just inside the main gate, to preserve the estate's pastoral quality. Two dozen galleries, including a 4-D Revolutionary War film offer insight into numerous aspects of Washington's family and professional life. You can see, for example, a scenario of the dinners Washington held every Thursday at 4 p.m. for invited members of Congress and other government officials.

The greatest treasure in the museum is the 1785 terra-cotta bust of Washington that French sculptor J. A. Houdon made from a life mask. The center also has

three life-size figures of Washington—at ages 19, 45, and 57—that were based on forensic research.

On-site dining facilities and shops at Mount Vernon have been expanded. If time allows, visit the re-creation of a 16-side barn and the 4-acre (1.6 ha) demonstration farm that depicts planting and crop experiments.

Woodlawn

George Washington gave Nelly Custis, his step-granddaughter, and Maj. Lawrence Lewis, his nephew, 2,000 acres (809 ha) of his estate in 1799 as their wedding present and asked William Thornton, first architect of the U.S. Capitol, to design a house for them. Thornton completed the late Georgian/ early federal–era two-story mansion in 1805. Typical of the period, the house is arranged symmetrically according to a five-part Palladian plan. There is no "front" or

Mount Vernon Estate & Gardens

Labels on map: Washington's Tomb · Slave Memorial · Wharf · Mansion · Lower Garden · Fruit Garden & Nursery · George Washington Pioneer Farm Site

"back," rather two formal facades for approach by land or river.

The Lewis family and more than 90 slaves lived on the estate for more than 40 years. The family sold the estate in 1846 to a Quaker community, which used the house as a nucleus for their growing abolitionist organization. The National Trust for Historic Preservation acquired the house and some of the land in 1951; the estate now comprises about 120 acres (48.5 ha). The house is furnished much as it was during the Lewises' occupation, although exhibits also give a strong emphasis to the lives of the slaves.

Tours are offered on the hour from noon until 4 p.m. Inside, the refined **first-floor interior** includes a dining room, a family sitting room, and a parlor. The ceilings reach 13.5 feet (4 m) high—the parlor excepted, which is a foot higher, in keeping with the grand proportions of the space. The second floor is divided into four graciously appointed chambers. In honor of its first patron, Woodlawn's **reception area** features a bust of Washington commissioned by Nelly Custis Lewis; it stands on a pedestal at 6 feet 2 inches (188 cm), the general's actual height.

Outside is a **formal garden** with lilacs, azaleas, and roses.

George Washington's Distillery & Gristmill

Washington had the largest distillery in early America, which provided revenue for Mount Vernon. On weekends from April through October, you can watch whiskey-making demonstrations. Adjacent to the distillery is a 1771 water-powered gristmill where cornmeal for use in the distillery was ground and where wheat was ground into flour for export. The site is 3 miles (4.8 km) south of Mount Vernon, on Route 235.

Gunston Hall

🏛 Map p. 219 B1

✉ 10709 Gunston Rd., Mason Neck, VA, 20 miles S of Washington, off I-95 & US 1

☎ 703-550-9220

💲 $$

gunstonhall.org

From the riverside portico you can make out the Potomac, although silting over the past two centuries has pushed the river back. On the eastern horizon, tall trees block your view of Mount Vernon.

Before leaving Woodlawn, you can also walk over to view the 1940 **Pope-Leighey House** (tel 703-780-4000, $$$). This Frank Lloyd Wright–designed house was moved in 1964 from Falls Church, Virginia, to save it from destruction. The low-ceilinged, flat-roofed dwelling is a classic example of Wright's Usonian style.

Gunston Hall

The farthest south of the three plantation houses, Gunston Hall anchors 550 magnificently lush acres (222 ha), with tree-lined lanes,

---

INSIDER TIP:

At Gunston, you can walk a 1-mile [1.6 km] trail through the woods to the river. You might spot deer, herons, and geese along the way.

—DIANA PARSELL
National Geographic writer

---

formal gardens, and farm animals. It was once a 5,500-acre (2,225 ha) tobacco and corn plantation. Its owner was Virginian George Mason (1725–1792), a lesser known but brilliant patriot and statesman.

Mason tried to quit public life after his wife's death in 1773, but the fledgling country would need him in the years ahead. Mason

penned the 1776 Virginia Declaration of Rights, advocating religious tolerance and freedom of the press. Thomas Jefferson picked up, in some cases almost word for word, the same sentiments for the Declaration of Independence. Mason holds distinction as one of three delegates who refused to sign the Constitution in 1787. In passionate orations, he maintained that the Constitution gave the government too much power, a sentiment that helped pave the way for the Bill of Rights.

Begin your tour at the **visitor center,** which holds several interesting exhibits, including assorted family objects; an 11-minute film presents Mason as a paradoxical man. Although an ardent supporter of human rights and intellectually opposed to slavery, Mason had up to 90 slaves and could not reconcile his desire to end slavery with a means to ensure the continued prosperity of his plantation.

In the two-story Georgian **brick house,** designed in 1755 by indentured servant and soon-to-be-prominent architect William Buckland, each room has its own distinctive style. The Chinese-style formal parlor and the neoclassic, Palladian-style dining room, with arches and painstaking embellishments, are works of art.

The **grounds** include a reconstructed kitchen yard where slaves toiled, plus a slave dwelling and the family cemetery, while the gardens feature a boxwood allée that runs between formal plantings to a hilltop with a view of the distant Potomac River. ∎

ANNAPOLIS

Yachts, midshipmen in crisp uniforms, streets lined with colonial architecture, and restaurants serving world-famous crab cakes: The colorful port of Annapolis, less than an hour's drive east of Washington, offers big-time history in a small-town setting.

Ego Alley in the heart of Annapolis is the place to show off your boat.

Puritans escaping persecution first settled at the strategic mouth of the Severn River, just off the Chesapeake Bay, in 1649. Named the Capital of the Proprietary of Maryland in 1694, the settlement grew to become one of the Colonies' most sophisticated towns by the eve of the American Revolution. As bales of tobacco flowed out of its port, in flowed European luxuries to adorn beautiful Georgian homes and their elegant inhabitants.

Annapolis's political high point occurred between November 1783 and August 1784, when it served as the fledgling nation's working capital. After the capital was moved to Trenton, New Jersey, in 1784, however, the city dozed for two centuries. The U.S. Naval Academy came in 1845, turning Annapolis into a sort of company town that catered to its guest institution. In the 1960s, interest in historic preservation brought about new life, as taverns, shops, restaurants, and museums moved into restored structures.

Today, Annapolis showcases more than a dozen architectural styles spanning three centuries; some 1,300 buildings—all meticulously maintained—predate 1900. Much of the small city's charm owes to the fact that it preserves its 1695 radial street plan, which gives the highest elevations to the church (St. Anne's) and state (State House)—and offers many vistas of the picturesque waterfront. ∎

Annapolis

Map p. 219 E4

Visitor Information

✉ Annapolis & Anne Arundel County Conference & Visitors Bureau, 26 West St.; seasonal information booth at City Dock

☎ 410-280-0445

🚎 Free downtown Circulator trolley; inquire at visitors bureau

visitannapolis.org

WALKING AROUND ANNAPOLIS

The narrow streets and brick sidewalks in the historic center of Annapolis will enchant you. Plan to spend at least half a day strolling around and visiting its sights. With limited street parking available, your best bet is to leave your car in one of the garages near the visitor center.

The Maryland State House (1779) anchors the city's captivating downtown.

Start your stroll at the friendly, information-packed **visitor center** ❶ *(Annapolis & Anne Arundel County Conference & Visitors Bureau, 26 West St., tel 410-280-0445)*. Just to the east, Church Circle features the Romanesque **St. Anne's Episcopal Church** ❷ *(tel 410-267-9333, stannes-annapolis.org)*, built in 1858–1859. The church still has the communion silver set sent by King William III in 1696. Standing at the intersection of Church Circle and Main Street, the venerable 1772 **Maryland Inn** *(tel 410-263-2641, historicinnsofannapolis.com)* features wood balconies and an award-winning restaurant, the Treaty of Paris.

Proceed six blocks down Main Street, attractively lined with two-story brick and wood buildings harboring boutiques, restaurants, galleries, and bars. At the end of the street is the **Historic Anapolis Museum** ❸ *(99 Main*

> ## NOT TO BE MISSED:
>
> **City Dock • U.S. Naval Academy Chapel • Hammond-Harwood House**

St., tel 410-267-7619, annapolis.org), occupying a redbrick house built in 1790 for German immigrant Frederick Grammar. In 1960, it became the first building restored on the waterfront. After another lengthy restoration, it reopened as a history museum in 2021.

The museum fronts Market Space and its busy waterfront, the **City Dock** ❹. This heart of the town bustles with cafés, shops, and restaurants. The number of yachts moored here attests to Annapolis's standing as one of the East Coast's great sailing centers. Stop by

To Baltimore, 25 miles

450

College Creek

Severn

BOWYER ROAD
RAMSAY RD.

ROSCOE C. ROWE BLVD.

KING GEORGE STREET

UPSHUR ROAD

MC NAIR RD.

DECATUR ROAD

PARKER ROAD

HOLLOWAY ROAD

BALCH ROAD

ST. JOHN'S COLLEGE

WAGNER ST.

Preble Hall, U.S. Naval Academy Museum

U.S. NAVAL ACADEMY **6**

COOPER ROAD

U.S. Naval Academy Chapel

Bancroft Hall

NORTHWEST ST.

CALVERT ST.

ST. JOHN'S STREET

BLADEN ST.

COLLEGE AVE.

NORTH ST.

Chase-Lloyd House
Hammond-Harwood House **7**

MARYLAND AVE.

HANOVER ST.

KING GEORGE

BUCHANAN ST.

PORTER ROAD

BRONSON RD.

Annapolis & Anne Arundel County Conference & Visitors Bureau **1**

St. Anne's Episcopal Church **2**

Maryland State House **8**

William Paca House and Garden

Old Treasury Building

EAST ST.

Gate

WEST ST.

CHURCH CIR.

SCHOOL ST.

STATE CIR.

PINKNEY ST.

Shiplap House **5**

Waterfront Warehouse

START

CATHEDRAL STREET

Maryland Inn

DUKE OF GLOUCESTER ST.

CORNHILL ST.

MAIN STREET

Market House

Middleton Tavern

Halsey Field House

Historic Annapolis Museum **3**

PRINCE GEORGE STREET

Ricketts Hall, U.S. Naval Academy Visitor Center

City Gate Ln.

SHAW STREET

MURRAY AVE.

SOUTH ST.

CHARLES STREET

STREET

UNION ST.

GREEN ST.

NEWMAN ST.

ST. MARY'S STREET

COMPROMISE STREET

City Dock **4**

FRANKLIN ST.

CONDUIT ST.

MARKET ST.

REVELL ST.

SHIPWRIGHT STREET

SOUTHGATE AVE.

TANEY AVE.

CHESTON AVE.

PRESIDENT PT. DR.

LOCKWOOD CT.

Spa Creek

Drawbridge

SEVERN AVENUE

5TH ST.

4TH ST.

3RD ST.

0 ———— 200 meters
0 ———— 200 yards

---

the dockside **Market House** for a sandwich and join a life-size bronze of *Roots* author Alex Haley by the water's edge, where he sits telling a story to a group of children on the same spot where his ancestor, Kunta Kinte, arrived in 1767 on a slave ship. For another dining option, head across Market Space to **Middleton Tavern** *(tel 410-263-3323, middletontavern.com)*, a cozy place dating from 1750 that welcomed the likes of George Washington, Thomas Jefferson, and Benjamin Franklin.

Just up Pinkney Street, step into the

🅰	See also area map p. 219
🅿	Visitor center
🕒	4 hours
🗓	1.8 miles (2.9 km)
🅿	Maryland State House

Waterfront Warehouse (ca 1815) to see the scale model of the waterfront as it was in the 1700s. A few doors up, **Shiplap House 5** *(18 Pinkney St.)* dates from 1715. Now go back down Pinkney and turn left on Randall; in

Sandy Point State Park

For a change from the cobblestones of Annapolis, drive to this Chesapeake Bay park *(9 miles/14.4 km E of Annapolis on U.S. 50, tel 410-974-2149, $)*. The sandy beach is great for swimming, as well as for views of the Bay Bridge. You can rent rowboats and motorboats, and 5 miles (8 km) of trails wind through woods and marshes.

two blocks turn right for the gates to the **U.S. Naval Academy** ❻ *(usna.edu, tours available by reservation)* and follow signs to the visitor center. Established in 1845, the academy is now a 338-acre (136 ha), four-year coed college. Flanking the tree-dotted central green to the southeast is the enormous beaux arts **Bancroft Hall,** one of the world's largest dormitories. The nearby copper-domed **U.S. Naval Academy Chapel** features a long, shiplike nave; don't miss the lavishly displayed marble tomb of Revolutionary War naval hero John Paul Jones in the crypt. Just to the northwest, Preble Hall houses the **U.S. Naval Academy Museum**, containing one of the world's finest collections of model warships, plus uniforms, armaments, ship's instruments, captured foreign flags, and more than 1,200 paintings.

Back at the gate turn northwest on King George Street, then southwest on Maryland Avenue. The 1774–1775 **Hammond-Harwood House** ❼ *(19 Maryland Ave., tel 410-263-4683, hammondharwoodhouse.org, closed Mon., closed Tues., $$)* is on the left. This national historic landmark house, considered by many to be the finest example of Georgian architecture in colonial America, was the last project of architect William Buckland, once an indentured servant, who also designed Gunston Hall (see p. 228). Continue down Maryland Avenue to Prince George Street and turn left to the Georgian **William Paca House and Garden** *(186 Prince George St., tel 410-267-7619, annapolis.org, $$),* built in 1765. Paca was a signer of the Declaration of Independence and a three-term governor of Maryland. The house and gardens have been meticulously restored to their colonial glory.

A block west on East Street is State Circle, where the Old Treasury Building and the **Maryland State House** ❽ *(State Circle, tel 410-946-5400, msa.md.gov)* sit. Completed in 1779, the state house is the nation's oldest continuously used capitol building. Two events of importance took place in its old Senate Chamber during the nine months when Annapolis served as the new country's working capital: George Washington resigned his commission as commander in chief of the Continental Army on December 23, 1783, and, three weeks later, Congress ratified the Treaty of Paris, ending the Revolutionary War.

The U.S. Naval Academy Band stays crisply in line—and in tune.

BALTIMORE

Only 40 miles (64 km) north of Washington, Baltimore would appear to have very little in common with the District. Baltimore's brick buildings, puffing factories, older ethnic neighborhoods, and heavy ship traffic give it more of a "real city" feel. But it also has its share of world-class museums, and the city's Inner Harbor, a showcase of urban revitalization, ranks as one of the East Coast's top travel destinations.

■ The Inner Harbor has led Baltimore into the limelight of urban revitalization.

Strategically placed at the mouth of the Patapsco River at Chesapeake Bay, the Inner Harbor has long been a major port for coal and grain. Also considered an urban eyesore, it was targeted for demolition and renewal as far back as 1963. Buildings began coming down in the late 1960s, and the first skyscrapers appeared in the early '70s. Restaurants, tourist attractions, and Oriole Park at Camden Yards followed thereafter, contributing to the harbor's vitality.

Today, a promenade lined with shops and restaurants edges the waterfront and offers a delightful stroll past the harbor's various museums. Water taxis will ferry you from sight to sight if you'd rather ride than walk.

On the harbor's north side, at Pier 3, the seven-story **National Aquarium** is Baltimore's biggest visitor draw. Inside, exhibitions span distinct aquatic habitats, from an Amazon rain forest to an Atlantic coral reef teeming with colorful fish, while sharks and rays glide through "Shark Alley." The aquarium's bottlenose dolphins were relocated to a Caribbean sanctuary in 2022.

The submarine U.S.S. *Torsk* and the lightship *Chesapeake* are moored alongside the aquarium. They, along with the Coast Guard cutter *Taney* and Seven Foot Knoll Lighthouse on Pier 5, form the **Historic Ships in Baltimore Maritime Museum** (*tel 410-539-1797, historicships.org, $$$*). The last Civil War–era vessel still afloat, the **U.S.S. Constellation** is

Baltimore
⊠ Map p. 219 D6

Visitor Information

✉ Baltimore Visitor Center, 401 Light St.

☎ 877-225-8466

baltimore.org

National Aquarium
✉ 501 Pratt St.
☎ 410-576-3800
$ $$$$$

aqua.org

Baltimore Museum of Art

 10 Art Museum Dr.

☎ 443-573-1700

🕐 Closed Mon.–Tues.

artbma.org

Walters Art Museum

 600 N. Charles St.

☎ 410-547-9000

🕐 Closed Mon.–Tues.

thewalters.org

Fort McHenry National Monument and Historic Shrine

 2400 East Fort Ave.

☎ 410-962-4290

💲 $$

nps.gov/fomc

moored at Pier 1. Climb aboard to learn about her past. Launched in 1854, she has caught slave traders off the coast of Africa, blockaded ports during the Civil War, and acted as a relief flagship of the U.S. Atlantic Fleet in World War II.

Walk past the cruise ship docks toward the harbor's south side and the **Maryland Science Center** *(601 Light St., tel 410-685-5225, mdsci.org, $$$),* which has exhibits, an IMAX theater, and a planetarium.

Located inland, on the harbor's north side, is the interactive **Port Discovery** *(35 Market Pl., tel 410-727-8120, portdiscovery.org, closed Mon.–Tues., $$$),* catering to kids with interactive exhibits and activities.

INSIDER TIP:

The Baltimore-based Morgan State University Choir [msuchoir.org] has performed as far afield as China. A hometown concert is a treat.

—SHEILA BUCKMASTER
National Geographic Traveler magazine editor at large

Impressionism lovers will not want to miss the Cone Collection—works by Matisse, Picasso, and others—on display at the **Baltimore Museum of Art,** which also has a sculpture garden. The **Walters Art Museum** offers a broad look at more than 55 centuries of art, including Roman sarcophagi, Asian ceramics, Old Master paintings, and art deco jewelry.

Fort McHenry sits southeast of the harbor. During the War of 1812, as American forces valiantly defended the fort against the British, a young lawyer named Francis Scott Key felt inspired to pen some words as he saw its flag still waving in the early dawn light. A tour of the monument to American freedom is not easily forgotten.

The heart of Baltimore is its historic **Charles Street district.** A stroll down the 12-mile (19 km) strip will take you past Mount Vernon Place, where you can check out Baltimore's Washington Monument (it predates the one in Washington) and climb 228 steps to the top for a great view of the city. Window-shop for collectibles before choosing among the restaurants that serve up crab cakes, steamed shrimp, and oysters.

Also worth a trip: the **B & O Railroad Museum** *(901 West Pratt St., tel 410-752-2490, borail.org, $$$$).* Its locomotive and rolling stock collection dates from 1830 to the present, while its small object collection includes pocket watches, lanterns, and dining car china. For a perspective on the struggles, accomplishments, and culture of African-American Marylanders, visit the **Reginald F. Lewis Museum** *(830 E. Pratt St., tel 443-263-1800, lewismuseum.org, closed Tue.–Wed.),* two blocks from the Inner Harbor.

At the end of the day, consider a jaunt to **Fells Point,** where the city took root in the early 1700s. Located east of the Inner Harbor, a short cab ride away, this waterfront district's brick row houses, congenial pubs, and snug restaurants have an enduring charm. ∎

TRAVELWISE

Eero Saarinen designed the Dulles International Airport terminal.

TRAVELWISE

PLANNING YOUR TRIP
When to Go
Climate

Until well into the 20th century, Washington was, because of its reputation for heat and humidity (plus the mosquitos that thrive in these conditions), classified as a hardship post for British diplomats. It is true that July and August in the capital are frequently hot and steamy, but Washington has relatively brief winters and often long and lovely springs and falls. Rain is fairly evenly divided throughout the year (an average of 3.31 inches/8.4 cm per month), except for afternoon thundershowers in June, July, and August.

The busy season for tourism starts in April with spring school vacation, when busloads of schoolchildren from all over visit the museums, monuments, and U.S. Capitol. Spring is also the time of the annual cherry blossoms display around the Tidal Basin; when the blossoms are at their peak, the area around the monuments is packed. Summer, of course, is family vacation time.

The average high and low temperatures are as follows:

January—44°F/30°F
February—46°F/29°F
March—54°F/36°F
April—66°F/46°F
May—76°F/56°F
June—83°F/65°F
July—87°F/69°F
August—85°F/68°F
September—79°F/61°F
October—68°F/50°F
November—57°F/39°F
December—46°F/32°F

What to Bring

Heavy winter coats are usually essential only in December, January, and February, but a light coat or jacket can come in handy in the cooler spring or fall months. Government buildings and museums have miles of corridors with marble floors, and there's lots of great city walking, so comfortable shoes are a must.

HOW TO GET TO WASHINGTON, D.C.
By Plane

Washington is served by three major airports: Ronald Reagan Washington National Airport (DCA) in Virginia, about 4 miles (6.4 km) from the city center; Washington Dulles International Airport (IAD), 26 miles (42 km) west of Washington; and Baltimore/Washington International Thurgood Marshall Airport (BWI), 25 miles (40 km) northeast of Washington. All three airports are served by SuperShuttle *(tel 800-258-3826, supershuttle.com)*.

Ronald Reagan Washington National Airport is the closest airport to the city and also the most convenient: Washington's Metro system has a station right there. Taxi fare to downtown Washington is about $20.

Dulles International Airport is served by its own Washington Flyer Taxi Service *(tel 703-572-8294, washfly.com)*, with 24-hour service to and from the airport. Taxi fare to downtown Washington is about $60. The Metro Silver Line extension from downtown D.C. to Dulles opened in early 2022 *(wmata.com)*. The best way to get to and from BWI Airport is by SuperShuttle or train. Both MARC's Penn Line *(tel*

410-539-5000) and Amtrak *(tel 800-872-7245)* provide frequent service between Union Station in downtown Washington and BWI's own rail station; a free shuttlebus connects the rail station and the airport terminal.

Airport Information

For general airport information: Reagan National *(tel 703-417-8000, flyreagan.com)*, Dulles *(tel 703-572-2700 , flydulles.com)*, and BWI *(tel 800-435-9294, bwiairport. com)*.

Airlines

The Washington, D.C., metropolitan area is served by the following non-stop:
Aer Lingus 800-474-7424, aerlingus.com
Aeroflot 866-879-7647, aeroflot.ru/cms/en
Air Canada 888-247-2262, aircanada.com
Air China 800-882-8122, airchina.us
Air France 800-237-2747, airfrance.com
Air India 888-634-1407, airindia.in
Alaska Airlines 800-252-7522, alaskaair.com
American Airlines 800-433-7300, aa.com
ANA 800-235-9262, ana.co.jp
Austrian 800-843-0002, austrian.com
Avianca 800-284-2622, avianca.com
British Airways 800-247-9297, britishairways.com
Brussels Airlines 866-308-2230, brusselsairlines.com
Copa Airlines 844-287-0304 copaair.com
Delta Air Lines 800-221-1212, delta.com

Egyptair 800-334-6787,
egyptair.com

Emirates 800-777-3999,
emirates.com

Ethiopian 833-923-2689,
ethiopianairlines.com

Etihad Airways 877-923-0767,
flights.etihad.com

Frontier Airlines 801-401-9000,
flyfrontier.com

Icelandair 800-223-5500,
icelandair.com

JetBlue Airways 800-538-2583,
jetblue.com

KLM 866-434-0320,
klm.com

Korean Air 800-438-5000,
koreanair.com

Lufthansa 800-645-3880,
lufthansa.com

Porter 888-619-8622,
flyporter.com

Qatar Airways 877-777-2827,
qatarairways.com

Royal Air Maroc 800-344-6726,
royalairmaroc.com

SAS 800-221-2350,
flysas.com

Saudia 800-472-8342,
saudiairlines.com

Southwest Airlines 800-435-
9792, southwest.com

TAP Air Portugal 800-221-7370,.
flytap.com

Turkish Airlines 800-874-8875,
turkishairlines.com

United Airlines 800-864-8331,
united.com

Virgin Atlantic 800-862-8621,
virgin-atlantic.com

Volaris 855-865-2747, volaris.com

By Train

Amtrak (tel 800-872-7245,
amtrak.com) trains arrive at
Washington's Union Station on
Capitol Hill.

Although locals use the train
mostly as a fast, convenient way
to get to New York on the Acela
and Northeast Regional trains,
Washington is a major rail hub,
and it is connected by train to
most U.S. destinations with rail

service. The Metro station at
Union Station provides easy access
to the rest of the city and beyond.

GETTING AROUND

By Metro

The Washington Metropolitan
Area Transit Authority operates
the bus and subway systems in
the metropolitan area. Metrorail
stations are marked by large
columns with brown "M" signs.

The clean and efficient rail
network makes it very easy to get
around the region, but mainte-
nance and repairs required means
there may be occasional delays or
outages on some sections of the
system. In such cases bus transfer
between stations is usually available. Metro posts regular updates
about routes, fares, and operating
status (tel 202-637-7000, wmata.
com). Most suburban stations have
lots for all-day parking, but go
early because they fill up fast.

Metro farecards are purchased
at vending machines in the stations or online. Fares range from
roughly $2 to $6 one way, based on
distance and time of day. (Plastic
SmarTrip cards, for extended travel
and easy bus transfer, are also available at CVS pharmacy locations in
the D.C. area.) Fare information is
available near the ticket machines.

Metrorail operates Monday
to Thursday 5 a.m. to 11:30 p.m.,
Friday 5 a.m.–1 a.m., Saturday 7
a.m.–1 a.m., and Sunday 8 a.m.-
11 p.m.

By Bus

Metrobus (tel 202-637-7000,
wmata.com) service covers the
city and the suburbs, with some
lines running 24 hours. The fare
for any destination within Washington is $2 or $7.50 for express
service. Exact fare is required.
For just $1 per ride, the DC
Circulator bus service operates
daily in central Washington, with

frequent stops. The five routes
extend from Dupont Circle to
Rosslyn; Georgetown to Union
Station; Union Station to Navy
Yard; Woodley Park to McPherson Square; and Potomac Ave.
to Skyland. Visit dccirculator.com
for route schedules and maps.

By Taxicab

Cabs in Washington are plentiful
and fairly inexpensive. It's usually
possible to hail a cab on a major
street. They run on a meter system, and there are surcharges for
each extra passenger, rush hour,
and baggage. Information on surcharges is posted in every cab.

By Bicycle

In 2008, the District of Columbia became the first jurisdiction
in North America to launch a
bikesharing system. Capital Bikeshare (capitalbikeshare.com) has
grown exponentially since then,
with more than 4,300 bikes offered at 500 stations throughout
the District and in Arlington,
Alexandria, and Montgomery
County. The distinctive bright-
red bikes can be found at most
Metro stations and at convenient locations downtown and
along the National Mall. Regular
users can buy a daily, monthly, or
annual membership online, while
visitors can use a credit card at
any Bikeshare station kiosk to
purchase a 24-hour pass for $8
or a 3-day pass for $17.

By Car

Visitors should consider the
possibility that a car will be more
of an annoyance than a convenience. Parking is difficult, and
parking garages are expensive.

Should you find on-street
parking, check the signs, since
many streets become no parking
zones during rush hour. If your car
is not where you left it, call 202-

541-6083 for information on its location.

Some streets are two-way most of the time, but during rush hour become one way—including Rock Creek and Potomac Parkway and 17th Street, N.W.

Car Rentals

Washington's airports are served by the following national car rental companies:
Alamo 844-648-1605, alamo.com
Avis 800-331-1212, avis.com
Budget 800-218-7992, budget.com
Dollar 800-800-4000, dollar.com
Enterprise 844-648-1602, enterprise.com
Hertz 800-654-3131, hertz.com
National 844-648-1604, nationalcar.com
Sixt 888-749-8227
Thrifty 800-541-7044, thrifty.com

Negotiating the City

When seeking a site, first check the quadrant address, which indicates where it lies vis-à-vis the Capitol. Are you looking for N.W., N.E., S.W., or S.E.? The city is laid out in these four quadrants, with the Capitol Building in the center. North Capitol, South Capitol, and East Capitol Streets radiate from this nucleus, separating the quadrants (the Mall runs west from the Capitol Building).

Be advised that many District addresses can be found in more than one quadrant (for instance, there is a 400 M St. in N.E., S.E., S.W., and N.W.—four different D.C. locations).

After locating the quadrant, note that there are three types of streets in Washington. First are the numbered streets—those that run in a north-south direction from the Capitol. First Street, for instance, is located one block east or west of North or South Capitol Street, respectively.

The second street type is the lettered or named streets laid out in an east-west direction. Starting from East Capitol Street or the Mall, the streets run through the alphabet (with the exceptions of J, X, Y, and Z). The ones nearest the Capitol are one-syllable words; when the alphabet has been run through, they become two syllables, then three. As such, you can tell how far a certain street is from the Capitol by the letter with which it begins and how many syllables it contains.

Finally, the avenues that are named after states run diagonally across the grid.

PRACTICAL ADVICE
Communications
Newspapers

Washington, D.C., is a city of news. Most national and international news agencies have Washington bureaus. The Washington-based daily newspapers are the *Washington Post* (washingtonpost.com) and the *Washington Times* (washingtontimes.com). For upcoming local events, check the Weekend section of the *Washington Post,* published on Fridays. Also of interest is the free weekly publication, the *Washington City Paper* (washingtoncitypaper. com), published on Thursdays. It provides an up-to-date listing of what's happening in the clubs and theaters around town.

Radio

WMAL (FM 105.9)
Talk shows and breaking news
wmal.com

WTOP (FM 103.5)
News and all-talk format
wtop.com

WAMU (FM 88.5)
Public radio programming
wamu.org

WPFW (FM 89.3)
Community issues, jazz
wpfw.org

WCSP (FM 90.1)
C-SPAN and public affairs
c-span.org

WETA (FM 90.9)
Classical music
weta.org

WKYS "Kiss" (FM 93.9)
Urban, hip hop
kysdc.com

WIAD "Drive" (FM 94.7)
Classic hits
audacy.com/947thedrive

WPGC (FM 95.5)
Hip hop, R&B.
audacy.com/wpgc

WHUR (FM 96.3)
Urban contemporary, black culture
whur.com

WASH (FM 97.1)
Soft-rock, classics
washfm.com

WMZQ (FM 98.7)
Country music
wmzqfm.com

WIHT "Hot" (FM 99.5)
Contemporary hits
hot995.com

WBIG (FM 100.3)
Classic rock
wbig.com

WWDC (FM 101.1)
Rock
dc101.com

WRXQ (FM 100.7)
Classic rock
wrxq.com

WMMJ "Majic" (FM 102.3)
R&B and urban oldies
mymajicdc.com

WKIK (FM 102.9)
Country music
country1029wkik.com

WWRC (AM 1260)
Progressive
am570theanswer.com

Telephone
Local and long-distance
information, 411
Toll-free directory information,
800-373-3411

The area code for Washington,
D.C., is 202; for Maryland, 240,
301, 410, 443, and 667; and for
Northern Virginia, 703 and 571.
You must dial the area code with
the number, even for local calls.
The prevalence of cell
phones has limited the availabil-
ity of public telephones; some
are available in public areas,
such as Metro stations. Local
calls cost 50 cents.

Crime
Crimes of all sorts have been
on the decrease in the last two
decades in Washington, but
precautions are advised.
Don't wander onto deserted
or ill-lighted streets or parks, particularly at night. If you're uncom-
fortable in a neighborhood, leave.
Stay with the crowds. There's
safety in numbers.
If someone tries to rob you,
give the robber whatever he or
she asks. Your life is more valuable
than your belongings.
Keep your wallet in a front
trouser pocket—less vulnerable to
pickpockets than rear pockets or
breast pockets.
Women should keep their purs-
es close—especially in restaurants.
Don't carry large amounts of cash.
Leave credit cards you don't
plan to use at home. Don't leave
valuables in your car. The trunk is
more secure than the space under
the seats.

Money Matters
Banks and automatic teller
machines (ATMs) are located
throughout the city, and most
major attractions and shopping
centers also have them.
Check with your home bank
to find out which system accepts
your card. Credit cards, debit
cards, and traveler's checks are
accepted almost everywhere;
make sure you have an official
I.D. with you as some places
require it before you can make a
transaction.

ATM Locations
MasterCard/Cirrus,
800-424-7787
Visa/Plus, visa.com/atmlocator

National Holidays
New Year's Day
Martin Luther King, Jr., Day
(3rd Mon. in Jan.)
President's Day
(3rd Mon. in Feb.)
Washington's birthday
(3rd Mon. in Feb.)
Easter Sunday
Memorial Day
(last Mon. in May)
Emancipation Day
(19th June)
Fourth of July
Labor Day
(1st Mon. in Sept.)
Columbus Day
(2nd Mon. in Oct.)
Thanksgiving Day
(4th Thurs. in Nov.)
Christmas Day

Sales Tax
Taxes will increase the cost of
your purchased goods by 6
percent, your hotel bill by 19.5
percent, your restaurant bill by
10 percent, and your rental car
bill by 10.25 percent.

Security
Security has become a major
issue in many places worldwide,
but is especially a concern in
and around Washington's public
areas and government buildings.
Streets are sometimes closed
down with or without notice,
and may be blocked off by
concrete barriers.
Government buildings are
generally open to the public, but
they may close for security reasons with little or no notice.
Be flexible, and call ahead.
Following the deadly storm-
ing of the Capitol by supporters
of President Trump on January
6, 2021, additional security mea-
sures, including a perimeter fence,
were put in place. However, a
new security fence and barricades
installed around the White House
at Trump's request in 2019 were
removed in July 2021.
Metal detectors are standard
equipment in most public
buildings. Be prepared to have
your belongings scanned and
searched. If you have a pace-
maker or other medical device
that might be affected, let the
guards know. And do not carry
anything that could be considered a weapon and might be confiscated—for example, Grandpa's
pocketknife.

Tipping
A standard tip is 15 percent
of the bill at restaurants. Taxi
drivers should receive 10 to
15 percent, bartenders 10
percent, hairdressers 15 percent,
porters at least a dollar a bag,
valet parking attendees
$2 or more, and doormen
a couple of dollars every
time they whistle you a cab.
Tip the hotel concierge or
restaurant maître d' at your
discretion, depending upon
services performed.

Air-conditioning Indoor Pool Outdoor Pool Health Club Wi-Fi Credit Cards

Travelers With Disabilities

D.C. is a very accessible place for travelers with disabilities.

The Washington Metropolitan Area Transit Authority also publishes a free pamphlet on Metro's bus and rail system accessibility for the elderly and physically disabled. It also offers door-to-door transit service called MetroAccess for the disabled. Call 202-962-1100 to order the guide, or download it on Metro's website at wmata.com.

Smithsonian museum buildings are accessible to wheelchair visitors. Find detailed information online at si.edu or call 202-633-2921.

Visitor Information

The best source of visitor information is Destination D.C. (washington.org), Washington's official tourism site. It publishes a free visitors guide twice a year with comprehensive listings of attractions and events. Order it or download it online.

EMERGENCIES

Health Care
Useful Numbers

- Emergencies (police/fire/ambulance), 911
- Washington, D.C., Police (non-emergency), 311
- Metro Transit Police (emergency), 202-962-2121
- U.S. Park Police (emergency), 202-610-7500
- Travelers Aid, 202-546-1127
- International Visitors Information Desk (offers multilingual information and assistance; located at Dulles), 703-572-2536

Lost Credit Cards

American Express, 800-867-5523
Diners Club, 800-234-6377
Discover Card, 800-347-2683
MasterCard, 800-627-8372
Visa, 800-847-2911

ANNUAL EVENTS

January

Martin Luther King, Jr.'s Birthday Mid-January. Lincoln Memorial *(tel 202-619-7222, mlkholidaydc.org)*. Birthday parade includes wreath-laying at the Martin Luther King, Jr. National Memorial and at the Lincoln Memorial, where King delivered his "I Have a Dream" speech on August 28, 1963.

Presidential Inauguration January 20, every fourth year. After the swearing-in on the Capitol steps, a parade follows down Pennsylvania Avenue to the White House.

Washington Auto Show Late January. In the Convention Center *(washingtonautoshow.com)*. Consumers get a chance to ogle more than 500 new models from car manufacturers worldwide.

February

Chinese New Year Parade Late January or early February, depending on the moon. Chinatown, H St., N.W. *(bet. 5th & 8th Sts., dcparade.com)*. Colorful parade with firecrackers, drums, and traditional dragon dancers.

Abraham Lincoln's Birthday February 12. Lincoln Memorial *(tel 202-619-7222)*. A reading of the Gettysburg Address and a wreath-laying at the memorial.

George Washington's Birthday February 22. Wreath-laying ceremonies at Mount Vernon *(mountvernon.org)* and at the Washington Monument *(washingtonbirthday.com)*.

March

Blossom Kite Festival Late March or early April *(tel 877-442-5666, nationalcherryblossomfestival.org)*. Professional and amateur kitemakers and kite flyers compete for prizes at a contest on the Washington Monument grounds.

April

National Cherry Blossom Festival Late March to early April. *(tel 877-442-5666, nationalcherryblossomfestival.org)*. The city celebrates with three weeks of performances, exhibitions, and activities. The Cherry Blossom Parade is usually held on the first or second Saturday in April.

Filmfest DC Two weeks of international and American films, shown at local theaters and other auditoriums around the city *(tel 202-234-3456, filmfestdc.org)*.

White House Easter Egg Roll Monday after Easter. This annual event dates back to 1878 during the Rutherford B. Hayes Administration. Children (chosen by lottery *recreation.gov/ticket/facility/250029*), ages 12 and under, have a chance to play on the South Lawn of the White House. This fun event includes storytelling, music, and costumed characters.

White House Gardens & Grounds Tour A chance to get beyond the gates and tour the lovely spring gardens of the White House's South Lawn *(tel 202-456-7041)*.

May

Evening Parade Friday nights, May–Aug. U.S. Marine Barracks *(8th and I Sts., S.E., tel 202-433-4073, www.barracks.marines.mil)*. The evening begins with an outdoor concert by the United States Marine Band. Following that is a demonstration of precision marching by Marine Drum and Bugle Corps, and the Marine Corps Silent Drill Platoon.

Memorial Day Celebrations
Events on Memorial Day weekend include ceremonies at the Vietnam Veteran's Memorial (tel 202-619-7222), the Tomb of the Unknowns at Arlington National Cemetery (tel 703-607-8000), and a concert by the National Symphony Orchestra on the West Lawn of the Capitol (tel 202-619-7222, pbs.org/national-memorial-day-concert).

June
Dupont-Kalorama Museum Walk Weekend 1st full weekend. Dupont Circle neighborhood (dupontkaloramamc.com). Visit several museums and enjoy interactive tours, textile-weaving demonstrations, workshops, and concerts.

Juneteenth Formalized as a national holiday in 2021, Emancipation Day celebrates the end of slavery with citywide concerts and cultural events (juneteenthdc.org).

July
Smithsonian Folklife Festival Late June/early July. On the National Mall (tel 202-633-6440, festival.si.edu). A popular annual two-week celebration of folk cultures—American and foreign—with music, food, storytelling, art exhibits, handicraft demonstrations, and special evening entertainment.

Fourth of July Celebrations The National Independence Day Parade takes place at 11:45 a.m. on Constitution Ave. between 7th and 17th Sts., N.W. The **National Symphony Orchestra,** with guest stars and soloists, performs at 8 p.m. on the West Lawn of

the Capitol. The **Fourth of July fireworks** show starts at about 9 p.m. over the Washington Monument grounds (tel 202-619-7222).

September
Labor Day Concert The National Symphony Orchestra closes its summer season with a concert on the West Lawn of the Capitol (tel 202-619-7222).

DC Blues Festival The annual festival (dcblues.org) closes out the summer with free performances and workshops. Check the website for venues.

National Book Festival Mid-September. Ten days of heaven for bibliophiles at the Washington Convention Center as authors, illustrators, and poets read from and sign books from an entire spectrum of genres (tel 202-707-5000, loc.gov/events/2021-national-book-festival).

Virginia Wine Festival Sample Virginia's emerging wines along with music, food, and entertainment (virginiawinefest.com).

October
Waterford Homes Tour and Craft Exhibit First full weekend (waterfordfoundation.org/waterford-fair). A celebration of colonial and Civil War–era America along the streets of a charming town. Music, food, home tours, and crafts (this is Virginia's oldest juried crafts fair). Waterford, VA, 47 miles (75 km) northwest of Washington.

Marine Corps Marathon Thousands of runners take part in this annual marathon (marinemarathon.com). It starts at 8 a.m. at the Iwo Jima Memorial in Arlington, VA, and follows a course through Washington past monuments on the Mall.

Smithsonian Craft Show National Building Museum (tel 202-272-2448, smithsoniancraftshow.org). A juried show of American crafts, including basketry, ceramics, fiber decorative and wearables, furniture, glass, jewelry, leather, metal, mixed media, paper, and wood.

November
Veterans Day Celebrations
Events honoring the service of U.S. military veterans occur November 11 at Arlington National Cemetery (tel 877-907-8585) and various memorials throughout the area.

December
Pageant of Peace/Lighting of the National Christmas Tree
On the Ellipse south of the White House (tel 202-208-1631). The official kickoff of the Christmas season in Washington, with concerts and a Christmas tree from each of the states.

Washington National Cathedral Christmas Services Massachusetts and Wisconsin Aves., N.W. (tel 202-537-6200, cathedral.org/christmas). Christmas Eve services; passes are required for admission.

FURTHER READING
The best book on Washington architecture is E. J. Applewhite's *Washington Itself.* Applewhite, a former CIA officer, has a keen eye for buildings and an ear for the details of history.

Fiction lovers should check out Margaret Truman's murder mysteries set in and around Washington, D.C. President Truman's daughter wrote dozens of suspense novels, including *Murder in the White House* and *Murder at the Watergate.* And Gore Vidal's novel *Washington, D.C.* offers an illuminating portrait of the republic from the time of the New Deal to the McCarthy era.

HOTELS & RESTAURANTS

When it comes to travel, where you sleep and eat can make all the difference. Washington, a city that regularly hosts guests from all nations, offers a panoply of hotel and restaurant selections in all price categories and styles.

Hotels

Washington hotels vary from the luxurious and very expensive—the Four Seasons in Georgetown and the Mandarin Oriental near the Mall being good examples—to the basic and still fairly expensive, such as the large downtown hotels that cater mostly to the convention and meeting trade. Small and charming is harder to find, but the past decade has seen an explosion of chic new boutique hotels.

Because every major business in the country is affected by government legislation and regulations, Washington hotels cater to business travelers on expense accounts. That means high prices during the week, when businesses are paying the tab, but it also means weekend bargains for leisure and family travelers.

Hotels in the city are expensive, so some visitors prefer to stay in less expensive places in suburban Virginia and travel into the city each day. Many hotels routinely offer rates cheaper than their posted rack rates, and many properties offer discounts through organizations such as AAA or AARP.

Most Washington hotels are nonsmoking establishments.

Restaurants

For many years, Washington was thought to hold little interest as a restaurant city. But a number of distinguished chefs running national-class restaurants now make Washington their home. Michel Richard at Central and Todd Gray at Equinox are at the top of the class, but their students, many of whom have stayed in Washington and opened their own restaurants, continue to enrich Washington dining, as do other top chefs who continue to come and open restaurants.

In addition to this wonderful but pricey dining, the Washington area has long been an attractive place for exiles to begin new lives. Refugees from Vietnam opened fine restaurants in the Virginia suburbs. Washington has more Ethiopian restaurants than any other city in the country. Thailand, India, Pakistan, and Malaysia have all given the city fine restaurants.

Unless otherwise noted, all restaurants are open daily and air-conditioned.

Smoking is prohibited in all bars and restaurants.

L=lunch
D=dinner

Credit Cards

Many hotels and restaurants accept all major credit cards. Smaller ones may accept some or none, as shown in their entry. Abbreviations used are: AE American Express, D Discover, DC Diners Club, MC MasterCard, and V Visa.

Organization

Hotels and restaurants are listed by chapter area, then by price category, then alphabetically. Hotel restaurants of note have been bolded in the hotel entries and indicated by a restaurant icon beneath the hotel icon (if they're unusually special, they are treated in a separate entry within the restaurant section).

PRICES

HOTELS

An indication of the cost of a double room in the high season is given by $ signs.

$$$$$	Over $300
$$$$	$225–$300
$$$	$150–$225
$$	$100–$150
$	Under $100

RESTAURANTS

An indication of the cost of a three-course meal without drinks is given by $ signs.

$$$$$	Over $75
$$$$	$50–$75
$$$	$35–$50
$$	$15–$35
$	Under $15

▶ **CAPITOL HILL**

HOTELS

🏨 **YOTEL**
🍴 **$$$$$**
415 NEW JERSEY AVE., N.W.
TEL 202-638-1616
yotel.com
Formerly the Liaison Capital Hill Hotel, this boutique hotel, located between Union Station and Capitol Hill, has been recently refurbished with a hip, minimalist vibe. It features a rooftop bar and seasonal pool. The **Art and Soul** restaurant's chef Danny Chávez creates fusion dishes inspired by his Latin roots.
ⓘ 343 🅿 📶 🚭 All major cards
Ⓜ Union Station

🏨 **HILTON WASHINGTON DC CAPITOL HILL**
$$$$–$$$$$
525 NEW JERSEY AVE., N.W.
TEL 202-628-2100
hilton.com
Rebranded and totally renovated in modern vogue in

🏨 Hotel   🍴 Restaurant   ⓘ No. of Guest Rooms   🅿 Parking   🕐 Closed   🛗 Elevator   🚭 Nonsmoking

2021, the former Washington Court Hotel has a dramatic four-story atrium lobby and sweeping city views from guest rooms.

[i] 267 [P] [V] [S] All major cards [M] Union Station

THE HOTEL GEORGE
$$$$–$$$$$
15 E ST., N.W.
TEL 202-347-4200 OR
800-576-8331
hotelgeorge.com
A completely renovated building (from 1928), the George is a Kimpton hotel with stylishly elegant decor, convenient to Capitol Hill offices and attractions. The restaurant **Bistro Bis** (see below) offers quality contemporary French bistro fare. Cigar-friendly Billiard Room.

[i] 139 [P] [V] [S] All major cards [M] Union Station

HYATT REGENCY WASHINGTON ON CAPITOL HILL
$$$$
400 NEW JERSEY AVE., N.W.
TEL 202-737-1234 OR
800-223-1234
hyatt.com
This large upscale convention hotel occupies a full city block on Capitol Hill. The hotel is centrally located to offer access to museums, monuments, and government buildings.

[i] 838 [P] [Z] [V] [S] All major cards [M] Union Station

PHOENIX PARK HOTEL
$$$$
520 N. CAPITOL ST., N.W.
TEL 202-638-6900 OR
855-371-6824
phoenixparkhotel.com
Named after the park in Dublin, this recently renovated Georgian hotel has a contemporary sophistication. The adjoining **Dubliner Pub** evokes a Gaelic setting and

offers good pub cooking and Irish entertainment.

[i] 149 [P] [V] [S] All major cards [M] Union Station

CAPITOL HILL HOTEL
$$$
200 C ST., S.E.
TEL 202-543-6000
capitolhillhotel-dc.com
Tucked behind the Library of Congress on the House side of the hill, Capitol Hill Hotel has been upgraded with stylish elegance.

[i] 153 [P] [V] [S] All major cards [M] Capitol South

RESTAURANTS

BISTRO BIS
$$$$
THE HOTEL GEORGE
15 E ST., N.W.
TEL 202-661-2700
bistrobis.com
Chef/owner Jeffrey Buben serves contemporary French bistro fare in this sleek Capitol Hill hangout. Consistently rated one of Washington's best restaurants.

[+] 115 [P] [S] All major cards [M] Union Station

BISTRO CACAO
$$$$
316 MASSACHUSETTS AVE., N.E.
TEL 202-546-4737
bistrocacao.com
Serving modern French cuisine under the helm of Chef Alex Merritt, this antique-filled gourmet restaurant with Richelieu-red curtains offers such indulgent treats as frogs' legs, sautéed snails, pan-seared duck breast, and warm chocolate fondant.

[+] 70 [S] [S] All major cards [M] Union Station

BIDWELL
$$$–$$$$
UNION MARKET
1309 5TH ST., S.E.
TEL 202-547-0172

bidwelldc.com
A cornerstone of the Union Market artisanal food emporium, Bidwell proudly sources its ingredients responsibly, with literal roof-to-table cuisine: Much of the restaurant's produce comes from aeroponic planters on the roof of Union Market. Chef John Mooney's signature dishes feature Southern flavors, especially his gin and tonic salmon, crispy deviled eggs, and suckling pig.

[+] 120 [C] Closed Mon.–Tue. [S] All major cards [M] NoMa–Gallaudet U

GRANVILLE MOORE'S
$$$
1238 H ST., N.E.
TEL 202-399-2546
granvillemoores.com
This delightfully rustic American/Belgian gastropub is a mainstay of the newly transformed H Street corridor and a favorite local watering hole. Slip into one of the wooden booths for Belgian-style beers and a plate of *moules-frites*.

[+] 90 [C] Closed L & Mon.–Wed. [S] AE, MC, V [M] Union Station, then trolley

JOSELITO CASA DE COMIDAS
$$$
660 PENNSYLVANIA, S.E.
TEL 202-930-6955
joselitodc.com
This intimate family-run Spanish restaurant dishes out lovingly-prepared tapas such as fried anchovies, plus such other Iberian favorites as velvety chicken liver terrine, and steamed Huelva shrimp, anchovies, and clams. Leave room for a decadent *sopa de chocolate blanco dessert*. Wash your meal down with sangria or a Spanish vermouth.

[+] 70 [S] [C] Closed L Mon.–Fri. [S] All major cards [M] Eastern Market

[S] Air-conditioning [Z] Indoor Pool [Z] Outdoor Pool [V] Health Club [W] Wi-Fi [S] Credit Cards

🍴 THE MONOCLE
$$$

107 D ST., N.E.
TEL 202-546-4488
themonocle.com
Its position as the closest
restaurant to the Senate side
of the Capitol means that
there's no better place for
sighting politicos. Run by the
Valanos family for more than
50 years, the Monocle serves
an all-American menu of
burgers, steaks, and seafood.
🔩 110 🕐 Closed Sat.–Sun.
🚭 AE, DC, MC, V 🚇 Union
Station

🍴 BELGA CAFÉ
$$–$$$

514-8TH ST., S.E.
TEL 202-544-0100
belgacafe.com
Award-winning chef Bart Van-
daele's vibrant Brussels-style
café serve authentic Belgian
cuisine and craft beers. The
menu offers such delights
as Flemish beef stew with
frites, but it's really all about
mussels, with seven dishes.
Afterward head up to its roof-
top bar, Betsy, for a signature
gin cocktail.
🔩 54 🚭 🕐 Closed L Mon.
🚭 All major cards 🚇 Eastern
Market

🍴 BANANA CAFÉ
$$

500 8TH ST., S.E.
TEL 202-543-5906
bananacafedc.com
This cheerful Latin American
and Cuban restaurant has a
bar and dining room on the
main level and a piano bar
above. Order from a small
selection of tapas to start,
but then dive into the Cuban
specialties. Don't miss the
mango margaritas.
🔩 100 🚭 All major cards
🚇 Eastern Market

🍴 GOOD STUFF EATERY
$$

303 PENNSYLVANIA AVE., S.E.
TEL 202-543-8222

goodstuffeatery.com
This family-run, nontradi-
tional burger joint has been a
hit among Capitol Hill staffers
ever since it was launched
in 2008 by "Chef Spike"
Mendelsohn, who worked in
Napa Valley and New York
City restaurants before com-
ing to D.C. The handcrafted
burgers, fries, shakes, and
salads are all made with top-
quality ingredients.
🔩 100 🚭 All major cards
🚇 Capitol South

🍴 MATCHBOX CAPITOL HILL
$$

521 8TH ST., S.E.
TEL 202-548-0369
matchboxrestaurants.com/
capitol-hill
Wood-fired pizzas with blis-
tery crusts and imaginative
toppings are a big draw at
this spacious and trendy spot,
which also features dishes
such as bacon-wrapped
shrimp with grits. Sister
locations are in Chinatown
(713 H St., N.W.) and U St.
(1901 14th St., N.W.).
🔩 150 🚭 All major cards
🚇 Eastern Market

SOMETHING SPECIAL

🍴 JIMMY T'S
$$

501 E. CAPITOL ST., S.E.
TEL 202-709-3557
jimmytsplace.business.site
The best greasy spoon in
Washington, this hole-in-the-
wall neighborhood diner in a
1860s redbrick row house is
a Hill institution, with kitschy
decor (including a collection
of souvenir snow globes)
that's unchanged since it
opened five decades ago.
Even the occasional drop-in
Senator or Supreme Court
Justice gets a mismatched
thrift store coffee mug with
"all-day" breakfast. Think
French toast, grits, waffles
and bacon, omelets, and

seasonal pumpkin pancakes.
The ridiculously cheap
cheeseburgers are to die for,
and its meatloaf and tuna
casserole specials are better
even than your mom made.
🔩 26 🚭 🚭 No credit cards
🚇 Capitol South, Eastern
Market

▶ THE MALL

HOTELS

🏨 MANDARIN ORIENTAL
🍴 $$$$$

1330 MARYLAND AVE., S.W.
TEL 202-554-8588
mandarinoriental.com
/washington
This super-luxury hotel
near the southeastern end
of the Mall, overlooks the
Tidal Basin and the Jefferson
Memorial. The marble baths,
lacquered furniture, silk fur-
nishings, and extensive spa
services make for a soothing
stay. Chef Stefan Kauth of
the hotel's Asian-inspired
Muze has been named one
of America's "best new
chefs."
🛏 400 🅿 📺 🍴 🚭 All major
cards 🚇 L'Enfant Plaza

🏨 RIGGS WASHINGTON D.C.
$$$$$

900 F ST., N.W.
TEL 202-638-1800
riggsdc.com
Occupying the 1891 former
Riggs Bank opposite the
National Portrait Gallery, this
swank newcomer opened
in 2020 with exuberant and
whimsical contemporary
furnishings. The boundary-
pushing rooftop cocktail bar
offers fabulous city views.
Chef Patrick Curran's **Café
Riggs** (see below) lobby
restaurant has a luxurious
atmosphere.
🛏 181 🅿 Valet 📺 🚇 Eastern
Market

🏨 **HILTON WASHINGTON D.C. NATIONAL MALL**
$$$$
480 L'ENFANT PLAZA, S.W.
TEL 202-484-1000
hilton.com
Close to the Smithsonian museums, this hotel is attractive to both business and leisure travelers. Dining options include a seafood-dominated brasserie and a brewpub. Formerly the L'Enfant Plaza Hotel, it reopened in 2019 after a complete renovation.
🛏 367 🉐 🏊 🈺 🆚 All major cards 🚇 L'Enfant Plaza

RESTAURANTS

🍽 **CAFÉ RIGGS**
$$$$
900 F ST., N.W.
TEL 202-638-1800
riggsdc.com
The airy, ground-floor café-restaurant at the exciting Riggs Washington D.C. evokes a stately European brasserie with its expansive coffered ceiling, marble Corinthian columns, and sumptuous velvet chairs in joyful colors. Chef Patrick Curran uses the freshest sustainable ingredients in his contemporary takes on classic dishes, such as decadent French toast with maple, bacon, and pecan; caviar grilled goat cheese; shellfish platter with lobster, oysters, shrimp, scallops, and caviar; and 13 vegan dishes.
🍴 74 🈁 🅿 Valet 🈵 Closed L Mon.–Fri. 🆚 All major cards 🚇 Eastern Market

🍽 **OLLIE'S TROLLEY**
$$–$$$
425 12TH ST., N.W.
TEL 202-770-8614
This colorful family-owned restaurant has been a D.C. institution for more than 30 years. Located just blocks from the National Mall, the menu of burgers, crab cakes, fish sandwiches, and milkshakes is a sure hit with kids after a day spent exploring the Smithsonian museums. Don't skip the famous Olliefries, tossed in the secret house blend of 26 herbs and spices.
🍴 30 🆚 Cash only 🚇 Metro Center

🍽 **NATIONAL GALLERY OF ART CAFÉS**
$–$$
6TH ST. & CONSTITUTION AVE., N.W.
TEL 202-737-4215
The Garden Café offers light lunch fare, while the large Cascade Café, in the concourse between the two buildings, has a varied cafeteria menu. The Sculpture Garden Pavilion Café serves pizzas, sandwiches, desserts, wine, and beer. Check out the weekend jazz brunches, and for a treat, don't miss the great gelato at the Espresso Bar.
🚇 Archives–Navy Memorial–Penn Quarter–Smithsonian

▶ **WHITE HOUSE & AROUND**

HOTELS

🏨 **FAIRMONT HOTEL**
🍽 **$$$$$**
2401 M ST., N.W.
TEL 202-429-2400 OR
866-540-4505
fairmont.com/washington
Built around a garden courtyard, the Fairmont is in the West End area of town near Georgetown. Rooms are luxurious, service is attentive. The fitness center, with pool, is one of the most complete and popular in the city. **Juniper** offers good modern American cooking, while the **Collonade** serves an elaborate holiday brunch.

🛏 415 🅿 🉐 🏊 🈺 🆚 All major cards 🚇 Foggy Bottom–GWU

🏨 **THE HAY-ADAMS**
🍽 **HOTEL**
$$$$$
800 16TH ST., N.W.
TEL 202-638-6600
hayadams.com
Built on the site where President Lincoln's secretary John Hay and John Adams's grandson Henry Adams lived. The hotel is just across Lafayette Square from the White House and exudes timeless elegance and luxury. The **Lafayette** dining room and guest rooms on the south side offer great views of the Executive Mansion, and *Forbes* named the lush Off The Record as one of the "World's Best Hotel Bars."
🛏 145 🅿 🈺 🆚 All major cards 🚇 Farragut West, McPherson Square

🏨 **JW MARRIOTT HOTEL**
$$$$$
1331 PENNSYLVANIA AVE., N.W.
TEL 202-393-2000 OR
800-393-2503
marriott.com
Centrally located and connected to the shops and boutiques of National Place, the newly stylish JW Marriott is a convenient hub for exploring the city.
🛏 777 🅿 🉐 🏊 🈺 🆚 AE, DC, MC, V 🚇 Metro Center

🏨 **PARK HYATT**
🍽 **$$$$$**
1201 24TH ST., N.W.
TEL 202-789-1234
hyatt.com
Located in Washington's West End, just three blocks from Georgetown, the Park Hyatt is comfortably IKEA-style modern. The lobby is decorated with an impressive collection of art. Rooms are large and luxurious. The distinguished restaurant,

Blue Duck Tavern (see p. 247), serves chef Sebastien Archambault's accomplished modern American cooking and a lavish weekend brunch.
🛈 220 🅿 📶 🚭 All major cards 🚇 Foggy Bottom–GWU

🏨 RITZ-CARLTON HOTEL
🍴 WASHINGTON, D.C.
$$$$$
1150 22ND ST., N.W.
TEL 202-835-0500
ritzcarlton.com
The elegant guest rooms of this luxury hotel offer a nice ambience in a neighborhood setting, with a courtyard view. The hotel's **Westend Bistro** has emerged as one of D.C.'s top-rated restaurants under chef Alvin de la Cruz.
🛈 300 🅿 📶 🚭 All major cards 🚇 Foggy Bottom–GWU

🏨 SOFITEL
🍴 LAFAYETTE SQUARE
$$$$$
806 15TH ST., N.W.
TEL 202-730-8800
sofitel-washington-dc.com
Housed in an 1880s building, this well-located hotel, near the White House, has the sophisticated elegance of its parent, the French Accor chain. **Opaline**, the hotel's brasserie restaurant, serves French cuisine, and **Le Bar** lounge is a popular meeting place.
🛈 237 🅿 📶 🚭 All major cards 🚇 McPherson Square

🏨 THE ST. REGIS
🍴 $$$$$
923 16TH ST. AT K ST., N.W.
TEL 202-638-2626 OR
888-627-8087
stregiswashingtondc.com
The posh St. Regis, located near the White House and museums, is built in Italian Renaissance style with fine plasterwork ceilings, antiques, and ornate chandeliers. The hotel offers butler service in its luxurious suites.
🛈 187 🅿 📶 🚭 All major cards 🚇 Farragut North

🏨 THE WESTIN GEORGE-TOWN
$$$$$
2350 M ST., N.W.
TEL 202-429-0100
marriott.com
This low-key hotel, located between Georgetown and the White House, is known for its friendly, attentive service. Comfortable rooms, recently renovated in modern vogue, and great location offer good value.
🛈 255 🅿 Valet 🏊 📶 🚭 All major cards 🚇 Foggy Bottom–GWU

🏨 WILLARD INTER-
🍴 CONTINENTAL HOTEL
$$$$$
1401 PENNSYLVANIA AVE., N.W.
TEL 800-424-6835
washington.intercontinental.com
A Willard Hotel has been located on this site since 1850. Abraham Lincoln stayed here before his Inauguration; Julia Ward Howe wrote the "Battle Hymn of the Republic" here. The hotel has been luxuriously updated in regal styling. **Café du Parc** features French bistro cuisine and exquisite pastries. The **Round Robin Bar** is one of the city's most popular gathering places.
🛈 335 🅿 📶 🚭 All major cards 🚇 Metro Center

🏨 W WASHINGTON D.C.
🍴 $$$$
15TH ST. & PENNSYLVANIA AVE., N.W.
TEL 202-661-2400
wwashingtondc.com
Italian Renaissance meets modern cool in this urbane, youthful hotel with amenities that include a Bliss spa and the rooftop POV bar, with a fabulous view of Washington. The **Living Room** combines gourmet fusion dining with artisanal cocktails and groovy DJ mixes.
🛈 317 📶 🚭 All major cards 🚇 Metro Center

<hr>

PRICES

HOTELS
An indication of the cost of a double room in the high season is given by **$** signs.

$$$$$	Over $300
$$$$	$225–$300
$$$	$150–$225
$$	$100–$150
$	Under $100

RESTAURANTS
An indication of the cost of a three-course meal without drinks is given by $ signs.

$$$$$	Over $75
$$$$	$50–$75
$$$	$35–$50
$$	$15–$35
$	Under $15

<hr>

🏨 ARC THE HOTEL
$$–$$$
824 NEW HAMPSHIRE AVE., N.W.
TEL 202-307-6620
arcthehoteldc.com
Opened in 2018, this new boutique hotel close to the Kennedy Center in tree-lined Foggy Bottom combines modern amenities and hip styling with old-world charm and panoramic views of the Potomac River.
🛈 136 🚭 🅿 Valet 📶 🚇 Foggy Bottom–GWU

RESTAURANTS

🍴 EQUINOX
$$$$
818 CONNECTICUT AVE., N.W.
TEL 202-331-8118
equinoxrestaurant.com
Chef Todd Gray has received numerous culinary awards for his innovative takes on American cuisine. A commitment to seasonal ingredients and sustainable farming has won this restaurant, established in 1999, a strong local following.
🍴 90 🕐 Closed Mon.–Wed.,

<hr>

🏨 Hotel 🍴 Restaurant 🛈 No. of Guest Rooms 🅿 Parking 🕐 Closed 🛗 Elevator 🚭 Nonsmoking

& Sat.–Sun. L 🍴 AE, DC, MC, V 🚇 Farragut West

🍴 MARCEL'S
$$$$
2401 PENNSYLVANIA AVE., N.W.
TEL 202-296-1166
marcelsdc.com
Chef Robert Wiedmaier's Belgian-influenced French cooking is both sophisticated and robust. You can choose from three- to seven-course meals, or have lighter fare from the pre-theater menu.
🪑 120 🅿 Valet 🕐 Closed L & all Mon.–Tues. 🍴 AE, DC, MC, V 🚇 Foggy Bottom–GWU

🍴 CAFÉ DU PARC
$$$–$$$$
1401 PENNSYLVANIA AVE., N.W.
TEL 202-942-7000
cafeduparc.com
Located in the Willard Intercontinental Hotel, this elegant and colorful bistro blends traditional French fare with a modern vibe. Sidewalk seating with a view of Pershing Park across Pennsylvania Avenue offers an excellent spot to unwind while sightseeing. Start off with coffee and a croissant or a full breakfast buffet, or enjoy an afternoon lunch of the cafe's famed French terrines or mussels *à la mariniere*.
🪑 202 (84 in winter) 🅿 Valet at Willard Hotel 🍴 All major cards 🚇 Federal Triangle, Metro Center

SOMETHING SPECIAL

🍴 BLUE DUCK TAVERN
$$$
24TH & M STS., N.W.
TEL 202-419-6755
blueducktavern.com
One of Washington's very best restaurants, the award-winning Blue Duck Tavern has a handsome ultra-contemporary wood and blue burlap interior that showcases chef Adam Howard's celebration of regional and artisanal American foods. The menu features simple but exquisitely prepared dishes such as jumbo crab cakes with cress, frisee, fennel, pickled onions, and lemon-caper remoulade; oven-fired prime New York strip with horseradish cream; and roasted halibut with artichokes, fava bean, baby radish, and beurre blanc.
🪑 100 🍴 All major cards 🚇 Foggy Bottom–GWU

🍴 CENTRAL MICHEL RICHARD
$$$
1001 PENNSYLVANIA AVE., N.W.
TEL 202-626-0015
centralmichelrichard.com
This low-key restaurant has Washingtonians flocking to its affordable takes on the innovative mastery of chef Michel Richard. The fare is French bistro with a twist, with such dishes as country pâté, bacon and onion tart, and scallops with sweet corn and mushrooms.
🪑 140 🅿 Valet 🕐 Closed Mon. 🍴 AE, D, MC, V 🚇 Metro Center, Archives–Navy Memorial–Penn Quarter

🍴 OLD EBBITT GRILL
$$$
675 15TH ST., N.W.
TEL 202-347-4800
ebbitt.com
Large, casual, and always crowded, the Old Ebbitt Grill feeds Washingtonians and out-of-towners with a menu that ranges from burgers to grilled fish in a historic saloon environment. There's no better place in town for oysters.
🪑 500 🅿 Valet 🍴 All major cards 🚇 Metro Center

🍴 RIS
$$$
2275 L ST., N.W.
TEL 202-730-2500
risdc.com
Esteemed local chef Ris Lacoste, trained in French cuisine, fulfilled a longtime dream in opening this cozy restaurant that features homey food with a deft touch, such as chicken pot pie, cider-glazed pork chops, and pasta with ramps.
🪑 180 🕐 Closed Sat., & Sun. L 🍴 All major credit cards 🚇 Foggy Bottom–GWU

▶ DOWNTOWN

HOTELS

🏨 EATON DC
🍴 $$$$$
1201 K ST., N.W.
TEL 202-289-7600
eatonworkshop.com
Opened in 2019 as a socially conscious, environmentally friendly hotel with a communal workspace, the Eaton infuses an artsy Asian aesthetic into its homey yet upscale "future-proofed" design. The influence extends to the hotel's **American Son** restaurant.
ℹ 209 🍴 🅿 Valet 🍴 All major cards 🚇 Metro Center, McPherson Square

🏨 GRAND HYATT WASHINGTON
$$$$$
1000 H ST., N.W.
TEL 202-582-1234
hyatt.com
Located near the Washington Convention Center and Verizon Center, this large hotel features a parklike atrium, cigar bar, and several dining options.
ℹ 897 🅿 🍴 🏊 🍴 All major cards 🚇 Metro Center

🍴 Air-conditioning 🏊 Indoor Pool 🏊 Outdoor Pool 🏋 Health Club 📶 Wi-Fi 🍴 Credit Cards

HENLEY PARK HOTEL
$$$$$
926 MASSACHUSETTS AVE., N.W.
TEL 202-638-5200
henleypark.com
Newly renovated in 2020 in the tradition of Europe's finest hotels, this hotel is one of D.C.'s most charming. Dozens of gargoyles and lead windows grace its exterior. The **Tavern** restaurant offers very good new American fare. Located near the Convention Center.
🛈 96 🅿 💺 🚭 All major cards 🚇 Mount Vernon Square 7th Street–Convention Center, Gallery Place–Chinatown

SOMETHING SPECIAL

HOTEL MONACO
$$$$$
700 F ST., N.W.
TEL 202-628-7177 OR
800-649-1202
monaco-dc.com
This luxury Kimpton boutique hotel is housed in the architecturally stately 1839 Tariff Building in Penn Quarter, within steps of the Capitol One Arena, Washington Convention Center, and 7th Street arts scene. The distinctive rooms with 15-foot (4.5 m) ceilings feature neoclassical furnishings and vivid colors. The edgy **Dirty Habit** restaurant and bar serves avant-garde fusion fare.
🛈 183 🅿 💺 🚭 AE, D, MC, V 🚇 Gallery Place–Chinatown

JEFFERSON HOTEL
$$$$$
1200 16TH ST., N.W.
TEL 202-448-2300
jeffersondc.com
Regarded by many as Washington's finest small hotel, the Jefferson—with many touches inspired by the third president—is even more exquisite after an extensive renovation in 2009 uncovered a previ-

ously unknown skylight. Dine at **The Greenhouse** restaurant, and don't miss breakfast or lunch in the gorgeous and sunny **Greenhouse.**
🍴 95 🅿 💺 🚭 All major cards 🚇 Farragut West

THE MADISON
$$$$$
1177 15TH ST., N.W.
TEL 202-862-1600
hilton.com
Formerly the Loews Madison and recently refurbished in boutique style by Hilton, the Madison offers a great location for exploring D.C. sights as well as the Dupont Circle area.
🛈 365 🅿 💺 🚭 All major cards 🚇 McPherson Square

MARRIOTT AT METRO CENTER
$$$$$
775 12TH ST., N.W.
TEL 202-737-2200 OR
800-393-2510
marriottmetrocenter.com
Conveniently located at the flagship station of the city's Metro system, the Marriott at Metro Center is attentive to both business and vacation guests.
🛈 459 🎦 💺 🚭 All major cards 🚇 Metro Center

THE MAYFLOWER
$$$$$
1127 CONNECTICUT AVE., N.W.
TEL 202-347-3000
themayflowerhotel.com
Once the home to many members of Congress and today part of Marriott's Signature collection, The Mayflower has been the site of many Inaugural Balls and the setting of many historic occasions. The gracious lobby runs an entire city block from Connecticut Avenue to 17th Street. Rooms are luxuriously modern and the bar is a favorite gathering spot.
🛈 657 🅿 💺 🚭 All major cards 🚇 Farragut North

MORRISON-CLARK INN
$$$$$
MASSACHUSETTS AVE. & 11TH ST., N.W.
TEL 202-898-1200; OR
800-332-7898
morrisonclark.com
This stately Victorian mansion on Massachusetts Avenue was built as two townhomes in 1864. A grand expansion in 2014 into the church next door doubled the room count. Chefs of the Morrison-Clark restaurant have won many awards for their New American cuisine.
🛈 114 🅿 💺 🚭 All major cards 🚇 Mount Vernon Square 7th Street–Convention Center

HOTEL HARRINGTON
$–$$
436 11TH ST., N.W.
TEL 202-628-8140 OR
800-424-8532
hotel-harrington.com
Low prices, a prime location, and very plain, clean rooms, make the Hotel Harrington popular with bus groups of students and other travelers on a tight budget.
🛈 242 🚭 All major cards 🚇 Metro Center

RESTAURANTS

TOSCA
$$$$
1112 F ST., N.W.
TEL 202-367-1990
toscadc.com
Cesare Lanfranconi opened this restaurant with a menu based on the food of his native Lake Como region. Now headed by chef Phil Marzelli, the sophisticated modern setting was completely redesigned while closed during the COVID-19 pandemic with widely spaced tables designed for privacy and conversation. The menu includes such temptations as wild scallops with corn pu-

---

 Hotel 🍴 Restaurant 🛈 No. of Guest Rooms 🅿 Parking 💺 Closed 🔀 Elevator 🚭 Nonsmoking ree, eggplant jam, and trout roe; classic veal and pork ragu; and olive-oil-poached salmon.

🍴 120 🅿 Valet 🕐 Closed Sat.–Sun. 🅢 AE, DC, MC, V 🚇 Metro Center

🍴 BRASSERIE BECK

$$$

1101 K ST., N.W.

TEL 202-408-1717

beckdc.com

This popular European-style brasserie allows Robert Wiedmaier, owner of the formal Marcel's (see p. 247), to offer robust food from his native Belgium—such as beef carbonnade and *moules* and *frites*—in a casual setting. The spacious bar features a huge array of Belgian beers.

🍴 165 🅿 Valet 🅢 All major cards 🚇 Metro Center

🍴 ZAYTINYA

$$–$$$

701 9TH., N.W.

TEL 202-638-0800

zaytinya.com

For more than two decades, sleekly modern Zaytinya has been satisfying diners with an innovative small-plate meze menu of Levantine dishes. Chef Michael Costa offers a tasting menu, and a four-course meze brunch with rosé flights on weekends.

🍴 204 🅢 🅢 All major cards 🚇 Metro Center, Gallery Place–Chinatown

🍴 BAAN SIAM

$$

425 I ST., N.W.

TEL 202-588-5889

baansiamdc.com

Chef Jeeraporn Poksupthon's roomy Thai restaurant delivers such complex soulful dishes as mild or hot-as-you-wish pork curry with dandelion leaves and stir-fried eggplant with chicken and salted fish.

🍴 84 🅢 🅢 All major cards 🚇 Gallery Place-Chinatown, Union Station

🍴 JALEO

$$

480 7TH ST., N.W.

TEL 202-628-7949

jaleo.com/dc

There are main courses at Jaleo, but most diners choose to make a meal of the large selection of tapas—wonderful Spanish cheeses and cold cuts, eggplant flan, spicy octopus, sausages and beans. It's a great place for a light dinner before a performance at the nearby Shakespeare Theatre.

🍴 145 🅿 Valet 🅢 All major cards 🚇 Gallery Place–Chinatown

🍴 OYAMEL

$$

401 7TH ST., N.W.

TEL 202-628-1005

oyamel.com

Mexican food goes upscale on a menu that invites grazing. Selections include cactus paddle salad, stuffed poblano peppers, and hominy soup. For something really different, there's a Oaxacan specialty of sautéed grasshoppers.

🍴 120 🅿 Valet 🕐 Closed Mon.–Tues. 🅢 All major credit cards 🚇 Gallery Place–Chinatown, Archives–Navy Memorial–Penn Quarter

🍴 RASIKA

$$

633 D ST., N.W.

TEL 202-637-1222

rasikarestaurant.com

This chic Indian restaurant, launched by the owner of the Bombay Club, has developed a loyal following for its modern takes on the classics, as well as inventive entrées such as tandoori lamb chops with cashews, ginger, and herbs. Dinner options include pre-theater and tasting menus.

🍴 120 🅿 Valet 🕐 Closed L Sat. 🅢 AE, MC, V 🚇 Gallery Place–Chinatown, Archives–Navy Memorial–Penn Quarter

▶ GEORGETOWN

HOTELS

SOMETHING SPECIAL

🏨 FOUR SEASONS

🍴 HOTEL

$$$$$

2800 PENNSYLVANIA AVE., N.W.

TEL 202-342-0444 OR

800-819-5053

fourseasons.com/washington

Located on the very eastern edge of Georgetown, this luxurious hotel with modern styling provides a nice link into the rest of the city. **Bourbon Steak** restaurant, overlooking the C & O Canal, is a favorite power breakfast spot. The three-level fitness center with an adjoining spa is one of the most opulent in town.

ℹ 222 🅿 🅢 🅥 🅢 AE, DC, MC, V 🚇 Foggy Bottom–GWU

🏨 THE GRAHAM GEORGETOWN

$$$$$

1075 THOMAS JEFFERSON ST., N.W.

TEL 202-337-0900

thegrahamgeorgetown.com

This recently revamped hotel is located in the center of Georgetown and is named for one-time neighborhood resident Alexander Graham Bell. It is close to the historic C & O Canal. It is now blessed with a hip boutique vibe. The Rooftop at The Graham bar and lounge offers panoramic views of the D.C. skyline.

ℹ 57 🅢 AE, D, MC, V 🚇 Foggy Bottom–GWU

🏨 RITZ-CARLTON

🍴 GEORGETOWN

$$$$$

3100 SOUTH ST., N.W.

TEL 202-912-4100

ritzcarlton.com

Built on the former site of a historic brick incinerator

building, complete with a 130-foot-high (40 m) smokestack, this hotel offers views of the Potomac waterfront. The rooms and suites offer luxury and soothing retreat. **Degrees** restaurant features innovative regional cuisine with international flavors, while the cozy **Living Room** lounge offers cocktails and free s'mores in front of the fireplace.

🛈 86 🅿 📺 🚫 AE, DC, MC, V 🚇 Foggy Bottom–GWU

🏨 🍴 **THE GEORGETOWN INN**
$$$$
1310 WISCONSIN AVE., N.W.
TEL 202-333-8900
georgetowninn.com
This pleasant redbrick hotel has contemporary-style colonial decor, large all-white rooms, and marble bathrooms. It's conveniently located for Georgetown shopping and entertainment. Chef Jenn Crovato's modern **130 Kitchen & Bar** offers fresh and flavorful fusion fare.

🛈 96 🅿 📺 🚫 AE, D, MC, V 🚇 Foggy Bottom–GWU

RESTAURANTS

🍴 **1789**
$$$$
1226 36TH ST., N.W.
TEL 202-965-1789
1789restaurant.com
One of Washington's loveliest and most beloved restaurants, housed in a federal town house. Chef Kyoo Eom sources ingredients from local farms for dishes such as pheasant ballotine foie gras, pickled tiny radishes, and mustard aioli. Downstairs is the **Tombs,** where generations of Georgetown students have drunk countless pitchers of beer.

🍴 300 🅿 Valet 🕐 Closed L & Mon.–Tues. 🚫 All major cards 🚇 Foggy Bottom–GWU

🍴 **LUTÈCE BY BONAPARTE**
$$$
1522 WISCONSIN AVE., N.W.
TEL 202-333-8830
lutecedc.com
A recent reboot of Café Bonaparte, this cozy bistro with whitewashed brick walls now has an open kitchen and a menu of innovative takes on French fare and American classics. Chef Matt Conroy's Parisian gnocchi comes with chanterelle, leeks, and Comté cheese; Berkshire pork chops with piquillo pepper echo his time at the Michelin-starred Mexican restaurant Oxomoco in Brooklyn.

🍴 30 🚫 🕐 Closed Mon.–Tues. & L Wed.–Thurs. 🚫 AE, MC, V 🚇 Foggy Bottom–GWU

🍴 **CLYDE'S**
$$
3236 M ST., N.W.
TEL 202-333-9180
clydes.com/georgetown
The founder of the Clyde's group of restaurants had the idea that he'd "rather eat in a bar than drink in a restaurant." This Georgetown original of the chain is built around a bar business, but offers an impressive menu of bar food, particularly in the summer when Clyde's makes a point of sending trucks to local farms for fresh produce. It's an excellent place for a restorative drink and a light meal while out shopping in Georgetown.

🍴 188 🅿 Georgetown Park Mall lot 🚫 All major cards 🚇 Foggy Bottom–GWU

🍴 **KAFE LEOPOLD**
$$
3315 CADY'S ALLEY, OFF M ST., N.W.
TEL 202-965-6005
kafeleopolds.com
This light and airy, tucked-away café-restaurant is known for its genteel European-style

---

PRICES

HOTELS

An indication of the cost of a double room in the high season is given by **$** signs.

$$$$$	Over $300
$$$$	$225–$300
$$$	$150–$225
$$	$100–$150
$	Under $100

RESTAURANTS

An indication of the cost of a three-course meal without drinks is given by $ signs.

$$$$$	Over $75
$$$$	$50–$75
$$$	$35–$50
$$	$15–$35
$	Under $15

---

pastries and breakfasts such as Belgian sugar waffle with whipped cream. Lunch and dinner may mean tuna niçoise, grilled salmon, or schnitzel. The brick patio is a lovely space on sunny days.

🍴 80 🚫 🚫 All major cards 🚇 Foggy Bottom–GWU

▶ **DUPONT CIRCLE & BEYOND**

HOTELS

🏨 🍴 **ROYAL SONESTA**
$$$$$
2121 P ST., N.W.
TEL 202-448-1800
sonesta.com
Sophistication and personalized service are the hallmarks of this former Kimpton Palomar Hotel, reinvented in 2020 with a moderne bohemian look. Exotic woods, bold art, and geometric touches abound. **Certo!** restaurant serves Italian cuisine.

🛈 335 🅿 ⛱ 📺 🚫 All major cards 🚇 Dupont Circle

🏨 Hotel 🍴 Restaurant 🛈 No. of Guest Rooms 🅿 Parking 🕐 Closed 🚻 Elevator 🚫 Nonsmoking

AMERICAN GUEST HOUSE
$$$$

2005 COLUMBIA RD., N.W.

TEL 202-588-1100

americanguesthouse.com

This fabulous B&B in an Adams Morgan 1893 townhome transports guests back in time with its wood floors, elegant colonial-style furnishings, and rich fabrics. Guests start the day with a gourmet breakfast.

🛈 12 🅢 🅢 AE, MC, V
🚇 Woodley Park–Zoo/Adams Morgan, U Street/African-American Civil War Memorial/Cardozo

THE CHURCHILL
$$$$

1914 CONNECTICUT AVE., N.W.

TEL 202-797-2000

thechurchillhotel.com

Located just north of the vibrant Dupont Circle area, near Embassy Row, the Churchill offers a variety of suites and rooms with separate studies, recently refurbished in chicly appealing 18th-century style. The **Chartwell Grill** offers suavely elegant dining.

🛈 173 🅿 🅦 🅢 All major cards 🚇 Dupont Circle

THE DUPONT CIRCLE HOTEL
$$$$

1500 NEW HAMPSHIRE AVE., N.W.

TEL 202-483-6000

doylecollection.com

Owned and operated by Ireland's Jurys Doyle Hotels, this recently remodeled hotel in Dupont Circle has beautiful 21st-century styling and is in one of the city's liveliest areas.

🛈 309 🅿 🅦 🅢 All major cards 🚇 Dupont Circle

FAIRFAX AT EMBASSY ROW
$$$$

2100 MASSACHUSETTS AVE., N.W.

TEL 202-293-2100

fairfaxwashingtondc.com

The hotel dates to 1924 and has been for many years the residential hotel favored by members of Congress. Former Vice President Al Gore grew up here. Guest rooms in Georgian style are luxurious, as one would expect from a hotel on Massachusetts Avenue's Embassy Row. Public areas, redesigned in 2019 in more contemporary vogue, include a chic games room. The **Sally** restaurant offers good bistro cuisine.

🛈 259 🅿 🅦 🅢 AE, D, MC, V
🚇 Dupont Circle

HOTEL MADERA
$$$$

1310 NEW HAMPSHIRE AVE., N.W.

TEL 202-296-7600

hotelmadera.com

This pampering boutique hideaway is like a B&B tucked in a quiet location near downtown office buildings and embassies. Part of the Kimpton chain, it has a sophisticated decor and the amenities of a big hotel. Revamped with lush new styling during the COVID-19 pandemic, **Firefly** restaurant offers American bistro fare.

🛈 82 🅿 🅢 All major cards
🚇 Dupont Circle

KIMPTON BANNEKER
$$$$

1315 16TH ST., N.W.

TEL 202-234-6399 OR 800-994-4654

thebanneker.com

In 2020, the Kimpton group shuttered its Hotel Rouge and invested $20 million to remake it as the Banneker, with a stand-out sophisticated minimalist design. The rooftop bar with a view straight down 16th Street, N.W., to the White House is a highlight.

🛈 144 🅦 🅢 AE, D, MC, V
🚇 Dupont Circle, McPherson Square

THE LINE DC
$$$$

1770 EUCLID ST., N.W.

TEL 202-588-0525

thelinehotel.com/dc

Occupying a former neoclassical First Church of Science building in Adams Morgan, this seriously cool, pet-friendly hotel launched in 2018. Divine decor hints at its ecclesiastical roots, although guest rooms are in a modern annex. Gourmands are served by four restaurants, and tipplers get two bars.

🛈 220 🅢 🅿 🅢 All major cards 🚇 Woodley Park–Zoo/Adams Morgan, Columbia Heights

VICEROY D.C.
$$$$

1430 RHODE ISLAND AVE., N.W.

TEL 202-742-3100

viceroyhotelsandresorts.com

Opened in 2020, the hip and artful Viceroy D.C. (formerly the Mason & Rook Hotel) features urbane oversized rooms with harmonious taupe, grey, and black with organ highlight color schemes and custom-curated jazz playlists. The contemporary **Dovetail** restaurant also plays up the Logan Circle jazz heritage, plus it has a café, wine bar, and seasonal rooftop lounge-bar.

🛈 178 🅿 🅦 🅢 AE, D, MC, V
🚇 Dupont Circle

TABARD INN
$$$

1739 N ST., N.W.

TEL 202-785-1277

tabardinn.com

This small hotel is greatly loved by those who consider it quaint and adore the Victorian clutter. Locals love the hotel's restaurant (see p. 253), which has a charming outdoor garden and imaginative food. The rooms vary widely in size, so look before you commit.

🛈 40 🅿 🅢 AE, D, MC, V
🚇 Dupont Circle

RESTAURANTS

SOMETHING SPECIAL

🍴 SUSHI TARO
$$$$
1502 17TH ST., N.W.
TEL 202-462-8999
sushitaro.com
A quintessential upscale Japanese ambiance pervades this famous and Michelin-starred restaurant, oddly-located behind a pharmacy. Book well in advance for a seat at the omakase counter, where chefs Nobu Yamazaki and Masaya Kitayama prepare elaborate and divine sushi, such as squid ink-tinted soft-shell crab tempura, for up to eight lucky diners. It also has a broad à la carte menu for other diners.
🔢 80 🚭 🚭 All major credit cards 🚇 Dupont Circle

🍴 FLORIANA
$$$$
1602 17TH ST., N.W.
TEL 202-667-5937
florianarestaurant.com
This homey, under-the-radar Italian bistro in a historic redbrick row house serves authentic, value-priced Italian and American classics using homemade pastas and fresh seasonal ingredients.
🔢 60 🚭 🚭 AE, MC, V
🚇 Dupont Circle

🍴 OBELISK
$$$$
2029 P ST., N.W.
TEL 202-872-1180
obeliskdc.com
At Obelisk, everything is small in scale except flavor. This tiny Italian restaurant in a 1930s rowhouse holds fewer than 40 people, which makes it one of the hardest-to-get reservations in town. The $75 fixed-price five-course menu, which changes too often to recommend specific dishes, offers two or three choices of antipasto, pasta, main course, and dessert. Chef Peter Pastan's cooking is simple but never precious, and is based around fresh ingredients.
🔢 30 🕐 Closed L & all Mon. –Tue. 🚭 DC, MC, V
🚇 Dupont Circle

🍴 THE PALM
$$$$
1225 19TH ST., N.W.
TEL 202-293-9091
thepalm.com
The downtown branch of this steakhouse chain is the epicenter of Washington power dining. The main attractions are the Palm's steaks and five-pound lobsters, served by an efficient and irreverent crew of wise-cracking waiters. The Italian food is also very good.
🔢 185 🅿 Valet 🕐 Closed Sat.–Sun. L 🚭 AE, DC, MC, V
🚇 Dupont Circle

🍴 BIRCH & BARLEY
$$$
1337 14TH ST., N.W.
TEL 202-567-2576
birchandbarley.com
Giant copper pipes dominating the brick-walled decor signal the focus of this hip beer-diner's place in the Logan Circle area. On offer are more than 500 beer varieties from 30 countries, including 50 on tap. Snagging a table can be tough in the downstairs dining room, where the food tends toward hearty fare such as loin of venison and miso-marinated black cod. ChurchKey, the upstairs bar, is casual and crowded.
🔢 80 🕐 Closed L & all Mon. 🚭 All major credit cards
🚇 Dupont Circle

🍴 BISTROT DU COIN
$$$
1738 CONNECTICUT AVE., N.W.
TEL 202-234-6969
bistrotducoin.com
It's not a place for quiet conversation, but Bistrot du Coin is a lot of fun–its motto is "French, fun, and friendly." Owner Michel Verdon and chef Yannis Felix strike a nice balance between good cheer and good cooking. Mussels are a tasty way to start a meal here. For a main course, it's hard to go wrong with steak *frites,* but the more adventurous can order tripes à la niçoise or a delicious stew of rabbit and mushrooms. The house wines offer good value.
🔢 150 🚭 AE, D, MC, V
🚇 Dupont Circle

🍴 DOYLE
$$$
1500 NEW HAMPSHIRE AVE., N.W.
TEL 202-448-4301
doyle.bar
This glamorous mid-century cocktail bar in the Dupont Circle Hotel has upped the ante with a shaded patio dining area and creative menu offered by chef Taylor Burlingame. For light fare, try the Maryland jumbo crab crakes or pork belly steam buns. Full entrées include a prime-aged burger with Irish cheddar, and seared Chilean sea bass with couscous and pea and mint purée. Still hungry? Then the "Chocolate Temptation" is a must.
🔢 120 🚭 🅿 🚭 All major credit cards 🚇 Dupont Circle

SOMETHING SPECIAL

🍴 IRON GATE
$$$
1734 N ST., N.W.
TEL 202-524-5202
irongaterestaurantdc.com
There's no more charming spot in Washington for outdoor dining than the terrace at the Iron Gate Inn, a former stable built after the Civil War. The menu is Mediterranean-inspired and

---

the kitchen, under the helm of chef Anthony Chittum, does a good job on Middle Eastern dishes—stuffed grape leaves, braised lamb shank, and grilled fish.

🍴 80 🕐 Closed Mon. & L Tues.–Sat. 🚇 Dupont Circle

SOMETHING SPECIAL

🍴 LITTLE SEROW

$$$

1511 17TH ST., N.W.

NO TEL

littleserow.com

James Beard award–winning chef Johnny Monis opened his subterranean northern Thai tasting room in 2011 and has never looked back. It takes no reservations: Diners happily line up for one of the best values and mouth-searingly masochistic experiences in town. The prix-fixe seven-course, family-style menu rarely changes, and such spice-packed Thai dishes as chili-laced laap salads and whiskey-marinated, fall-off-the-bone pork short ribs are staples. Gewürztraminer and Normandy cider are among the eyebrow-raising offerings on the drinks list.

🍴 28 🅂 🕐 Closed Sun.–Mon. 🅂 MC, V 🚇 Dupont Circle

🍴 PERRY'S

$$$

1811 COLUMBIA RD., N.W.

TEL 202-234-6218

perrysadamsmorgan.com

Despite its meat-and-potatoes name, Perry's serves sushi and new takes on familiar fare such as scallops and soft-shell crabs. The Sunday brunch, with lip-synched entertainment by glamorous drag queens, is an Adams Morgan institution. The roof deck is pleasant for dinner.

🍴 90 outdoors, 90 indoors 🅿 Valet 🕐 Closed Mon.–Sat. L 🅂 All major cards 🚇 Woodley

Park–Zoo/Adams Morgan, Dupont Circle plus 15-minute walk

🍴 TABARD INN

$$$

1739 N ST., N.W.

TEL 202-785-1277

tabardinn.com/dining

The restaurant of this quaint hotel south of Dupont Circle serves new American cuisine in a well-appointed dining room that's a popular lunch spot. Sunday brunch is a favorite, and the pleasant brick-walled garden is a good place for a drink and dinner on a spring evening. Similarly, the lounge, with fireplace and creaky wood floors, is cozy on winter evenings.

🍴 80 (30 summer patio) 🅿 Valet Fri.–Sat. 🅂 AE, MC, V 🚇 Dupont Circle

🍴 COMPASS ROSE

$$–$$$

1346 T ST., N.W.

TEL 202-506-4765

compassrosedc.com

Compass Rose offers international flavors in a chic neighborhood tavern setting, with exposed brick walls and wood accents. After traveling the world for three years, owner Rose Previte was inspired to share her culinary discoveries, transforming the first floor of her 125-year-old row house near hopping 14th Street into a bar and restaurant. Favorite dishes are sourced from Brazil, Turkey, Morocco, and Peru, while the extensive drinks list features craft beers, wine, and inventive cocktails. The small patio strung with lights provides delightful outdoor seating on warm summer nights.

🍴 65 🕐 Closed Mon.–Tue. & L Wed.–Sat. 🅂 All major cards 🚇 U Street/African American Civil War Memorial/Cardozo

🍴 ALA

$$

1320 19TH ST., N.W.

TEL 202-717-1166

ala-dc.com

Former Turkish restaurant Ankara revamped in 2021 as Ala, meaning "mix of all colors." An invitingly dark industrial space splashed with color, it serves Levantine dishes with raki and rare Palestinian wines. Menu highlights include pomegranate-flecked tabbouleh and smoked cured mackerel with sumac cream. Leave room for pistachio baklava dessert with rose cream and petals.

🍴 80 🅂 🅂 All major cards 🚇 Dupont Circle

🍴 CORK WINE BAR

$$

1720 14TH ST., N.W.

TEL 202-265-2675

corkdc.com

Conceived as a casual but elegant neighborhood tasting room, Cork offers some 50 wines by the glass and 160 bottles from small producers around the world. The menu consists of cheese and charcuterie selections, salads, and hot plates such as duck confit with lentils, plus an excellent brunch.

🍴 70 🕐 Closed Mon.–Sun. 🅂 All major credit cards 🚇 U Street/African American Civil War Memorial/Cardozo, Dupont Circle

🍴 HANK'S OYSTER BAR

$$

1624 Q ST., N.W.

TEL 202-462-4265

hanksoysterbar.com

After laboring in several Washington restaurants, chef Jamie Leeds opened this restaurant in her own neighborhood near Dupont Circle to offer the kind of New England beach seafood cherished by her fisherman father, Hank. The crowded tables and eclectic decor were designed for joviality. Lobster rolls, clam chowder, steamed mussels, fish and chips, oysters, and ceviche are on offer, along with signature dishes such as Leeds's molasses-braised short ribs.

🔢 65 🕐 Closed Mon. & L Tues.–Thurs. 🚫 AE, MC, V 🚇 Dupont Circle

🍴 LAURIOL PLAZA
$$

1835 18TH ST., N.W.
TEL 202-387-0035
lauriolplaza.com
There's almost always a wait to get into this well-run Tex-Mex restaurant that offers much more than the usual burritos and enchiladas. The roof deck is a wonderful place to spend a summer evening over a pitcher of sangria or a few bottles of Dos Equis.

🔢 330 🅿 🚫 All major cards 🚇 Dupont Circle

🍴 SETTE OSTERIA
$$

1666 CONNECTICUT AVE., N.W.
TEL 202-483-3070
setteosteria.com
A companion restaurant of Washington's popular Café Milano, this casual eatery was fashioned on traditional trattorias of Naples. Pizzas from a wood-burning oven are the star attraction, along with homemade pastas, a range of appetizers, and a few grilled entrees. Brunch features a smoked salmon platter and uovo cotto. Patio dining in season.

🔢 75 🅿 Valet 🚇 Dupont Circle

🍴 PIZZERIA PARADISO
$

2003 P ST., N.W.
TEL 202-223-1245
eatyourpizza.com
This small pizza parlor, with sister locations in Georgetown and Old Town Alexandria, makes the best pizzas in Washington. The crust,

which tastes like good bread, is thin but supports the sparely applied toppings. If you don't want pizza, there are also superb panini, Italian sandwiches, and salads.

🔢 35 🚫 DC, MC, V 🚇 Dupont Circle

▶ CLEVELAND PARK & BEYOND

HOTELS

🏨 OMNI SHOREHAM HOTEL
$$$$

2500 CALVERT ST., N.W.
TEL 202-234-0700
omnishorehamhotel.com
Opened in 1930 on 11 landscaped acres (4.4 ha) near Rock Creek, the Shoreham is a frequent convention site and location for large events. Its location gives it convenient access to the jogging trails and paths of Rock Creek Park.

🛏 834 🏊 🍴 🚫 All major cards 🚇 Woodley Park–Zoo/ Adams Morgan

🏨 GLOVER PARK HOTEL
🍴 GEORGETOWN
$$$–$$$$

2505 WISCONSIN AVE., N.W.
TEL 202-638-1800
gloverparkhotel.com
Despite its name, this hotel overlooks the U.S. Naval Academy, just off Embassy Row, in Glover Park. Calming taupe color schemes dominate in contemporary guest rooms, many with superb views. The Glover Park Grill offers fine dining.

🛏 154 🚫 🅿 🍴 🚇 Woodley Park–Zoo/Adams Morgan

🏨 KALORAMA GUEST HOUSE
$$

2700 CATHEDRAL AVE., N.W.
TEL 202-588-8188
kaloramaguesthouse .com

This and a companion guest house in Adams Morgan offer B&B-style accommodation in the European tradition, with some shared baths and continental breakfast, afternoon lemonade, and sherry in the evening. The many repeat customers can help attest to its comfortable atmosphere.

🛏 19 🚫 All major cards 🚇 Woodley Park–Zoo/ Adams Morgan

RESTAURANTS

🍴 NEW HEIGHTS
$$$$

2317 CALVERT ST., N.W.
TEL 202-234-4110
newheightsrestaurant.com
A gracious second-floor dining room with large windows overlooking Rock Creek and a menu of creative new American cooking make this restaurant a perennial favorite.

🔢 92 🅿 Valet 🕐 Closed L 🚫 All major cards 🚇 Woodley Park–Zoo/Adams Morgan

🍴 MACON BISTRO
$$$

5520 CONNECTICUT AVE, N.W.
TEL 202-248-7807
maconbistro.com
Macon, Georgia, meets Mâcon, France, at this family-friendly restaurant that blends old-fashioned Southern cooking with European flair. The bistro, which features vintage fixtures, an open kitchen, and a 20-stool bar, is located in the historic 1925 Chevy Chase Arcade building. The dinner menu uses seasonal, local ingredients in classic dishes such as fried green tomatoes, short ribs, and hand-cut pommes frites. Pick up packaged house-made items like cheese coins and sea-salt caramels in the Macon Larder.

🔢 60 🚫 All major cards 🕐 Closed Mon. 🚇 Friendship Heights

🏨 Hotel 🍴 Restaurant 🛏 No. of Guest Rooms 🅿 Parking 🕐 Closed 🔁 Elevator 🚫 Nonsmoking

🍴 CACTUS CANTINA

$$

3300 WISCONSIN AVE., N.W.

TEL 202-686-7222

cactuscantina.com

This many-chambered cantina, usually noisy and crowded, serves very good Tex-Mex food, both large combination platters and specialties from its mesquite grill. The tamales are a terrific way to begin, but for a main course, order from the grill: crispy quail, great grilled shrimp, or full-flavored spareribs.

🍴 130 inside, 30 outside 🅿 All major cards 🚇 Tenleytown–AU plus a 15-minute walk

SOMETHING SPECIAL

🍴 LEBANESE TAVERNA

$$

2641 CONNECTICUT AVE., N.W.

TEL 202-265-8681

lebanesetaverna.com

There's no better place in Washington to experience the legendary hospitality of the Middle East—and its wonderful cooking—than at this busy Lebanese restaurant. It's possible to order a traditional three-course meal here, but you'll get to try a larger variety of dishes if your party makes a meal from mezes, the small appetizer plates that precede a Middle Eastern meal: spicy beef sausages, stuffed vine leaves, tart hummus, baba ghanoush, Lebanese "pizzas"—count on about three dishes per person. The restaurant has several locations around town.

🍴 100 🅿 AE, DC, MC, V 🚇 Woodley Park–Zoo/Adams Morgan

🍴 MEDIUM RARE

$$

3500 CONNECTICUT AVE., N.W.

TEL 202-237-1432

mediumrarerestaurant.com

Located just across the street from the Cleveland Park Metro station, Medium Rare adheres to the tradition of classic French steak-and-*frites* restaurants and its prix-fixe dinner menu serves up virtually one thing: delicious culotte steak and hand-cut fries. The more expansive weekend brunch menu offers steak and eggs and the house eggs benedict, with sliced steak and portobello mushrooms.

🍴 120 including patio 🕐 Closed Mon.–Fri. All major cards 🚇 Cleveland Park

🍴 SIAM HOUSE

$$

3520 CONNECTICUT AVE., N.W.

TEL 202-363-7802

siamhousedc.com

A local favorite, this Thai restaurant offers flavorful dishes as hot as you wish. The menu sizzles with such unusual dishes as clams with roasted chili sauce and basil, as well as pad Thai and other Thai standbys.

🍴 24 MC, V 🚇 Cleveland Park

▶ ACROSS THE POTOMAC

HOTELS

ALEXANDRIA, VA

🏨 🍴 MORRISON HOUSE

$$$$$

116 S. ALFRED ST.

TEL 703-838-8000

morrisonhouse.com

A Kimpton hotel designed to evoke the atmosphere of Old Alexandria, the Morrison resembles an 18th-century manor house. Recently refurbished, it traded in its federal-period reproductions for a stylish moderne boutique look. Dinner is offered at the hotel's very good **Grille** restaurant.

ⓘ 45 🅿 AE, MC, V 🚇 King Street–Old Town, then bus to Old Town

🏨 HAMPTON INN OLD TOWN

$$$

1616 KING ST.

TEL 703-299-9900

hilton.com

Located in the heart of historic Old Town and near Metro, this well-run hotel combines comfort and value with convenience. Walk to many restaurants in the area.

ⓘ 80 AE, D, MC, V 🚇 King Street–Old Town

🏨 🍴 KIMPTON LORIEN HOTEL & SPA

$$–$$$$

1600 KING ST.

TEL 703-894-3434 OR

877-956-7436

lorienhotelandspa.com

A 2018 redesign infused a recherché modernity to this boutique hotel. Behind its ungainly redbrick exterior, a soft blue, white, and taupe color scheme lends a welcoming touch. Rooms offer minimalist decor and sumptuous Frette linens; some have claw-foot tubs. Its **Brabo** restaurant serves fine European fare.

ⓘ 107 🅿 All major cards 🚇 King Street–Old Town

ARLINGTON, VA

🏨 🍴 RITZ-CARLTON PENTAGON CITY

$$$$$

1250 S. HAYES ST.

TEL 703-415-5000

ritzcarlton.com

A part of the Fashion Centre mall, this high-rise hotel offers luxury with the added advantage of shopping. It is minutes from Reagan National Airport. Modern globally-inspired fusion cuisine is offered in the **Fyve Restaurant Lounge**. Afternoon tea is popular.

ⓘ 366 🅿 All major cards 🚇 Pentagon City

🏨 CRYSTAL CITY MARRIOTT
$$$$

1999 JEFFERSON DAVIS HWY.
TEL 703-413-5500
marriott.com
Located a mile (1.6 km) from
Reagan National Airport, this
hotel connects to the Crystal
City Metro stop, so access to
the memorials and Smith-
sonian museums is easy. It
was recently refurbished in
contempo vogue.

🛏 343 🅿 ♿ 🚭 All major
cards 🚇 Crystal City

🏨 🍴 KEY BRIDGE MARRIOTT
$$$$

1401 LEE HWY.
TEL 703-524-6400
marriott.com
Just across the river from
Georgetown, the high-rise
Key Bridge Marriott offers
easy access by Metro to
downtown and its sites. The
Capital View Ballroom offers
an indulgent Sunday brunch
with stunning views of
Washington.

🛏 582 🅿 🚭 AE, D, DC,
MC, V 🚇 Rosslyn

🏨 🍴 LE MÉRIDIEN ARLINGTON
$$$$

1121 19TH ST. N.
TEL 703-351-9170 OR
888-627-7101
marriott.com
Close to the Metro, this stylish upscale modern high-rise
has contemporary furnishings
and neutral color schemes.
The **Amuse** restaurant serves
innovative French and Italian
cuisine and has good views
over the Potomac River to
Georgetown.

🛏 154 🚭 🅿 Valet 🚭 All
major cards 🚇 Rosslyn

🏨 🍴 HOTEL PENTAGON
$$

2480 S. GLEBE RD.
TEL 703-979-4400
hotelpentagon.net

Formerly the Best Western,
this newly renovated hotel
has modestly furnished
rooms with faux wood floors
and royal blue-and-white
color schemes. It provides a
courtesy shuttle to Reagan
National Airport, Pentagon
City Metro station, and the
Fashion Centre Mall. The
restaurant **Monuments**
serves dinner, and breakfast
is served daily in the **Capital
Ballroom**.

🛏 205 🅿 ♿ 🚭 All major
cards 🚇 Pentagon City

RESTAURANTS

ALEXANDRIA, VA

🍴 NASIME JAPANESE RESTAURANT
$$$$

1209 KING ST.
TEL 703-457-0146
nasimerestaurant.com
An upscale cubbyhole
Japanese restaurant with a
destination-worthy tasting
menu, it focuses on a sea-
sonal five-course lineup that
includes a traditional soup, a
grilled dish, and melt-in-your-
mouth sashimi prepared by
chef/owner Yuh Shimomura.

🪑 20 🚭 🅿 🕐 Closed
Sun.–Mon. 🚭 MC, V 🚇 King
Street–Old Town

🍴 BLACKWALL HITCH
$$$–$$$$

5 CAMERON ST.
TEL 703-739-6090
blackwallhitchalexandria.com
Named for a mariner's knot,
this nautical-inspired restau-
rant overlooking the harbor
opened in 2019 turns out
classics such as filet mignon
and grilled pork chop. More
creative dishes include crab-
stuffed rockfish. It draws a
bar crowd for live music.

🪑 160 🚭 🚭 All major credit
cards 🚇 King Street–Old Town

🍴 BASTILLE
$$$

606 N. FAYETT
TEL 703-519-3776
bastillerestaurant.com
Now in a new location
close to downtown, chefs
and owners Christophe and
Michelle Poteaux accent
French bistro food with
Mediterranean and global
influences. You'll find dishes
such as black truffle and
mushroom risotto and duck
with spiced pineapple sauce.
Michelle Poteaux's pastry
and desserts are among the
best in the area. The indoor
decor is warm and inviting,
but on a gorgeous day, opt
for the charming courtyard
patio.

🪑 50 🕐 Closed Mon. & L
Tues.–Sat. 🚭 All major credit
cards 🚇 Braddock Road

🍴 EVENING STAR CAFÉ
$$$

2000 MT. VERNON AVE.
TEL 703-549-5051
eveningstarcafe.net
An ambitious seasonal Ameri-
can comfort-food menu and
an impressive wine program
raise this appealing eatery out
of the neighborhood
restaurant category. A bar has
more than 1,500 labels and
small plates for snacking. In
fair weather, there's outdoor
seating.

🪑 70 🕐 Closed Mon.–Tues.
& L Wed.–Fri. 🚭 All major
cards 🚇 Braddock Road

🍴 THE MAJESTIC
$$$

911 KING ST.
TEL 703-837-9117
themajesticva.com
First established in 1932, the
Majestic opened on this King
Street spot in 1949 and still
boasts its signature neon-lit
façade, coffered-ceiling,
and terrazo floor. After the
building had been left vacant

for many years, chef Susan Lindeborg reopened the historic restaurant in 2000, modernizing the interior while preserving its art deco elements. Now run by chef/owner Gaby Hakman, the local landmark serves creative American dishes such as roasted parsnip angolotti and Amish roast chicken. The family-style "Nana's Sunday Dinner," served Sunday nights, is a popular draw.

🛏 72 🕐 Closed L Mon.–Thurs. 🏧 All major cards 🚇 King Street–Old Town, then DASH bus or Metro shuttle

ARLINGTON, VA

🍴 SER
$$$
1110 N GLEBE RD.
TEL 703-746-9822
serrestaurant.com
Javier Candon's airy and colorful Spanish restaurant is a hidden gem beloved by locals for its tapas and full plates, from *pulpo a la gallega* and grilled sardines to paella and smoked pork shoulder.

🛏 90 🅢 🏧 All major credit cards 🚇 Ballston–MU

🍴 BIG BUNS DAMN GOOD BURGERS
$
4401 WILSON BLVD.
TEL 703-276-3032
eatbigbuns.com
Delicious burgers with customizable options such as caramelized onions are the name of the game at Big Buns, accompanied by ice cream shakes and local brews and signature cocktails. It also serves ahi tuna burgers, chicken sandwiches, and vegetarian options.

🛏 60 🅢 🏧 MC, V 🚇 Ballston–MU

▶ EXCURSIONS

RESTAURANTS

ANNAPOLIS, MD

🍴 CANTLER'S RIVERSIDE INN
$$
458 FOREST BEACH RD.
TEL 410-757-1311
cantlers.com
A short drive from downtown Annapolis, Cantler's—owned by a family of watermen—is one of the city's most popular seafood restaurants. You eat at benches at communal tables, or at picnic tables on the deck, overlooking the docks and beautiful creek. Begin with a cup of she-crab soup. There are meat and chicken dishes, but the best main courses feature seafood from Maryland waters—crab cakes, softshell crabs, and rockfish.

🛏 318 🅿 🏧 AE, D, DC, MC, V

BALTIMORE, MD

🍴 THE BLACK OLIVE
$$$$–$$$$$
814 S. BOND ST.
TEL 410-276-7141
theblackolive.com
The cobblestoned streets of Baltimore's historic Fells Point neighborhood lend quiet charm and elegance to this family-run restaurant. Whitewashed brick walls and wooden tables deliver the atmosphere of the Greek islands. The menu boasts seafood such as Dover sole and grilled octopus, organic produce from local farms, and an immense wine list with more than 3,000 bottles in the private wine cellar. Fresh fish is filleted tableside. Be sure to sample the succulent baklava ice cream. The accompanying Black Olive Inn offers spacious rooms

with organic materials and views of the Inner Harbor.

🛏 90 🅿 Valet 🕐 Closed L & Sun.–Mon. 🏧 All major cards

🍴 CHARLESTON
$$$$
1000 LANCASTER ST.
TEL 410-332-7373
charlestonrestaurant.com
Chef Cindy Wolf's Charleston in the Inner Harbor is Baltimore's most praised restaurant. As the name suggests, this is low-country Southern cooking. Starters have included Charleston she-crab soup, cornmeal-crusted oysters, and fried green tomatoes with lobster. Wolf frequently features traditional Carolina dishes such as seafood Perlau, or southern improvisations such as venison medallions with spoonbread or duck breasts with Madeira-poached pears and pecan rice. The wine selection is well chosen and well priced.

🛏 130 🅿 Valet 🕐 Closed L 🏧 AE, D, DC, MC, V

SHOPPING

Washington is the place to pick up that perfect political souvenir—from campaign buttons to White House Easter eggs to presidential seal mouse pads. But just as there is more to the city than what goes on atop Capitol Hill, there is more to Washington shopping than political paraphernalia. The museum stores, for starters, have wonderful inventories of unique books, arts and crafts, jewelry, and artifact reproductions. It's natural that in such a highly educated city you'll find countless excellent bookstores. And local markets feature interesting bric-a-brac.

For a real shopping experience, however, wander into the neighborhoods, which harbor neat little one-of-a-kind shops and boutiques. Georgetown's two main arteries—M Street and Wisconsin Avenue—have many fashionable boutiques, bookstores, art galleries, antiques stores, and contemporary clothing stores. Dupont Circle is much funkier, with its eclectic boutiques, vintage clothing stores, and antique furniture shops. Adams Morgan resembles Berkeley, California, perhaps more than anyplace else on the East Coast, with its down-to-earth selection of African goods, items from India, and curious New Age paraphernalia. Across the river, Old Town Alexandria's historic core along King Street showcases a slew of antiques shops, art galleries, and carpet stores in charming 18th-century buildings.

This listing covers some of the more unique shopping experiences in the Washington, D.C., area.

Antiques

Georgetown overflows with antique shops, especially on Wisconsin Avenue between P and S Streets, and along M and O Streets. Store after store features gorgeous furniture and such accessories as grandfather clocks, 19th-century paintings, and sterling tableware. **Adams Morgan** and **Dupont Circle** also offer a good selection of antiques.

In **Kensington, Maryland,** Howard Avenue is one of the foremost antique districts in the mid-Atlantic, with prices being better than those in Georgetown. Head to the lower, warehouse end of the street for serious antiques shopping. The downtown Antique Row has cute, smaller shops full of collectibles.

Old Town Alexandria has dozens of antiques shops, purveying authentic Persian rugs, as well as French, English, and American period furniture.

Arts & Crafts Galleries

The best places to look for handmade works of art are Adams Morgan, Georgetown, Dupont Circle, and Old Town Alexandria. Seventh Street, N.W., between D Street and the Capitol One Arena, has become a mecca of galleries.

Addison/Ripley Fine Art, 1670 Wisconsin Ave., N.W. (Georgetown), tel 202-338-5180, addisonripleyfineart.com. One of Washington's foremost galleries, established in 1981, featuring painting, sculpture, photography, and fine arts prints.

Torpedo Factory Art Center, 105 N. Union St., Alexandria (Across the Potomac), tel 703-746-4570, torpedofactory.org. More than 80 working artists' studios (each one selling their works) and six galleries showcase sculpture, pottery, paintings in watercolor, acrylic, and oil, plus much more.

Zenith Gallery, 1429 Iris St., N.W. (Excursions), Silver Spring, MD, tel 202-783-2963, zenithgallery.com. One of the Washington area's top galleries for contemporary fine art sales, it's well worth the journey out of town.

Books

Capitol Hill Books, 657 C St., S.E. (Capitol Hill), tel 202-544-1621, capitolhillbooks-dc.com. Opposite Eastern Market, this long-established icon has books spanning all genres, dispersed in a warren of rooms on two floors.

Kramerbooks & Afterwords Café, 1517 Connecticut Ave., N.W. (Dupont Circle & Beyond), tel 202-387-1400, kramers.com, open 24 hours on weekends. Small but good selection of books. Late-night dining and entertainment at the café.

Mahogany Books, 1231 Good Hope Rd., S.E. (East & North of the Capitol), tel 844-279-6239, mahoganybooks.com. This independent bookstore in Anacostia specializes in books by and about African Americans and the African Diaspora.

Politics and Prose Bookstore & Coffeehouse, 5015 Connecticut Ave., N.W. (Cleveland Park & Beyond), tel 202-364-1919, politics-prose.com. Popular with Washington's intelligentsia. Frequent author readings and book signings. Café downstairs.

Second Story Books, 2000 P St., N.W. (Dupont Circle & Beyond), tel 202-659-8884, secondstory books.com. A large shop with used and rare books, including first editions, fine bound volumes, and just plain secondhand. Stays open late.

Clothing

Hu's Wear, 2906 M St., N.W. (Georgetown), tel 202-42-2020, husonline.com. Avant-garde high-end items for forward-thinking fashionistas, including latest runway items in the basement.

Rag & Bone, 3067 M St., N.W. (Georgetown), tel 202-295-9072, rag-bone.com. This well-known chain store sells gritty staples, from T-shirts to blazers, and glamorous classic cuts. Check out its panchromatic range of denim jeans.

Read Wall, 1875 Connecticut Ave., N.W. (Dupont Circle & Around), tel 202-733-1913, readwall.com. Upscale men's boutique for ready-made and bespoke-tailored shirts, sports coats, and suits. Excellent selection of handcrafted American and Italian neckwear.

Lou Lou Clothing, 1623 Connecticut Ave., N.W. (Dupont Circle & Around), tel 202-817-2089, loulouboutiques.com. What began as a small Washington store has become a national chain for the popularity of its colorful dresses, whimsical tops, and other womenswear, including both bohemian and glamourous pieces.

Department Stores & Malls

Crystal City Shops, Crystal Dr. bet. 15th & 23rd Sts., Arlington (Across the Potomac), tel 703-413-7900, thecrystalcityshops.com. More than 200 stores and eateries.

Fashion Centre at Pentagon City, 1100 S. Hayes St., Arlington (Across the Potomac), tel 703-415-2400, simon.com. Four-story mall with 130 shops, including Macy's and Nordstrom. Dining and cinema as well.

Mazza Gallerie, 5300 Wisconsin Ave., N.W., tel 202-966-6114, mazzagallerie.com. This complex of exclusive shops, restaurants, and theaters showcases Neiman Marcus, Saks Fifth Avenue Men's Store, and Williams-Sonoma.

Potomac Mills Outlet Mall, 2700 Potomac Mills Circle, Woodbridge, VA (Excursions), tel 703-496-9330, simon.com. Off I-95 about 30 miles (48 km) south of Washington. Said to be Virginia's number one tourist attraction, the 152-acre (61 ha) shoppers' paradise has some 250 discount and outlet stores, including Nordstrom Rack, Coach, and Neiman Marcus. IKEA, the popular Swedish furniture store, has recently expanded to twice its original enormous space.

The Shops at Chevy Chase Pavilion, 5335 Wisconsin Ave., N.W. (Cleveland Park & Beyond), tel 202-686-5335, chevychase pavilion.info. Stores at this popular mall include J. Crew, H & M, and World Market.

Shops at Georgetown Park, 3222 M St., N.W. (Georgetown), tel 202-965-1280, georgetown park.com. Several shops and boutiques in a restored tobacco warehouse, including Anthropologie, J. Crew, H&M, and Olivia Macaron's.

Tyson's Corner Center, 1961 Chain Bridge Rd., McLean, VA (Excursions), tel 703-893-9400, tysonscornercenter.com. Washington's largest mall, with more than 300 shops and boutiques, including Nordstrom, Bloomingdale's, and Lord & Taylor. With many dining options.

Union Station, 50 Massachusetts Ave., N.E. (Capitol Hill), tel 202-289-1908. An interesting mix of dozens of stores on three levels, plus a food court, in an active, historic train station.

Farmers & Flea Markets

Alexandria Farmers Market, 301 King St., Alexandria (Across the Potomac), alexandriava.gov/ FarmersMarkets, Sat. a.m. only. Traditional farmers market with the freshest fruits and vegetables, preserves, just-baked breads and pastries, and flowers. Opens at 5 a.m.; locals love to show up early.

Dupont Circle Farmers Market, see p. 168.

Eastern Market, 225 7th St., S.E. (Capitol Hill), easternmarket.org, closed Mon. Washington's last remaining public market, dating from 1870, has been beautifully renovated and looks better than ever. The location also features a farmers market and flea market (Sat.–Sun.). Popular breakfast and lunch grill (Tues.–Sat.).

Georgetown Flea Market, 1819 35th St., N.W., at Hardy Middle School (Georgetown), Sun. Vendors offer a museum's worth of antique musical instruments, rugs, clothes, furniture, new jewelry and sunglasses, old cameras and books, and much more.

Maine Avenue Fish Market, Washington Channel, S.W., wharfdc.com/fish-market.

Canopied dockside barges hold beautiful, gleaming piles of recently swimming rockfish, bluefish, shad, catfish, swordfish, pompano, crabs, clams, and just about any other catch you can name. A couple of stands sell hot cooked crabs, for those who just can't wait to get home or are just visiting and hungry.

Gourmet Foods & Wine

Balducci's, three locations in the Washington area, including 600 Franklin St., Alexandria, VA, tel 703-549-6611, balduccis.com. Modeled on European markets, featuring specialty foods and wines.

Calvert Woodley Fine Wines & Spirits, 4339 Connecticut Ave., N.W. (Cleveland Park & Beyond), tel 202-966-4400, calvertwoodley .com. This family-owned emporium, in business for over 30 years, offers deluxe cheeses from beaufort to brie and a vast selection of beer, wines, and spirits. The expert wine staff assists customers in finding the perfect varietal.

Museum Shops

Decatur House museum shop, 1610 H St., N.W. (White House & Around), tel 202-218-4333. Small and elegant, with reproductions of home accessories from the 18th and 19th centuries, including presidential china, books, and children's selections.

Hillwood Museum, 4155 Linnean Ave., N.W. (Cleveland Park & Be-Beyond), tel 202-243-3931. The former home of Marjorie Merriweather Post, cereal heiress, has a shop with French and Russian decorative arts and reproductions.

Hirshhorn Museum, 700 Independence Ave., S.W. (The Mall) tel 202-633-0126, hirshhorn. si.edu. Unusual items, including contemporary jewelry that's fun and quirky.

John F. Kennedy Center for the Performing Arts, 2700 F St., N.W. (White House & Around), tel 202-416-8000, shop.kennedy-center.org. Good selection of gifts with music, dance, theater, and opera themes, plus books and memorabilia of JFK.

Mount Vernon Estate, George Washington Memorial Pkwy., Alexandria (Across the Potomac), tel 703-799-6301, shops.mount vernon.org. Reproductions of the Washingtons' belongings, including china and silver, as well as toys and souvenirs, plus estate-produced honey and roasted peanuts.

National Air and Space Museum, 7th St. & Independence Ave., S.W. (The Mall), tel 202-633-1000. Freeze-dried ice cream (just like what the astronauts eat), kites, books, models, and videos for aspiring pilots and astronauts.

National Archives Museum Store, 7th St. & Constitution Ave., N.W. (Downtown), tel 202-357-5000, nationalarchivesstore. org. Copies of the Charters of Freedom, posters, and cards.

National Building Museum, 401 F St., N.W. (Downtown), tel 202-272-2448. Well-chosen architecture-related books, prints, posters, toys, and gifts.

National Gallery of Art, 600 Constitution Ave., N.W. (The Mall), tel 202-737-4215, shop. nga.gov. Several shops in the museum feature quality prints and posters, art reproductions, gifts, and art books.

National Geographic Society, 1145 17th St., N.W. (White House & Around), tel 202-857-7700. Wall maps, books, globes, and educational children's toys.

National Museum of African Art, 950 Independence Ave., S.W. (The Mall), tel 202-633-4600. Books for adults and children on history, travel, culture, and the natural world. Also African crafts, posters, dolls, jewelry, and tapes.

Phillips Collection, 1600 21st St., N.W. (Dupont Circle & Beyond), tel 202-387-2151, phillipscollec tion.org/music. Jewelry, ceramics, glassware, and other objects by contemporary artists, plus hand-painted scarves, reproductions, books, stationery, and more.

Renwick Gallery, Pennsylvania Ave. at 17th St., N.W. (White House & Around), tel 202-633-6856, americanart.si.edu. Features contemporary crafts of fiber, metal, ceramic, wood, and more.

Smithsonian American Art Museum & the National Portrait Gallery, 8th & G Sts., N.W. (Downtown), tel 202-633-1589, American Art Museum. Souvenirs and gifts inspired by the collections in the museums.

Textile Museum, G & 21st Sts., N.W., George Washington University's Foggy Bottom Campus (White House & Around), tel 202-994-5200, museum.gwu.edu. Tapestries, clothing, gift items, and books related to fiber arts.

ENTERTAINMENT

After traipsing around all day from site to site, be sure to save some energy for Washington after dark. Your choices are many: theater, a movie, dancing, or just hanging out at one of the local bars. Check the Friday Weekend section of the *Washington Post* for goings-on, as well as the weekly *Washington City Paper*. *Washingtonian* magazine is another good source of information.

Dance

Dance Place, 3225 8th St., N.E., tel 202-269-1600, danceplace.org. Metro: Brookland. Dance Place presents programs of modern and ethnic dance most weekends.

Washington Ballet, tel 202-677-5193, washingtonballet.org. The nationally recognized Washington Ballet presents a full season between September and May at the Kennedy Center as well as *The Nutcracker* each Christmas at the Warner Theatre.

Film

American Film Institute Silver Theatre and Cultural Center, tel 301-495-6720, afisilver.afi.com. The AFI screens hundreds of films every year at its AFI Silver Theatre and Cultural Center. Actors and directors often are present to discuss their work at these showings.

Filmfest DC, tel 202-234-3456, filmfestdc.org. The DC International Film Festival, held in late April and early May, screens American and international films in a variety of local theaters and auditoriums.

National Gallery of Art East Building, 4th St. & Constitution Ave., N.W., tel 202-842-6799, nga.gov. Metro: Archives–Navy Memorial–Penn Quarter. The National Gallery shows free classic films and films relating to exhibitions in the galleries. It also has a special children's film calendar (tel 202-789-3030).

Reel Affirmations, facebook. com/reelaffirmation. D.C.'s gay and lesbian film festival, held in October each year, shows films of gay and lesbian interest at various Washington area theaters. Between festivals, films are screened at the E Street Cinema *(555 11th St., N.W.)* and other locations.

Music
Chamber Music
Library of Congress, 1st St. & Independence Ave., S.E., tel 202-707-5502, loc.gov/concerts. Metro: Union Station, Capitol South. Broad range of classical music and modern performers.

Phillips Collection, 1600 21st St., N.W., tel 202-387-2151, phillips collection.org/music. Metro: Dupont Circle. Sunday concerts in the Phillips mansion's music room from October to May.

Choral Music
Choral Arts Society of Washington, tel 202-244-3669, choralarts.org. Between September and May, this 200-voice ensemble, directed by Scott Tucker, presents frequent classical programs in the Kennedy Center Concert Hall.

Opera
Washington Opera, Kennedy Center Opera House, tel 202-467-4600, kennedy-center.org/ wno. Metro: Foggy Bottom-GWU. During its lengthy season, the Washington Opera, directed by Francesca Zambello, produces up to eight operas, sung in their original languages with English subtitles.

Orchestra
National Symphony Orchestra, Kennedy Center Concert Hall, tel 202-467-4600, kennedy-center. org/nso/home. Metro: Foggy Bottom–GWU. From September to June, the NSO performs at the Kennedy Center. In the summer, there are concerts at Wolf Trap *(tel 703-255-1900, wolftrap.org),* **Carter Barron Amphitheatre,** and other locations in and around town.

Nightlife
The Birchmere, 3701 Mount Vernon Ave., Alexandria, VA, tel 703-549-7500, birchmere .com. Buses: 10A, 10B, 23B. The Birchmere takes music very seriously—the club's no-talking policy is strictly enforced. But the performers and the sound are terrific; the food, from Alexandria's King Street Blues, is very good.

Blues Alley, 1073 Wisconsin Ave., N.W., tel 202-337-4141, bluesalley.com. Metro: Foggy Bottom–GWU, then walk or bus to Georgetown. All the legends of blues have played at this small club—Dizzy Gillespie, Wynton Marsalis, Nancy Wilson, Charlie Byrd. There are usually 8 p.m. and 10 p.m. shows, and sometimes on weekends a midnight set. Reservations are essential.

Café Citron, 1343 Connecticut Ave., N.W., tel 202-530-8844, cafecitrondc.com. Metro: Dupont Circle. Riotously colorful Latin fusion restaurant segues into a neon-lit dance club at 10 p.m. DJs spin Latin house, plus pop, reggaeton, salsa, and even bachata. Check out the free salsa lessons Wed.–Sat. 8–10 p.m. Dress code Friday and Saturday.

Eighteenth Street Lounge, Blagden Alley, N.W., 18thstlounge.com. Metro: Mount Vernon Square 7th Street–Convention Center. Popular nightclub with eclectic music relocated in 2021, with a rooftop deck. DJs predominantly spin funk, jazz, Latin, and reggae tunes, and live acts perform.

Harlot DC, 2001 11th St., N.W., tel 202-986-7159, harlotdc.club. Metro: U Street/African-Amer Civil War Memorial/Cardozo. Occupying the ground floor of the former Bohemian Club, this hip, sultry lounge bar and nightclub has a nightly DJ, plus a Saturday brunchtime drag show that packs 'em in for over-the-top portrayals of such celebs as Beyoncé and Miley Cyrus.

Jojo Restaurant and Bar, 1518 U St., N.W., tel 202-319-9350, jojodc. com. Metro: U Street/African-Amer Civil War Memorial/Cardozo. One of D.C.'s top spots for jazz and blues, this two-level brick-walled restaurant draws top local and international artists and stays true to the soulful spirit of U Street.

Madam's Organ, 2461 18th St., N.W., tel 202-667-5370, madamsorgan.com. Metro: Woodley Park–Zoo/Adams Morgan. The popular Madam's Organ has a full schedule of bluegrass, R&B, and blues. Try to arrive before 10 p.m. Thursday through Saturday—after 11 p.m., be ready to wait in line.

Mister Henry's, 601 Pennsylvania Ave., S.E., tel 202-546-8412, mrhenrysdc.com. Metro: Eastern Market. Robert Flack got her break at this iconic venue, which still has its cozy upstairs live jazz supper club on Wednesday through Saturday nights. Thursday is for Latin jazz, and it sometimes has bluegrass and karaoke.

9:30 Club, 815 V St., N.W., tel 202-265-0930, 930.com. Metro: U Street/African-Amer Civil War Memorial/Cardozo. A great sound system makes this crowded club the best place in town to hear top-tier rock, punk, hip-hop, and country performances.

Sax Dinner Theater & Lounge, 734 11th St., N.W., tel 202-737-0101, saxwdc.com. Metro: Metro Center. Sumptuous Versailles-inspired restaurant and cabaret lounge transforms into a late-night dance club on weekends. It plays a mix of house and Top 40. Live entertainment spans aerialists to acrobatic pole ballet.

The Kennedy Center, 2700 F St., tel 202-467-4600, kennedy-center. org. Metro: Foggy Bottom–GWU. Now in a cabaret-style lounge the REACH, the KC Jazz Club maintains its annual calendar of jazz, hip-hop, and contemporary music performances, Thurs.–Sat., Jan.–April.

Theater

Arena Stage, 1101 6th St., S.E., tel 202-488-3300, arena stage.com. Metro: Waterfront. This respected resident theater company presents a busy season on its three stages.

Ford's Theatre, 511 10th St., N.W., tel 202-347-4833 or 888-616-0270 (tickets), fordstheatre. org. Metro: Metro Center. See p. 140.

Howard Theatre, 620 T St., N.W., tel 202-803-2899, theho wardtheatre.com. Metro: Shaw–Howard University. See p. 177.

Lincoln Theatre, 1215 U St., N.W., tel 202-888-0050, thelincolndc. org. Metro: U Street/African-Amer Civil War Memorial/ Cardozo. See p. 177.

National Theatre, 1321 Pennsylvania Ave., N.W., tel 202-628-6161, thenationaldc.org. Metro: Federal Triangle, Metro Center. See pp. 145–146.

Shakespeare Theatre, 450 7th St., N.W., tel 202-547-1122, shakespearetheatre.org. Metro: Archives–Navy Memorial–Penn Quarter, Gallery Place–Chinatown. See pp. 138–139.

Signature Theatre, 4200 Campbell Ave., Arlington, VA, tel 703-820-977, sigtheatre.org. Metro: Pentagon City Station + Buses. Especially known for its productions of modern musical theater.

Studio Theatre, 1501 14th St., N.W., tel 202-332-3300, studiotheatre.org. Metro: Dupont Circle. Presents the best of contemporary theater. It is the home of Studio Theatre Acting Conservatory, which runs a widely respected school for the theater arts.

Warner Theatre, 13th & E Sts., N.W., tel 202-783-4000, warnertheatredc.com. Metro: Metro Center. See p. 146.

Woolly Mammoth, 641 D St., N.W., tel 202-393-3939, woollymammoth.net. Metro: Gallery Place–Chinatown. *Variety* comments on Woolly Mammoth's "fierce dedication to the offbeat," a dedication that is pursued with genuine devotion and solid production values for more than 25 years. See p. 134.

ACTIVITIES

From boating to golfing to ice skating, Washington offers an amazingly diverse selection of options for outdoor enthusiasts. If you're in the mood to watch others do the work instead, you have a number of big-name sports teams from which to choose, including the Capitals, Nationals, Wizards, Washington Football Team (formerly the Redskins), and D.C. United. For something a little different, join one of the many specialty tours—a chance to see the city from a different point of view, by walking, boating, or even by bike.

Outdoor

Boating

Key Bridge Boathouse, 3500 Water St., N.W., tel 202-337-9642, boatingindc.com. Open April–Oct. Located under Key Bridge in Georgetown, rents canoes and kayaks.

Thompson Boat Center, 2900 Virginia Ave., N.W., tel 202-333-9543, thompsonboatcenter.com. Open April–Oct. Canoes, rowing shells, and kayaks for rent. Lessons available. Also, all-terrain and cruiser bike rentals.

Golf

The National Park Service operates the following three public golf courses in Washington. Check the website (playdcgolf.com) for amenities and details.

East Potomac Park Golf Course, 972 Ohio Dr., S.W., tel 202-554-7660. This public course near the Mall consists of one 18-hole, par-72 course and two 9-hole courses.

Langston Golf Course, 26th St. & Benning Rd., N.E., tel 202-397-8638. The Langston Golf Course is an 18-hole, par-72 public course that also offers a golf school, golf shop, driving range, putting green, and snack bar.

Rock Creek Park Golf Course, 16th & Rittenhouse Sts., N.W., tel 202-882-7332. This 4,798-yard, par-65 public course has a hilly and challenging terrain.

Amenities include a golf school, golf shop, putting green, and snack bar. The course is open every day from dawn to dusk.

Ice Skating

National Gallery of Art Sculpture Garden Ice Skating Rink, 7th St. & Constitution Ave., N.W., tel 202-216-9397. Open mid-Nov.–mid-March. This charming rink right on the Mall affords skaters views of modern sculpture in the museum garden.

Tennis

East Potomac Tennis Center, 1090 Ohio Dr., S.W., tel 202-554-5962, eastpotomactennis. com. Indoor and outdoor courts, seasonal membership as well as walk-in court rental, tennis lessons, and racquet stringing.

Rock Creek Park Tennis Center, 16th & Kennedy Sts., N.W., tel 202-722-5949, rockcreektennis .com. The facility has 25 outdoor courts: 15 hard courts and 10 clay courts. Five indoor courts are heated and available for play in colder weather.

Spectator Sports

D.C. United, tel 202-587-5000, dcunited.com. Professional MLS soccer team at RFK Stadium.

Washington Capitals, tel 202-628-3200, capitals.nhl.com. Professional hockey right in D.C., at the Capitol One Arena.

Washington Mystics, tel 877-324-6671, wnba.com/mystics. Professional women's basketball played at the Verizon Center.

Washington Nationals, tel 202-675-6287, washington. nationals.mlb.com. The Nationals Park stadium is located near the Washington Navy Yard in Southeast (see p. 67).

Washington Football Team, tel 301-276-6800, washington football.com. NFL football at FedExField.

Washington Wizards, tel 202-661-5100, nba.com/wizards. Professional men's basketball at the Capitol One Arena.

Specialty Tours

Bus & Trolley Tours

Take a spin around town to get your bearings and figure out just where you want to spend more time exploring.

Big Bus Tours, tel 877-332-8689, bigbustours.com. The National Park Service authorizes these comprehensive tours. The **Patriot Tour** covers D.C. then heads across the river to Arlington Cemetery.

City Sights DC, tel 202-650-5444, citysightsdc.com. See the sights from the vantage of an open-top double-decker bus.

Old Town Trolley, tel 202-832-9800, historictours.com. Find out all the local history during a two-hour narrated tour.

Bicycle Tours
Bicycling is a cool way to explore Washington, D.C., especially in spring and autumn.
Capital Bikeshare (capitalbike share.com) makes it easy with 4,500 bikes at more than 500 stations throughout the metropolitan area. Simply buy a pass, unlock a bike, then return it to any station when you're finished. You can unlock an e-bike for an extra $1 per ride.

Bike N Roll DC, tel 202-842-2453, bikeandrolldc.com. This venture offers family-oriented tours that combine bicycle riding and walking. Bike and child trailer rentals are available, as are tandems, electric-bikes. It also has Segway tours. Bike and Roll has outlets at 998 Main Ave., S.W., in Washington, and at 1 Wales Alley in Old Town Alexandria.

Walking Tours
A number of self-guided walking heritage tours have been established around the city including **Roads to Diversity: Adams Morgan, City Within a City: Greater U Street,** and **River Farms to Urban Towers: Southwest** as well as the **African American Heritage Trail.** For information on these as well as many other biking and walking tours contact Cultural Tourism DC *(cultural tourismdc.org)* for their free brochures.

Walk of the Town, tel 240-672-6306, walkofthetowndc.com. Licensed tour guide and former teacher Tim Stewart leads 4-hour walking tours that take in the major sites between Capitol Hill and the Lincoln Memorial. **Washington Walks,** tel 202-

484-1565, washingtonwalks. com. Offered April–Oct. Among the walks to choose from are **Memorials: The Journey to Civil Rights,** which visits the memorials of personalities in the struggle for independence, equal rights, and justice. **Embassy Row,** Washington's grandest boulevard; **Georgetown;** and **Memorials by Moonlight,** which is as its name reflects a tour of Washington, D.C., at its most beautiful.

Boat Tours & Cruises
City Cruises by Hornblower, Gangplank Marina, 600 Water St., S.W., tel 703-684-0580 or 800-459-8105, cityexperiences. com. The two- to three-hour cruises feature innovative meals, an excellent wine list, and live music, while taking in the sites of the nation's capital. It operates two vessels: the low-lying *Odyssey DC,* a climate-controlled, glass-enclosed vessel that can pass under the low bridges for up close views of the monuments, while the sleek *Spirit of Washington* has three levels, each with outdoor observation decks.

Potomac Riverboat Company, tel 703-684-0580, potomac riverboatco.com. Now operated by City Cruises by Hornblower, this outfit provides water taxi service that will take you to National Harbor for a day of shopping or Nationals Park for an evening of baseball and hot dogs. Traditional cruises also available.

Other
D.C. Design Tours, tel 202-229-6795, dcdesigntours.com. Get an insider scoop on Washington's architectural marvels and the development of our Capital City on any of eight walking tours, including a "Dupont Circle & Embassy Row Tour," with plenty

of juicy gossip included at no extra charge.

Nonpartisan Pedicab, tel 703-231-9882, nonpartisanpedicab. com. Sit back and relax as your guide pedals you around the major sights in a pedicab. A popular option is the "Smithsonian Museums & Pennsylvania Avenue" tour along the presidential inaugural route from the Capitol to the White House.

Scandal Tours, tel 202-770-6917, gnpcomedy.com. This irreverent tour of Washington's infamous scandal sites is hosted by the critically acclaimed comedy group Gross National Product, which gives you an impudent commentary on some of Washington's most embarrassing moments. Find out the gossip while taking in the city's beauty. Reservations required. Offered from April Fool's Day through Labor Day. Pickup is at the Old Post Office Pavilion, 1100 Pennsylvania Ave., N.W.

Spy Tours, (garypowers.com). Author Gary Powers leads half- and full-day bus tour to espionage sites in and around Washington, D.C., including the Cold War Museum and International Spy Museum.

Washington Photo Safari, tel 202-669-8468, washington photosafari.com. Professional photographer David Luria offers half- and full-day photography workshops in English, French, and Spanish designed to improve amateur photographers' shooting skills as well as showcase some of Washington's most photogenic subjects. Tour options include "Full Moonrise over the Jefferson Memorial," "Monuments at Night," and "Sunrise on the National Mall."

INDEX

Bold page numbers indicate illustrations.
CAPS indicates thematic categories.

ILLUSTRATIONS CREDITS

National Geographic

TRAVELER

Washington, D.C.

SIXTH EDITION

Since 1888, the National Geographic Society has funded more than 14,000 research, exploration, and preservation projects around the world. National Geographic Partners distributes a portion of the funds it receives from your purchase to National Geographic Society to support programs including the conservation of animals and their habitats.

National Geographic Partners, LLC
1145 17th Street NW
Washington, DC 20036-4688 USA

Get closer to National Geographic explorers and photographers, and connect with our global community. Join us today at nationalgeographic.org/joinus

For rights or permissions inquiries, please contact National Geographic Books Subsidiary Rights: bookrights@natgeo.com

Sixth edition edited by White Star s.r.l.
Licensee of National Geographic Partners, LLC.
Update by Christopher P. Baker

Map illustrations drawn by Chris Orr Associates, Southampton, England.
Cutaway illustrations drawn by Maltings Partnership, Derby, England.

The information in this book has been carefully checked and to the best of our knowledge is accurate. However, details are subject to change, and the publisher cannot be responsible for such changes, or for errors or omissions. Assessments of sites, hotels, and restaurants are based on the author's subjective opinions, which do not necessarily reflect the publisher's opinion.

ISBN: 978-88-544-1800-4

Printed in Poland

NATIONAL GEOGRAPHIC TRAVELER
THE BEST GUIDES BY YOUR SIDE

More than 80 destinations around the globe

ARIZONA · AUSTRALIA · CALIFORNIA · COASTAL ALASKA · COSTA RICA
CUBA · HAWAII · IRELAND · ITALY · JAPAN
LONDON · NEW YORK · PERU · PORTUGAL · PUGLIA
ROME · SCOTLAND · VIETNAM · WASHINGTON, DC